G000143590

Lessons in Licensing

Microsoft 70-705: Exam Preparation Guide

By Louise Ulrick

Published by Licensing School.

Copyright © 2018 Licensing School.

All rights reserved.

ISBN: 978-1-911530-02-2.

No part of this publication may be reproduced or transmitted in any form or by any means, electronic or mechanical, without permission in writing from Licensing School.

Third Edition February 2018.

Dedicated to the
memory of the late,
and the great,
JDY.

The cleverest man I know,
an all round good chap,
and, above all,
my Daddy.

Table of Contents

PART 1: INTRODUCTION

The Microsoft Certified Professional Certification

The Microsoft Certified Professional (MCP) certification validates IT professional, developer, and licensing specialist expertise through industry-recognized exams. There is just one exam aimed at licensing professionals and passing this exam gives MCP status:

- 70-705: Designing and Providing Microsoft Volume Licensing Solutions to Large Organizations

Achieving this certification demonstrates that you have a good understanding of the Microsoft products and their licensing, and can ultimately recommend the right licensing solutions to a range of customers. It's ideal both for people who work for Microsoft partners selling software solutions, or someone who works for a customer organization and needs to know about Microsoft licensing. The certification is valid worldwide and is great to have on your CV or résumé.

Exam 70-705 Syllabus

You can find the full list of the requirements for the exam at this link: https://www.microsoft.com/en-us/learning/exam-70-705.aspx.

However, in summary, the exam covers the three key areas below, and in Part 7 of this book we'll look in detail about what these mean and which sections will help you with the knowledge that you'll need:

- Recommend the appropriate technology solution
  (Determine the right on-premises, Online Services or Azure solution to meet a customer's needs)

- Recommend the appropriate Software Assurance benefits
  (Determine the right SA benefits to meet a customer's needs)

- Recommend a licensing solution
  (Determine the right Microsoft licensing program to meet a customer's needs)

Using this Book

The primary aim of this book is to help you to prepare for the 70-705 exam and, of course, to ultimately pass it. The book is designed to help you to pass the exam by teaching you the things that you need to know – it's not a list of all the exam questions that I and my many licensing acquaintances can remember from when we took the exam – you'll find plenty of resources on the Internet if that's the way you want to go! Learning the topics to pass the exam will also stand you in good stead in real life afterwards as well of course; the knowledge in this book is relevant and useful for when you need to advise any customers about licensing solutions.

I would recommend that you start at the beginning of this book and work your way through the sections in order. These sections cover all the topics that you'll need to know about to answer the exam questions based on the syllabus above, and give you lots of tips on how you should apply your knowledge in the exam. There are also summary tables throughout this book, and these are the things that you should try and learn for the exam.

At the end of each section you'll find some revision questions on the topics covered and you can choose how you use these; if you're pretty experienced with Microsoft licensing and you want to see how good your existing knowledge is, you could work through those questions and then read appropriate sections if you discover any particular weaknesses. You may want to do the questions as you work through the book, or you may want to do a big revision session when you've finished reading.

The final section consists of a sample scenario; this gives you a good flavor of the type of scenario that you can expect to find in the exam, and will help you to see if you've got any remaining gaps in your knowledge.

And finally, throughout the explanations I've used the words such as "typically" and "generally". This is not me being imprecise so much as showing you how specific you need to be and what level of detail you need to know for the exam. If something disturbs you in my simplifications do email us at info@licensingschool.co.uk with suggestions to help make things

© Licensing School 2018

clearer for others! You may also know other things about the licensing of the products that I haven't included – I've tried to keep to just the level of detail that is included in the exam, rather than attempting to create an exhaustive guide on the licensing of all the Microsoft products.

Product Versions

The exam that you will be taking was first made available in November 2017 and the following products and versions are covered in the exam:

On-premises products:
- Windows 10
- Office 2016
- Windows Server 2016
- System Center 2016
- Exchange Server 2016
- SharePoint Server 2016
- Skype for Business Server 2015
- Project Server 2016
- SQL Server 2016
- Dynamics 365 Server
- Dynamics 365 for Operations Server

Online Services products:
- Office 365
- Enterprise Mobility + Security (EMS)
- Microsoft 365
- Dynamics 365
- Microsoft Azure

Of course, there are always changes in Microsoft licensing, but any that have been implemented after September 2017 are not included in the exam, or in this book.

An Overview of the Exam

Although we take a more extensive look at the exam and the final preparation that you will want to do for it at the end of this book, I think it's worth having a quick overview here so that you know what you're aiming for as you work through the different sections.

The exam is closed-book and proctored. That is to say, you can't take any resources into the test room with you and it will be invigilated – either by a person in the room with you or via CCTV. In some countries there may be the opportunity to take the exam as an online proctored exam which means that you take the exam in your home or office and are monitored by a proctor via a webcam and microphone.

The exam has two main sections: one section will have a whole series of individual questions and the other, two customer scenarios.

The individual questions section is composed of a whole range of questions on any aspect of licensing as defined in the syllabus above. Many of these will be multiple choice questions but there are also some different question types and you should make sure that you're familiar with these by working through Part 7 of this book. You can expect to get around 35 questions in this section.

In the customer scenarios you'll be given the background to the customer and told their current software situation, how they've acquired any current licenses, and their business goals. You'll be asked to recommend products, licenses, and then the programs to purchase those licenses through. You can expect to get around eight questions on each scenario.

You'll have up to two hours to work through both the questions and the scenarios and to pass, you'll need 700 points.

© Licensing School 2018

PART 2: LICENSING ON-PREMISES PRODUCTS

For the exam, you need to be able to identify which on-premises product might meet a company's business needs, and be confident in selecting the right licensing model for that product. This section takes you through all the key products and how they're licensed, as well as giving you some tips as to how you should apply the knowledge in the exam.

If you already have a good knowledge of the Microsoft on-premises products and their licensing models, why not skip to the Recap Questions on page 80 and test yourself?

Some Fundamental Concepts

Before we leap into the world of the Microsoft on-premises products and their licensing, there are a couple of key concepts that we should cover first.

The first: what is a license? It's obviously a fundamental question! A Microsoft license gives a customer rights to use the software and we'll see throughout this book that the rights differ dependent on how they've purchased the software – it could be as a boxed product, pre-installed, or through a Microsoft licensing program. All licenses give the customer the rights to install (where needed) and use the software, but additional rights, such as virtualization rights, are often only included when the licenses are purchased through one of the Volume Licensing agreements such as an Enterprise Agreement.

The second concept is the notion of versions and editions of Microsoft software – terms that I'll be using throughout this section. A version is a particular release of a piece of software and it often corresponds to a year – Office 2016, for example. An edition is a way of differentiating between different sets of functionality that are included in the product – Office Standard 2016 does not include as many components as Office Professional Plus 2016, for example.

© Licensing School 2018

Windows Server 2016

Windows Server 2016 is the Microsoft server operating system product and there are two editions aimed at larger customers: Standard and Datacenter editions. You need to know how these editions are licensed and to be able to work out how many licenses are required for a given server, and you also need to be able to calculate the licenses needed in a virtualized infrastructure. You do need to be able to recommend an edition of Windows Server 2016 based on a customer's requirements, but you shouldn't worry about the technical differences between the editions and in reality, your recommendation will be based solely on how heavily they want to virtualize their infrastructure.

Licensing Windows Server 2016

Both Windows Server 2016 Standard and Datacenter editions are licensed with the Per Core and CAL model. Licenses are assigned to a server based on the number of physical cores in the server, with a minimum of eight Core licenses required per processor and a minimum of 16 Core licenses required per server. So, a single processor machine with four cores would need 16 licenses assigned to it, and a server with four 2-core processors would need 32 licenses. All cores in the server must always be licensed. The diagram below shows the required licenses assigned to the servers in the examples we've just looked at, with the licenses in groups of eight for easy counting.

Figure 1: Windows Server 2016 Per Core Licensing

Then, any clients accessing the services of the server need to be licensed with a Client Access License – a CAL, as shown in the following diagram:

Figure 2: Windows Server 2016 Per Core and CAL Licensing

CALs almost always come in two types – a User CAL or a Device CAL, and both are available for Windows Server 2016.

Organizations buy User CALs when a single user will use multiple devices to access the services of the server. The CAL is assigned to the user, and that user may use any device to access the services of the server as shown in the diagram below:

Figure 3: Windows Server 2016 User CAL

© Licensing School 2018

Organizations buy Device CALs when a single device will be used by many users to access the services of the server. The CAL is assigned to a device, and any user may use that device to access the services of the server as shown in the diagram below:

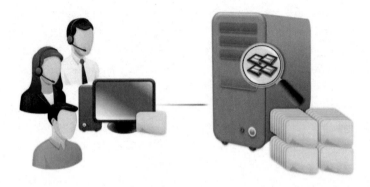

Figure 4: Windows Server 2016 Device CAL

Organizations can generally mix and match these CALs if required, but it does become more difficult to ensure compliance.

Once users or devices have been assigned CALs they may access any of the servers on the network; for example, if an organization has purchased Windows Server CALs for all users, then those users may access any licensed Windows Server on the network. The caveat to this is that the version of the CAL must be the same or higher than the version of the server. In other words, a Windows Server 2016 CAL may access a Windows 2016 server and/or a Windows 2012 server, but a Windows Server 2012 CAL may only access a Windows 2012 server, not a Windows 2016 server.

Windows Server 2016 Core licenses are actually purchased in 2-packs or 16-packs but in the exam you'll always be asked to recommend the actual number of licenses required rather than the number of 2-packs that are bought.

Licensing Virtualized Environments

Technology within Windows Server called Hyper-V enables customers to create and manage virtual machines on their physical servers, allowing them to consolidate servers and to gain some ease of manageability.

Let's take a look at how the licensing for Windows Server 2016 works in a virtualized environment by considering a server with two 4-core processors on which six virtual machines need to be run. We know that the physical cores must always be licensed so, starting with the Datacenter edition, we would need to assign 16 licenses to this device, following the minimums of assigning eight licenses for each processor. Having assigned the licenses to the machine the customer then receives rights to run a certain number of virtual machines, and in the case of the Datacenter edition, it's an unlimited number.

The licensing of Standard edition in a virtualized environment works in a similar way in that you have to license the physical server completely but that just gives rights to run up to two virtual machines. In our example we'd assign 16 licenses to the physical server to run the first two virtual machines and then you license the server again to run the next two virtual machines and so on. This means that to license Windows Server 2016 Standard to run six virtual machines on the server with two 4-core processors you would need to assign 48 Core licenses to the server.

So how do you decide between using Standard and Datacenter licenses? From a cost perspective, Standard licenses are about 15% of the price of a Datacenter license and there's a break-even point when it's more cost-effective to assign Datacenter licenses rather than Standard licenses. This varies dependent on the capacity of the physical server, but for the purposes of the exam, consider this to be at about when you need to run ten or more virtual machines. However, it's much easier to ensure compliance if you license with Datacenter edition since you can run an unlimited number of virtual machines without having to worry about specifically assigning additional licenses as additional virtual machines are added to the infrastructure. In real life, customers will weigh up the costs against the convenience in the context of their future plans for their server farms.

© Licensing School 2018

Licensing External Users

An organization licensing a server infrastructure will license its servers and its users and then potentially needs to license its external users. There are official definitions of what constitutes an external user, but for the purposes of the exam consider that these users are people who aren't employees of the organization but do need to access some internal solution.

For Windows Server 2016, the organization can choose to buy CALs for its external users, but it's generally more cost-effective, and easier to manage, to buy an External Connector license, since an External Connector license is a single license that allows an unlimited number of external users to access a server. An External Connector license is an Additive license – in other words, it can never be purchased alone, it needs to be purchased in conjunction with the underlying server licenses. For Windows Server 2016 there is a single External Connector license that is applied to a server device regardless of which edition of Windows Server 2016 is powering that server.

The diagram below shows a network infrastructure with three servers, all of which have the required number of Windows Server Core licenses assigned to them. The shaded server at the top also has an External Connector license assigned to it allowing any number of external users to access it:

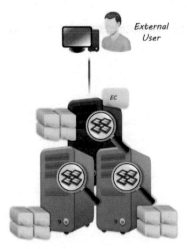

Figure 5: Windows Server 2016 External Connector License

Applying your knowledge in the exam:

- Look out for business goals that specify how many devices users will use; if they are using multiple devices you are likely to recommend User CALs, whereas if they are sharing devices, recommend Device CALs

- Look out for business goals that state that an organization needs to give access to its external users. Although they do have the choice of assigning CALs to these users, in almost all cases it is going to be more cost-effective to buy an External Connector license and that should be in your mind as your first recommendation

- Remember that External Connector licenses need to be applied to individual servers so if the customer's current situation or future plans involve allowing external users to access their multi-server infrastructure, you would need to recommend an External Connector license for each server

- Make sure that you're comfortable with calculating the licenses required for a given server in a physical environment

- When you're calculating the licenses required in a virtual infrastructure remember that the physical server needs to be fully licensed regardless of how many virtual machines are running. Don't forget that Standard edition gives rights to run two virtual machines and for further virtual machines you need to license the server completely again

- If a customer will only lightly virtualize their infrastructure – say run less than ten virtual machines on an individual physical server – then Windows Server 2016 Standard edition will be the right recommendation for them, otherwise, above that, they should use Datacenter edition. Don't try to read too much into the exam questions – if you're being given the steer that virtualization is key, then take that as a hint that you should be recommending Datacenter edition

© Licensing School 2018

Windows Server 2016 Services

Windows Server 2016 includes two important services that you need to know about for the exam: Remote Desktop Services and Rights Management Services.

Remote Desktop Services (RDS)

Remote Desktop Services was previously known as Terminal Services and very often in real life (and certainly for the purposes of the exam) it allows an organization to install Office on a server and to have users access it from their client devices over the network. All of the application processing is done on the server, and it's been a great way for organizations to continue to use older hardware since the client device does not need to be powerful enough to run Office.

There are some important concepts to be aware of in the licensing of Remote Desktop Services and we're going to take the example of running Office on the server, as it's the one you're most likely to come across in the exam. For this scenario, from a server perspective, the server needs to be licensed with the required number of Windows Server Core licenses – there are no other licensing requirements for the RDS component on the server. Then, all of the client devices need to be licensed with Windows CALs and, in addition, if they're using the services of RDS (which they are in our scenario) with RDS CALs too. Since Office will be used on the client devices, there needs to be an Office license assigned to the device too. Office will actually be installed and running on the server and there's just one licensing requirement associated with this – that the Office license has to be purchased through a Volume Licensing agreement since this gives the rights which allow an organization to install the software on a server and have the client devices access it remotely. Note that you don't need an extra license to install Office on the server; if you've got 350 PCs accessing the copy on the server you simply need 350 Volume Licensing licenses for the devices.

There is an External Connector available to license RDS for external users.

Active Directory Rights Management Services (AD RMS)

AD RMS can be used to protect documents using information rights management (IRM) which allows a user to attach access permissions to a particular document which can prevent it from being opened, forwarded or printed by unauthorized people, for example.

In common with RDS, there are no additional licensing requirements for the Windows Server itself, but every user or device that accesses the AD RMS services of the server must be covered with an AD RMS CAL.

Again, for external users there is an AD RMS External Connector available.

Applying your knowledge in the exam:

- The business goals may state quite specifically that the organization wants to use Office applications with RDS, or may describe a need for users to access Office remotely. Make sure that you don't fall into the trap of recommending that they acquire their Office licenses through OEM, since OEM licenses don't include the required remote access rights. Also ensure that you recommend a Volume Licensing Office license for each of the devices that will access Office on the server

- Although RDS is a service of Windows Server, remember that it is licensed with CALs, so don't forget to include both Windows Server and RDS CALs when recommending licenses in an RDS scenario

- Likewise, although there are no additional server licensing requirements when utilizing IRM, remember to include both Windows Server and AD RMS CALs in your licensing recommendations

- The components of the Core and Enterprise CAL Suites are listed on page 43 and you'll see that the AD RMS CAL is included as part of the Enterprise CAL Suite. Therefore, if you're recommending what licenses a customer needs to license an IRM solution check whether or not they already have this suite license

© Licensing School 2018

System Center 2016

The Microsoft products that enable organizations to manage their client and server infrastructure are all part of the System Center family.

System Center Licensing Model

In the diagram below the large server represents the management server where the System Center management product is installed, and this server manages a variety of client and server devices. We'll see that every device that is managed by that server needs to have either Client or Server Management Licenses assigned to it. Note that although software is installed on the management server there is no requirement to purchase a license for it – the rights to install the software here are included in the Management Licenses. Likewise, SQL Server is required to support the management server, and rights to install that are also included.

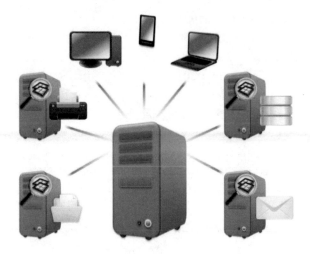

Figure 6: System Center 2016

Licensing System Center 2016 for Servers

Server Management Licenses (MLs) are assigned to server devices following the same Per Core licensing model as Windows Server 2016. As a reminder, every physical core needs to be licensed, with a minimum of eight Core licenses assigned to each processor. Thus, in Figure 6 all the servers would need to have 16 System Center 2016 Server Management Licenses assigned to them.

In common with Windows Server 2016 there are two editions of System Center 2016 – Standard and Datacenter edition – and again, from a licensing perspective, it's the virtualization rights that differ between them.

And finally, again like Windows Server 2016, System Center 2016 Server Management Licenses are sold in 2-packs or 16-packs but you should focus on the actual number of licenses required for the exam.

Licensing Virtualized Environments

The rules for licensing servers in a virtualized environment are exactly the same as for Windows Server 2016 but let's have a look at an example specifically for System Center 2016. In the diagram below, there's a physical server running four virtual machines with various workloads which we want to license so that each of the virtual machines may be managed by System Center 2016. You can see that 32 Core licenses have been assigned to the physical server and this would make the server compliant for the Datacenter edition since licensing the physical server completely allows an unlimited number of virtual machines to be managed.

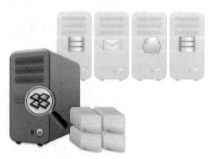

Figure 7: System Center 2016 Datacenter Virtualization Licensing

© Licensing School 2018

However, as we saw with Windows Server 2016 Standard, licensing the physical server completely with System Center 2016 Standard Server Management Licenses only allows two virtual machines to be managed. Thus, to license this scenario you would license the physical server again and thus assign 64 System Center 2016 Standard Core licenses to the server.

Core Infrastructure Server Suites

It's worth covering the Core Infrastructure Server Suites at this point. These suites are available in Standard and Datacenter editions and are a way of buying licenses for both Windows Server 2016 and System Center 2016. As you can imagine, the CIS Standard Suite includes the Standard edition of Windows Server and System Center, and CIS Datacenter includes the Datacenter edition of both products. The CIS Suites follow the same licensing rules as the individual products with the requirement to license all cores in the physical server and to assign a minimum of eight Core licenses to a processor, and with the same virtualization rules that we've already discussed.

As you might expect, buying the products together as a Suite attracts a discount when they're purchased through the Volume Licensing agreements, the largest of which is available when they are purchased with an enterprise-wide commitment through the Server and Cloud Enrollment and we'll look at the specific details for that in Part 5 of this book.

Licensing System Center 2016 for Clients

Client Management Licenses (CMLs) must be purchased for any client devices managed by System Center 2016, but these are split into different offerings rather than the single "System Center 2016" licenses that are available for the servers:

- System Center Configuration Manager 1606 CML

- System Center Endpoint Protection 1606 SL

- System Center 2016 Data Protection Manager CML

- System Center 2016 Operations Manager CML

- System Center 2016 Orchestrator CML

- System Center 2016 Service Manager CML

Many customers will acquire their Client Management Licenses through the CAL Suites, and both the Core and Enterprise CAL Suites include the first two licenses. These are the most popular System Center CMLs and the ones you should focus on for the exam.

Applying your knowledge in the exam:

- Remember that although management software and SQL Server are required and installed on the management server, there are no licensing requirements for this server since the rights to both of these products are included in the Management Licenses. Hence any licensing recommendations you make should take account of this

- Be prepared to calculate the System Center 2016 Server Management Licenses required for a server in both physical and virtual environments

- You may need to recommend the right edition of System Center 2016 – Standard or Datacenter – and remember that it's the virtualization rights that differ between the two editions. So, if the customer's environment is hinting at heavy virtualization then recommend the Datacenter edition

© Licensing School 2018

- Remember that the Core CAL Suite has the System Center Configuration Manager (SCCM) CML included in it. This is important when you're recommending licenses for an organization and you know they need to license SCCM for client machines but you can't see the CMLs called out specifically in the answer choices. Look instead for a choice with the Core CAL Suite

- If you're asked to recommend how a customer should acquire their System Center 2016 licenses, don't forget to check whether they also have a requirement for Windows Server 2016, since this would lead you to recommend acquiring licenses through the Core Infrastructure Server Suites

SQL Server 2016

SQL Server, as a quick definition, is Microsoft's enterprise database solution which shouldn't be confused with Microsoft Access which is a database solution for end users. There are several editions of SQL Server 2016 available to purchase, but only two that you need to know about for the exam: Standard and Enterprise editions. You need to be clear on how each edition is licensed and, given a sample server, what licenses you should assign to it, which may vary depending on a customer's specific needs.

There are two licensing models that are used to license the Standard and Enterprise editions of SQL Server 2016 – the Server/CAL model and the Per Core model. You can choose either model if you're deploying the Standard edition, whereas the Enterprise edition is always licensed with the Per Core model. Let's get some detail on how these licensing models work.

Server/CAL Licensing Model

In the Server/CAL licensing model a SQL Server 2016 Standard Server license is assigned to the server and then users or devices are licensed with SQL Server 2016 User or Device CALs, as shown in the diagram below:

Figure 8: SQL Server 2016 Server/CAL Licensing

© Licensing School 2018

Per Core Licensing

The second licensing model is the Per Core licensing model. You can choose to license SQL Server 2016 Standard edition with Core licenses if you wish, but for Enterprise edition it's the only option.

In this model, you count the number of cores in the physical server and assign that number of Core licenses to the server, making sure that you assign at least four Core licenses to each processor. You can see in the diagram below that there's a physical server with two 4-core processors and so eight Core licenses are assigned to the server. There's no need for separate CALs for users accessing the server, the Core licenses are all that is required.

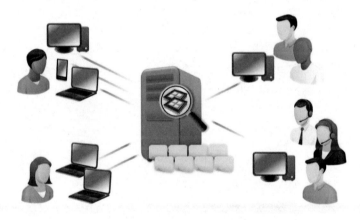

Figure 9: SQL Server 2016 Core Licensing

SQL Server 2016 Core licenses are purchased in 2-packs but again you should focus on the actual number of licenses needed rather than the number of 2-packs you would buy when you're answering questions in the exam.

External Users

There are no External Connector licenses available for SQL Server 2016. If a customer has chosen to license with the Server/CAL model, then they must buy CALs for external users and this does become expensive when there are many external users. It is generally more cost-effective to choose to license with the Per Core model if there is a large number of external users, since this will cover all internal users and any number of external users.

Licensing Virtualized Environments

In this section we'll look at how the different editions of SQL Server 2016 are licensed in a virtual infrastructure. There are different rules dependent on the edition of SQL Server 2016 – you either license at the individual virtual machine level and calculate the number of licenses required, or assign licenses to the physical server and receive rights to run a specific number of SQL Server virtual machines on that server.

Let's start with the simplest set of rules – when SQL Server 2016 is licensed with the Server/CAL model.

Virtualization Licensing: Server/CAL (Individual Virtual Machines)
If SQL Server 2016 Standard is licensed with the Server/CAL model, then you follow the same rules as you would for licensing separate physical servers. Look at the diagram below: it shows a physical server and then four virtual machines, two of which are running SQL Server 2016 (depicted by the database icon). Looking at the physical server you can see that two Server licenses have been assigned to it.

Figure 10: Virtualization Licensing – SQL Server 2016 Server Licenses

So, what's the rule here? You simply count the number of virtual machines running SQL Server and buy that number of SQL Server licenses. Those licenses are assigned to the physical server and you get rights to run a virtual machine with SQL Server for each license. If you want to run more virtual machines with SQL Server, then you would simply assign more licenses to the physical server.

© Licensing School 2018

Virtualization Licensing: Per Core (Individual Virtual Machines)

Let's take a similar example to the one above to see how the Per Core licensing model works in a virtual environment. The diagram below is again a physical server with four virtual machines, two of which are running SQL Server 2016. You can see that we need some extra information in this example, and this is the number of virtual cores that are assigned to each virtual machine. You may call these "virtual processors" rather than virtual cores, and that's probably the language that you'd use if you were setting them up technically, but I think it's easier to call them virtual cores as we have a Per Core licensing model. So, you can see that there are two virtual cores assigned to each virtual machine and the licensing rules are that you need to assign Core licenses to the virtual machines based on the number of virtual cores, with a minimum of four Core licenses per virtual machine. Again, the licenses are assigned to the physical server and you can see that there are eight Core licenses assigned to the physical server.

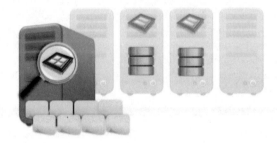

Figure 11: Virtualization Licensing – SQL Server 2016 Core Licenses

Virtualization Licensing: Per Core (Rights per Server)
With SQL Server 2016 Enterprise edition there is additional flexibility in licensing a virtualized environment. If you license the physical server completely then you can run SQL Server 2016 in a virtual machine for each Core license that you have assigned to the server. Consider the diagram below where you see a server with two 4-core processors. To license that server completely you need to assign eight Core licenses to the physical server and then you can run SQL Server in eight virtual machines, as shown:

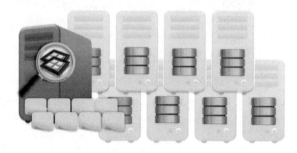

Figure 12: Virtualization Licensing – SQL Server 2016 Enterprise Core Licenses

If you need to run further virtual machines, you can simply add further Core licenses to the physical server to increase the number of virtual machines that you're allowed to run, at a rate of one per license.

Virtualization Licensing: Per Core (Unlimited Virtualization)
And the final part of virtualization licensing to consider is that of licensing for unlimited virtualization. This is only available for the Enterprise edition and is actually a Software Assurance benefit, but I think it makes sense to include it here. The rules are simple: if you license a physical server with Enterprise Core licenses with Software Assurance then you can run an unlimited number of virtual machines with SQL Server on that server.

© Licensing School 2018

The server below has, again, two 4-core processors and so eight Core licenses with SA need to be assigned to the server. You can see ten virtual machines running SQL Server, but an unlimited number would be allowed:

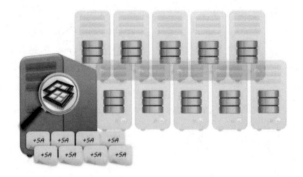

Figure 13: Unlimited Virtualization – SQL Server 2016 Enterprise Core Licenses

Applying your knowledge in the exam:

- Look out for business goals that specify that an organization wants to allow a large or unknown number of people to access their SQL Server; this is a clear steer to make a recommendation of Core licensing for SQL Server, whereas a small deployment for an organization wanting to keep costs as low as possible is likely to be a recommendation for the Server/CAL model

- Look out for business goals that state that an organization wants to give access to their SQL Server to external users – there is no additional External Connector license for SQL Server, and Core licenses are (certainly for the exam!) the best way to license these external users

- You are likely to be given a virtualized environment to specify the licenses for and this is likely to include the more complex Core licenses. So, make sure that you know how Standard edition works (based on virtual cores in individual VMs), Enterprise edition (1 VM per Core license), and how a customer gets unlimited virtualization rights (Enterprise Core licenses with SA)

Project Server 2016

Project Server 2016 is a project management server solution that allows project managers, key stakeholders, and other team members to collaborate on a project. The project plans themselves are created in Project Professional 2016 by a project manager and then saved to the Project Server. It's quite likely that no one else on the project will then use Project Professional, they'll just use a web browser to connect to the server to either see what tasks they've been assigned (as a team member) or to see whether the project is progressing to time and budget (as a key stakeholder).

Licensing Project Server 2016

Project Server 2016 is licensed with the Server/CAL licensing model. As we saw with SQL Server 2016, in this model there's a Project Server 2016 license assigned to the server and then users or devices are licensed with Project Server 2016 User or Device CALs, as shown in the diagram below. All users, whether they are accessing Project Server 2016 from a browser or Project Professional, must be licensed with a CAL.

Figure 14: Project Server 2016 Licensing

There's a special exception for customers who purchase Project Professional 2016 – they are deemed to have one Project Server 2016 Device CAL, so do bear that in mind when you are making licensing recommendations.

© Licensing School 2018

Licensing Virtualized Environments

The rules here are exactly the same as we saw with SQL Server when it's licensed with the Server/CAL model: a Project Server license is assigned to a physical server and this allows the software to be run in a single virtual machine. Extra licenses can be assigned to a physical server to allow Project Server to run in multiple virtual machines.

Licensing External Users

There is no External Connector license available for Project Server 2016, so an organization must buy Project Server CALs for its external users to access the services of their Project Servers.

Required Infrastructure Products

There are three products that are required pieces of the technology infrastructure for Project Server: SQL Server, SharePoint Server and, of course, Windows Server. Therefore, any licensing recommendations you make for Project Server should also include licenses for these products. From a SQL Server perspective, this can be covered with either Core licenses or Server licenses and CALs, and for SharePoint, the Server licenses and both Standard and Enterprise CALs are required.

Note that if external users are being licensed they need to be licensed for these products too, with the Windows Server element likely to be covered by an External Connector license.

Applying your knowledge in the exam:

- Remember to include CALs in your licensing recommendations for users who access Project Server 2016 through their browsers

- Many products now license external users via the Server license but Project is not one so make sure that you include Project Server CALs in any licensing recommendations for external users

- Learn the required infrastructure products for Project Server 2016 and make sure you include them in your licensing recommendations

Exchange Server 2016

Exchange Server 2016 is the Microsoft email server. Users can access their email, as well as calendar and contact information from Outlook, from Outlook on the Web, or from a mobile device through a variety of apps.

Licensing Exchange Server 2016

Exchange Server 2016 is licensed with the Server/CAL model but rather than there just being one level of CAL, there are two CALs available for organizations to purchase. These CALs allow access to different levels of functionality, which means that customers can be licensed for whatever functionality their users need to use.

The two CALs are Standard and Enterprise CALs. The Standard CALs are often known as Base CALs and the Enterprise CALs as Additive CALs. An Additive CAL may only ever be purchased in addition to a Base CAL, never solely alone. This means that customers must purchase Standard CALs for all users accessing an Exchange Server and then, additionally, Enterprise CALs for those users who need access to the higher-level functionality.

The diagram below shows some users licensed with just Standard CALs, and others licensed with both Standard and Enterprise CALs. The Standard CAL and the corresponding server functionality is shown in the darker color, and the Enterprise CAL and corresponding functionality is shown in the lighter color:

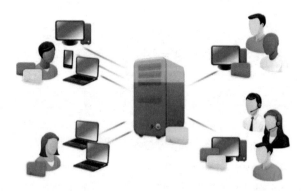

Figure 15: Exchange Server 2016 Licensing

© Licensing School 2018

Exchange 2016 Standard and Enterprise CALs are available as either User or Device CALs.

For the exam, you need to be able to recommend the right level of CAL for a particular customer so it's worth learning the key functionality that is licensed by the Standard and Enterprise CALs as detailed in the next couple of paragraphs.

Exchange Standard CALs allow users to access the basic functionality of Exchange and this includes accessing their email, calendar, contacts and tasks from a variety of clients including Outlook, Outlook on the Web, or an app on a mobile device. Note that if users are accessing Exchange from a free app they do still need to license the access with a CAL. As you would expect, if users have several devices that they access the Exchange Server from, then User CALs are a good recommendation.

An Enterprise CAL adds on access to some more sophisticated features, and the most well known is perhaps Unified Messaging which allows users to receive both emails and voicemails into their Inboxes.

In addition, the Enterprise CAL is available "with Services". You should assume for the purposes of the exam that the Enterprise CAL includes these services which licenses users for the following:

- **Data Loss Prevention (DLP):** enforces compliance requirements for sensitive data so that important data can't be emailed, or it's checked against a template before emailing, for example

- **Exchange Online Protection:** provides anti-malware and anti-spam services

Exchange Server 2016 Server Editions

Exchange Server 2016 is available in Standard and Enterprise editions. The Standard edition is the base level edition with the Enterprise edition offering a greater level of scalability.

Note that the edition of the Server license is a completely separate purchasing decision for the customer from the CALs. They do NOT need Enterprise CALs with an Enterprise Server license for example! When you're making a recommendation in the exam, consider the scalability needs first and decide on the server edition, then consider the functionality required by the users and decide on the CALs required.

Licensing Virtualized Environments

As with Project Server 2016, an Exchange Server 2016 license is assigned to a physical server and can be used to license Exchange Server 2016 running in a single virtual machine.

Licensing External Users

The Server license itself covers an unlimited number of external users for access to the basic functionality of the server. If external users require access to the advanced functionality of the server then they must be licensed with Standard and Enterprise CALs.

Applying your knowledge in the exam:

- Be ready to recommend Server and CAL editions confidently. You may be asked to recommend licenses for a large company utilizing a fundamental set of technology, for which you'd need to choose the Enterprise Server (for the scalability) and Standard CALs (for the functionality)

- Remember, there is no situation where the Additive CALs can be purchased without a Base CAL. However tempting a particular answer looks, always make sure that your recommendation includes the Standard CALs

© Licensing School 2018

- Look out for a business need for Unified Messaging since this drives a requirement for Exchange Standard and Enterprise CALs,

- Also look out for business goals that relate to Data Loss Prevention or a specific need for anti-malware as this will also lead you to recommend the Enterprise CAL

- Make sure that you're confident with the rules for licensing Exchange 2016 in a virtualized environment so that you can calculate the licenses required for a given scenario

- Remember that there is no External Connector for Exchange 2016, the Server license covers external users for basic access. If the external users need access to advanced functionality, then recommend Standard and Enterprise CALs, and in either case don't forget to include a Windows Server External Connector in your recommendations

- Don't be misled by information about the existing infrastructure of a customer that states that users are using a free app to access the services of the Exchange Server – they will still need CALs

- Look out for information that would steer you to recommend either User or Device CALs and don't forget that it's OK to mix them across an organization

SharePoint Server 2016

SharePoint Server 2016 is a content management, workflow automation, and collaboration portal, which also allows a single infrastructure for Internet, intranet and extranet sites. Users typically connect to the SharePoint sites or portals through a web browser.

Licensing SharePoint Server 2016

SharePoint Server 2016 is licensed with the Server/CAL model and, as with Exchange Server 2016, there are Standard and Enterprise CALs available to license access to different functionality.

SharePoint Standard CALs allow access to a base level of functionality across the SharePoint workloads. Key features that are enabled when users have Enterprise CALs are the full set of Search functionality and the Business Intelligence (BI) functionality, and these are key words to look for when you're deciding which CALs to recommend.

Licensing Virtualized Environments

In common with the other products that we've looked at licensed with a Server/CAL model, a SharePoint 2016 Server license is assigned to a physical server and this allows SharePoint to run in a single virtual machine.

Licensing External Users

As with Exchange Server 2016, the Server license covers any number of external users for any level of access. However, there's another nuance with SharePoint Server licensing that you need to know about – how intranet, extranet, and Internet scenarios are licensed.

In an **intranet** scenario, a Server license is assigned to the server and all internal users (or devices) are licensed with CALs. There are no licensing requirements for the external users since they do not have access to the SharePoint content.

In an **extranet** scenario, a Server license is again assigned to the server and all internal users (or devices) are licensed with CALs. This time external

© Licensing School 2018

users do have access, but there are again no licensing requirements because access to the server is covered by the Server license.

In an **Internet** scenario, a Server license is, as usual, assigned to the server, and in this scenario there are no additional licensing requirements for either the internal or the external users. This relaxing of the licensing requirements is allowed since external users have access to all of the content on the SharePoint server.

Required Infrastructure Products
SQL Server is a required infrastructure product for SharePoint Server, and so any licensing recommendations you make for SharePoint Server should also include licenses for SQL Server which can be covered with either Core licenses or Server licenses and CALs.

Applying your knowledge in the exam:

- Remember, as with Exchange Server 2016, that customers can never have Enterprise CALs without Standard CALs, and may mix Device and User CALs as required

- Look out for business goals for a content management, workflow automation, or collaboration solution which will lead you to recommend SharePoint as a product

- Learn the licenses required for Internet, intranet and extranet scenarios so that you can confidently recommend the right solution

- Business goals for advanced Search capabilities or a Business Intelligence solution will lead you to recommend the Enterprise CALs

- If you're asked to make a licensing recommendation for the whole technology stack make sure you include SQL Server

Skype for Business Server 2015

Skype for Business Server 2015 is the server solution for instant messaging, presence information, web conferencing, and enterprise telephony. There are a variety of clients that users can use to access the services of Skype for Business Server 2015, but for the purposes of the exam you should assume that they are using the full Skype for Business 2016 client, most commonly acquired as part of Office Professional Plus 2016.

Licensing Skype for Business Server 2015

Skype for Business Server 2015 actually has three CALs available for customers to purchase. There's the Base CAL which is the Standard CAL, and then two Additive CALs called the Enterprise and Plus CALs. All Skype for Business Server users need to be licensed with the Standard CAL and then the organization can choose to purchase them Enterprise and/or Plus CALs dependent on what functionality those users need to use.

The diagram below shows users licensed with a variety of CALs dependent on what they will be doing with Skype for Business Server, with the Standard CAL and corresponding server functionality shown in the darkest color, the Plus CAL and functionality shown in the lightest color, and the Enterprise CAL and functionality in the color in between.

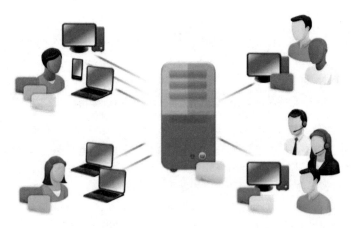

Figure 16: Skype for Business Server 2015 Licensing

© Licensing School 2018

Organizations purchase Skype for Business Standard CALs when they want to license their users for the instant messaging and integrated presence functionality of Skype for Business Server. If they want their users to be able to set up web conferences they optionally purchase the Skype for Business Enterprise CAL. And finally, the Plus CAL licenses users for enterprise telephony functionality.

Licensing Virtualized Environments
Again, a single Skype for Business Server 2015 license is assigned to a physical server and Skype for Business is then licensed to run in a single virtual machine.

External Users
The Skype for Business Server 2015 license is assigned to a physical server and an unlimited number of external users can access the services of the server.

Required Infrastructure Products
SQL Server is a required infrastructure product for Skype for Business Server 2015, and so any licensing recommendations you make for Skype for Business Server should also include licenses for SQL Server which can be covered with either Core licenses or Server licenses and CALs.

Applying your knowledge in the exam:

- Remember that there are three CALs, but the Enterprise and Plus CALs are both additive to the Standard CAL. If a customer wants enterprise telephony to manage phone calls you can recommend the Standard CAL and the Plus CAL – they don't need the Enterprise CAL as well

- Make sure that you're familiar with the product descriptions for all of the productivity servers (Project, Exchange, SharePoint, Skype for Business) so that you can pick out the right product against a set of business goals and requirements. Be particularly careful with business goals that state that there is a need to collaborate – is it on a document (choose SharePoint) or is it real-time person-to-person collaboration (choose Skype for Business)?

- Learn the points outlined above regarding what the different CALs give access to; you may be asked, for example, what an organization would need to purchase if they wanted all their users to have access to setting up web conferences. You need to feel confident that this is Skype for Business as a product, and that this particular functionality is licensed with the Standard and Enterprise CALs

- Finally, remember to include SQL Server in your licensing recommendations if you are asked to detail licenses for the whole technology stack

© Licensing School 2018

Dynamics 365

Dynamics 365 as a brand was launched by Microsoft in November 2016 representing a single Online Service which replaced the separate CRM Online and AX Online solutions. Later, the on-premises versions of these products (CRM Server 2016 and AX Server 2012 R3) were also rebranded as Dynamics 365 products.

For the exam you need to focus mainly on the Online Services solutions, but you do need to have a fundamental understanding of the on-premises licensing so that you can make recommendations in hybrid environments. There are Enterprise and (some) Business versions of the Dynamics 365 products but for the exam you just need to be familiar with the solutions that a larger organization would use, which are the Enterprise ones.

Let's start by being clear about what's offered by Dynamics 365 as a whole. Essentially, it's CRM or ERP functionality, available as either an on-premises or an online solution. You don't need to be any kind of an expert on CRM and ERP but you do need to know what sort of users would be licensed for each product, so an overview knowledge is useful.

Let's start with CRM, standing for Customer Relationship Management, a flavor of which is given by the diagram below.

Figure 17: Customer Relationship Management

Customer Relationship Management is about managing all aspects of relationships with customers; for example, it's knowing what they're interested in and when you last spoke to them and what about, it's tracking your sales pipeline and having a way of following up on opportunities, it's managing queries and problems via service requests, it's running targeted marketing campaigns to the right customers at the right time, and it's about tracking sentiment via social media – what are your customers saying about you or your services at any time? You can imagine that in a larger organization, different people will be doing front line sales roles from those who are running the marketing campaigns, and they will need software functionality relevant to their jobs. From an organizational point of view, we want the different people to have what they need, but we want everything to be integrated too so that we can get a holistic view about what's happening across our customers. And, as you might expect, this is what CRM functionality in Dynamics 365 delivers.

And ERP is Enterprise Resource Planning, again a flavor of which is given by the diagram below.

Figure 18: Enterprise Resource Planning

© Licensing School 2018

Enterprise Resource Planning is all about managing processes and departments within and across an organization itself, whether it's the finance department, HR, supply chain and logistics operations, or a retail function. Again, individuals working in these functional areas need software relevant to their role, but the software used by these people needs to be part of an integrated solution so that information can flow between different parts of the business and insights can be gathered across the organization.

We said earlier that these CRM and ERP solutions are available either on-premises or online so let's use the diagram below to see how they all fit together.

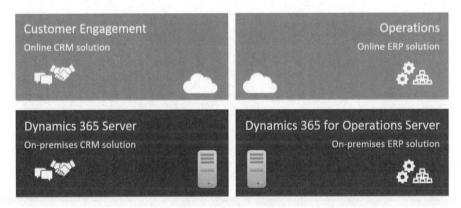

Figure 19: Dynamics 365

So, looking at the bottom of this diagram, at the on-premises part, we can see that the CRM solution is called Dynamics 365 Server, and the ERP solution is called Dynamics 365 for Operations Server. Let's look at how these two products are licensed.

Licensing Dynamics 365 Server

Dynamics 365 Server is licensed with the familiar Server/CAL model – with one difference you may perhaps spot in the diagram below.

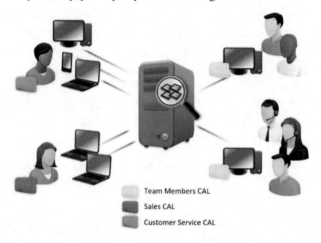

Figure 20: Dynamics 365 Server Licensing

And the difference? Although this product is officially licensed with a Server/CAL model there is no Server license available to purchase; the rights to install the server product are included when you buy one of the three CALs shown. You need to be able to choose the right CAL for a particular user in the exam so let's look at the CALs in a bit more detail now.

The Sales and Customer Service CALs are aimed at professionals who work in those fields. So, if you're a Customer Service agent and your organization has invested in Dynamics 365 Server then it's likely you'll be licensed with a Customer Service CAL. If you have more of a supporting role – you could be asked to look something up for a Sales person for example, then the (much cheaper) Team Members CAL is likely to be an appropriate license. The Team Members CAL licenses a user for light access to both Sales and Customer Service functionality.

 © Licensing School 2018

Dynamics 365 for Operations Server

Dynamics 365 for Operations Server is also licensed with the Server/CAL model, and this time it's exactly as you would expect with Server and CAL licenses as shown in the diagram below.

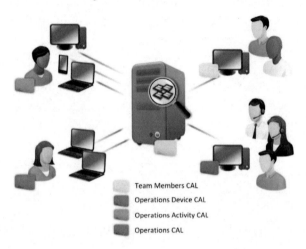

Team Members CAL
Operations Device CAL
Operations Activity CAL
Operations CAL

Figure 21: Dynamics 365 for Operations Server Licensing

Again, you need to be able to recommend the right license for a particular user in the exam. Let's start with the Team Members CAL since this is exactly the same sort of user as with Dynamics 365 Server – someone in a support role who needs light access to all functionality across the solution. The full Operations CAL is for someone whose main role is in the finance and operations part of a business, and the Activity CAL is (at a simple level) for the user who needs to do more than would be allowed via a Team Members CAL but doesn't need a full Operations CAL. And, finally, the Device CAL is primarily for licensing devices in a retail environment where several people will use the same device where it's being used as a point of sale device, shop floor device, warehouse device or store manager device.

Applying your knowledge in the exam:

- You need to be confident with the (slightly confusing) names of the products so that if you get a question about Dynamics 365 CRM functionality then you know it's the licensing of Dynamics 365 Server, and if it's Dynamics 365 ERP functionality then it's all about Dynamics 365 for Operations Server

- Remember that there is no Server license for Dynamics 365 Server, and make sure that you are happy recommending the rights CALs for users based on their roles. Words like "specialist" or "professional" will guide you to recommend a Sales or Customer Service CAL, and for support staff or those who need light access to the functionality you'd choose a Team Members CAL

- Likewise, for Dynamics 365 for Operations Server, make sure you can recommend the right CAL for given users. Look for similar words as described above for the Operations and Team Members CALs, and watch out for retail devices guiding you to a recommendation for the Operations Device CAL

© Licensing School 2018

The CAL Suites

Many customers buy one of two suites of CALs for convenience and cost-effectiveness. These suites are the Core CAL Suite and the Enterprise CAL Suite and it's worth being confident with the components of these suites for the exam. The components of the Core and Enterprise CAL Suites do change and what is listed below are the components that were part of the CAL Suites when the exam was created. CAL Suites can be purchased for Users or Devices.

	Core Infrastructure	Productivity Servers
Core CAL Suite	• Windows Server 2016 CAL • System Center Configuration Manager 1606 Client Management License (CML) • System Center Endpoint Protection 1606 Subscription License (SL)	• Exchange Server 2016 Standard CAL • SharePoint Server 2016 Standard CAL • Skype for Business Server 2015 Standard CAL
Enterprise CAL Suite	• Windows Server 2016 Active Directory Rights Management Services CAL • Advanced Threat Analytics 2016 CML	• Exchange Server 2016 Enterprise CAL with Services • SharePoint Server 2016 Enterprise CAL • Skype for Business Server 2015 Enterprise CAL • Exchange Online Archiving for Exchange Server SL

Figure 22: The Core and Enterprise CAL Suites

There are a couple of components in the table above that we haven't covered yet: the Advanced Threat Analytics 2016 CML, and the Exchange Online Archiving for Exchange Server SL.

Advanced Threat Analytics is security technology which uses machine learning to learn what's normal behavior for users and devices so that it can identify suspicious behavior which may indicate a malicious attack.

Exchange Online Archiving for Exchange Server is (as its name indeed suggests!) an online archive for an on-premises deployment of Exchange Server and offers two key benefits:

- **In-place archive:** allows users to store messages in an archive mailbox rather than a personal store (pst) file

- **In-place hold:** preserves all mailbox content, including deleted items and original versions of modified items, a feature important in the event of litigation

Applying your knowledge in the exam:

- As well as knowing the components that ARE in the suites, it's worth noting a couple that are omitted. In particular, be aware that a SQL CAL, a Remote Desktop Services (RDS) CAL and the Skype for Business Plus CAL would all be additional purchases outside of the suites for organizations that need the functionality licensed by these CALs

- If one of the fictional organizations needs to make use of the basic functionality in the productivity servers (Exchange, SharePoint and Skype for Business) then they will need the Standard CALs which are all in the Core CAL Suite. As soon as advanced functionality is mentioned you will need to recommend Enterprise CALs and thus the Enterprise CAL Suite

- Look carefully at the organization's requirements for CALs; typically you should be recommending the Core CAL Suite, rather than purchasing individual CALs, if the customer has a requirement for three or more of the components

© Licensing School 2018

Windows 10

Windows 10 is the Microsoft client operating system. This section of the book covers the general licensing of this product.

The Editions

Windows 10 is available in four editions for businesses:

- **Windows 10 Pro**
  Consider this the entry level product for businesses

- **Windows 10 Enterprise LTSB**
  Adds features such as DirectAccess (enabling users to work remotely without needing a VPN connection) and App-V (for application virtualization)

- **Windows 10 Enterprise E3**
  Adds extra rights such as Virtual Desktop Access (for VDI desktops) and additional MDOP tools (such as MED-V for enterprise desktop virtualization)

- **Windows 10 Enterprise E5**
  Adds Windows Defender Advanced Threat Protection (a security service that helps organizations detect, investigate, and respond to advanced attacks on their networks)

Licensing Model

Historically, Windows has always been a device licensing model, but now user licenses are also available for some editions. Note in the table below that some of the licenses are only available as Subscription Licenses, which means that the software may only be used while the subscription is active.

	Device	User
Windows 10 Pro	License	
Windows 10 Enterprise LTSB	License	
Windows 10 Enterprise E3	License	Subscription License
Windows 10 Enterprise E5	Subscription License	Subscription License

Figure 23: Windows 10 Licenses

Device licenses are assigned to a device and the software is licensed to be used on that device by any user. Licenses acquired through a Volume Licensing must be assigned to a device that is already licensed with a qualifying operating system. This qualifying operating system must be a business operating system, and although there are some exceptions, focus on the following ones for the exam: Windows 10 Pro or Enterprise, Windows 8.1 Pro or Enterprise, or Windows 7 Professional or Enterprise.

User licenses are (naturally) assigned to a user. However, there are some device requirements: the user must be the primary user of a device licensed with one of the operating systems above, and this device must also be the user's primary work device. The licensed user may then also install Windows 10 Enterprise E3/E5 on other devices that are licensed with one of these qualifying operating systems.

© Licensing School 2018

Additional Licenses

Now that there is quite a variety of Windows 10 licensing options you can imagine that an organization may want to move from a Windows 10 Enterprise E3 license to an E5 one, or from a device license to a user one. The diagram below shows the options that are available to change editions and licensing models. All of these licenses are Subscription Licenses and must be assigned to users or devices already licensed with Windows 10 Enterprise E3.

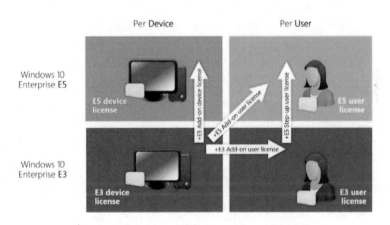

Figure 24: Windows 10 Add-on and Step-up Licenses

Software Assurance

There's a whole section on Software Assurance in this book and at this point all I want to say is that SA is included in some Windows licenses and enables an organization to gain access to an additional set of use rights. All of the Windows 10 Enterprise E3/E5 licenses acquired through a Volume Licensing agreement include Software Assurance.

Windows 10 Servicing Channels

The Windows 10 Servicing Channels control how often feature updates are available for Windows 10 devices. There are two channels:

- **Semi-Annual Channel**

  This channel makes feature update releases available twice a year in March and September, and each update is supported for 18 months. This channel is aimed at the typical end-user PC

- **Long-Term Servicing Channel**

  These are less frequent releases, probably every 2-3 years with the next one expected in 2019, and they are supported for 10 years. This channel is designed for special-purpose PCs such as those used in point-of-sale systems or controlling factory or medical equipment where it's not possible or desirable to have features updated regularly

Windows 10 Pro is always on the Semi-Annual Channel and Windows 10 Enterprise LTSB is always on the Long-Term Servicing Channel. Customers who buy Windows 10 Enterprise E3 or E5 User or Device licenses through a Volume Licensing agreement can choose their preferred channel for their deployments of Windows 10 Enterprise E3/E5.

License Reassignment Rights

Typically there are restrictions on how often a device license may be moved between different devices; Windows 10 Pro licenses acquired through either the OEM channel or through Volume Licensing agreements may not be moved, and the same is true for Windows 10 Enterprise LSTB licenses purchased through a Volume Licensing agreement.

Windows 10 Enterprise E3 and E5 User and Device licenses may be assigned to another user or device as long as changes are made no more frequently than every 90 days.

© Licensing School 2018

Downgrade and Down Edition Rights

One of the benefits of acquiring licenses through a Volume Licensing agreement is the availability of downgrade rights. However, OEM licenses do give some downgrade rights as the table below shows, and typically, this right is to the last two versions of the product.

The different flavors of Windows 10 Enterprise also give down edition rights – not only can you install an earlier version of the same edition (Windows 7 Enterprise, for example) but you can also install different editions – Windows 8.1 Pro or Windows Vista Business, for example.

	Windows 10 Pro (OEM)	Windows 10 Pro (VL)	Windows 10 Enterprise LTSB/E3/E5 (VL)
Windows 8/8.1 Enterprise			✔
Windows 8.1 Pro	✔	✔	✔
Windows 7 Enterprise			✔
Windows 7 Professional	✔	✔	✔
Windows Vista Enterprise			✔
Windows Vista Business		✔	✔
Windows XP Professional		✔	✔
Windows 2000 Professional		✔	✔
Windows 95/98/NT		✔	✔

Figure 25: Windows 10 Downgrade and Down Edition Rights

Availability

In Part 5 of this book we'll talk in detail about the different ways that customers can acquire licenses and so if you're not familiar with the MPSA, EA and CSP programs then all will become clear then! As a summary, all of the Windows 10 licenses we've talked about are available through the MPSA, those with Software Assurance included are available in the EA, and only some of the User licenses are available through CSP.

		MPSA	EA	CSP
Device	Windows 10 Pro Device license	✔		
	Windows 10 Enterprise LTSB Device license	✔		
	Windows 10 Enterprise E3 Device license	✔	✔	
	Windows 10 Enterprise E5 Device SL	✔	✔	
User	Windows 10 Enterprise E3 User SL	✔	✔	✔
	Windows 10 Enterprise E5 User SL	✔	✔	✔
Additional	Windows 10 Enterprise E3 Add-on User SL	✔	✔	
	Windows 10 Enterprise E5 Add-on Device SL	✔	✔	
	Windows 10 Enterprise E5 Add-on User SL	✔	✔	
	Windows 10 Enterprise E5 Step-Up User SL	✔	✔	

Figure 26: Availability of Windows 10 Licenses

© Licensing School 2018

Applying your knowledge in the exam:

- Look for business goals that state that the organization needs a high level of functionality in their client operating system since this would drive a requirement for one of the Enterprise editions of Windows 10. Make sure that you learn the key difference between Windows 10 Enterprise E3 and E5: Windows Defender Advanced Threat Protection

- If you are asked to recommend the number of licenses required for a Windows 10 deployment where you're given the number of users and devices, remember that Windows can be licensed by user or device now, so choose a variety of licenses appropriate to the scenario

- Remember that Windows 10 licenses acquired through Volume Licensing agreements require an underlying qualifying operating system license. These are the ones to remember for the exam: Windows 10 Pro or Enterprise, Windows 8.1 Pro or Enterprise, or Windows 7 Professional or Enterprise

- Make sure you're familiar with the options that exist for moving to a different edition or licensing model with the Windows 10 Enterprise E3/E5 Add-on and Step-up licenses

- If you identify that a customer has a need for Software Assurance on their Windows licenses then you need to recommend Windows 10 Enterprise E3 or E5 licenses acquired through a Volume Licensing agreement

- If you're asked to recommend a servicing channel for a Windows 10 Enterprise deployment your first thought should be to choose the Semi-Annual Channel unless there are strong hints about special-purpose PCs

- Learn the availability of the different licenses in Figure 26 so that you can make a recommendation as to how a customer should acquire their Windows licenses. In particular note that there are only User licenses available in CSP and they don't include Software Assurance

Office 2016

Office 2016 is the Microsoft suite of desktop productivity tools and is a cost-effective way for organizations to license all of these products.

The Office Products

The Office suite products are the following products:

- **Word 2016:** a word-processing tool
- **Excel 2016:** a spreadsheet tool
- **PowerPoint 2016:** a graphics and presentation tool
- **Outlook 2016:** the email client with calendar, tasks and contacts functionality
- **OneNote 2016:** a note-taking and information gathering application
- **Publisher 2016:** a desktop publishing tool
- **Access 2016:** the end user database solution
- **Skype for Business 2016:** the client application for the Skype for Business Server product

In addition, there are two Office-branded products that are also available as separate purchases:

- **Visio 2016:** an Office family product for creating sophisticated diagrams
- **Project 2016:** an Office family product for creating project plans

Licensing Model

Office 2016 is licensed by device: a license is assigned to a device and the software is licensed to be used on that device.

© Licensing School 2018

The Editions and Availability

Office 2016 is available in a number of different editions, and the availability of these differs by the channel that Office is purchased through. For instance, there are two business editions of Office available through the Volume Licensing agreements – Standard and Professional Plus, and just one edition – Professional, that is available to be pre-installed on a new device via the OEM channel.

The diagram below shows which products are in which editions. For many years, the difference between Office Standard and Office Professional has been Access, and this is still the case. Office Professional Plus 2016 then has the Skype for Business client in addition.

	Office Standard 2016	Office Professional 2016	Office Professional Plus 2016
Word 2016	✔	✔	✔
Excel 2016	✔	✔	✔
PowerPoint 2016	✔	✔	✔
Outlook 2016	✔	✔	✔
OneNote 2016	✔	✔	✔
Publisher 2016	✔	✔	✔
Access 2016		✔	✔
Skype for Business 2016			✔

Figure 27: Editions of Office 2016

License Types

Office licenses are a special type of license called a Suite license. This means that a license is assigned to a device and then all of the Office products must be installed on that single device rather than being split across a number of devices.

Software Assurance

Software Assurance may be added to Office 2016 licenses acquired through a Volume Licensing agreement or OEM. If the licenses have been acquired through a Volume Licensing agreement then it must be added at the time of purchase, and if Office has been purchased pre-installed then it must be added within 90 days of the purchase of the device. Note that Software Assurance can only be purchased through a Volume Licensing agreement so an organization would need to have an active agreement to make SA purchases through.

There's one other quirk that you need to know about SA. When you add SA to an OEM Office Professional 2016 license you actually add Office Standard 2016 SA within the Volume Licensing agreement.

License Reassignment Rights

Office licenses that are purchased through the OEM channel may never be reassigned to another device – they live and die on the machine with which they were purchased. Office licenses acquired through the Volume Licensing agreements may be assigned to another device – as long as it is no more frequently than every 90 days.

Downgrade and Down Edition Rights

Downgrade rights for Office are only available if licenses are purchased through the Volume Licensing channel. So if a customer buys a license for Office Professional Plus 2016 then they can install Office Professional Plus 2013 if that suits their business needs better. Note however that there are NO down edition rights for Office, even when it's purchased through Volume Licensing. This means that a license for Office Professional Plus 2016 does NOT permit you to install Office Standard 2016 in its place.

© Licensing School 2018

Portable Use Rights

When Office is acquired through some Volume Licensing agreements then portable use rights for Office are available; if a customer has purchased an Office license for a device, then he is also allowed to install Office on a second portable device for the exclusive use of the main user of the originally licensed device. Note that this is not a way to reduce the licenses required in all situations; customers wouldn't be compliant, for example, if they used portable use rights to license the use of Office on a portable device for a second user. Note also that where there is a requirement within a Volume Licensing agreement to license all devices in an organization, these rights are not available.

Server Usage Rights

Another right that is granted when an Office license is acquired through a Volume Licensing agreement is the right to install Office on a server and use it from there. This means that in RDS and VDI scenarios (see the following sections for more details) an Office license is assigned to each device that will access Office, but the right to install Office on the server and access it there is included in the license rights. This right is not part of an Office OEM license.

Office 365 ProPlus

Although Office 365 ProPlus is covered in detail in Part 3 of this book, it needs a quick mention here before we tackle the Virtual Desktop Infrastructure section. Office 365 ProPlus contains the same products as Office Professional Plus 2016 but it's licensed with a User Subscription License rather than a device license. It has some different rights to an Office Professional Plus license – no downgrade rights for example, but some similar rights too, and one of those is being able to install and use the software on a server as described above.

Applying your knowledge in the exam:

- Remember that Office Professional Plus 2016 is licensed by device, so when you're asked to recommend the required number of licenses in a particular situation, it's the number of devices that the products will be used on that is important, not the number of users using them

- Although Office licenses purchased through a Volume Licensing agreement can be reassigned to a different device, don't forget the 90-day rule

- Make sure that you're familiar with the products in the key Office editions mentioned above; you could be given a scenario with a list of products that are required and you need to be able to recommend the correct edition of Office to meet these business goals

- Equally, make sure you know which editions are available through which channel – if you're asked to recommend how customers should acquire some Office Professional Plus 2016 licenses there is no choice – it's just through the Volume Licensing agreements

- Don't forget that Visio and Project, although Office branded, are not part of the Office suites themselves, so a customer licensed for Office Professional Plus 2016 would need to make additional license purchases if they wanted to use either of these products

- Remember that the Office components can't be split between machines, so when you're asked to count up the number of licenses required, make sure that you take this into account

- On the same note, remember that portable use rights can't be allocated to more than one user. So if the scenario you're given details that five people use a desktop machine and another five people use portable devices, you would need to recommend ten licenses since there are ten different individuals using Office on the ten devices

© Licensing School 2018

- If a customer scenario involves running Office from a server in either an RDS or VDI environment, don't forget that this right is only part of a Volume Licensing license

- Remember that there are no down edition rights through any channel, so if a customer wants to deploy Office Standard 2016 then those are the licenses that they need to acquire

- If the customer scenario involves attaching SA to an Office license, remember that it must be done at point of purchase if it's a Volume Licensing license whereas a customer has 90 days to attach it to an OEM license where Office Standard 2016 SA may be attached to Office Professional 2016

Virtual Desktop Infrastructure

So far, we've covered the licensing of Windows and Office in a physical infrastructure – in other words, the products were installed directly onto client devices. As an alternative, an organization may want to set up virtual desktops on their servers and to have their users access them from their desktop machines – a setup known as a Virtual Desktop Infrastructure (VDI).

The diagram below shows a server at Spring Green Grocers' head office running personalized Windows 10 Enterprise E3 and Office Professional Plus 2016 desktops that are being delivered to the end user desktop machines:

Figure 28: Virtual Desktop Infrastructure

Although the desktop machines do not have Windows and Office installed on them, they do still need to be licensed for both Windows and Office. The licensing changes dependent on the particular scenario and we'll cover these scenarios in the next few pages. Users do need to be licensed for server access too and we'll look at that in the final part.

Licensing VDI for x86 Devices

The first scenario we'll take is one where Spring Green Grocers want to license x86 devices for VDI desktops. Consider an x86 device to be a PC-type device rather than an iPad which doesn't run a full version of Windows. Each user at Spring Green Grocers has a device allocated to him or her and doesn't use any other devices to access their virtual desktop.

 © Licensing School 2018

As we've said, these devices will be running Windows and Office in the VDI infrastructure and so need to be licensed for both of these products. Let's look at the licensing of each in turn.

A Windows 10 Enterprise E3 device license purchased through a Volume Licensing agreement includes Software Assurance which gives the added deployment flexibility of being allowed to create, store and run virtual desktops on a server. This right is known as Virtual Desktop Access rights. So, Spring Green Grocers assign a Windows 10 Enterprise E3 license to each of the devices.

An Office Professional Plus 2016 license is also assigned to the device and, actually, that's all you need for this scenario. If you refer back to the Server Usage Rights section on page 55 you may remember that an Office license acquired through a Volume Licensing agreement gives the rights to install Office on a server and use it from there – which is what we're doing in this scenario.

So, in summary, both Windows 10 Enterprise E3 and Office Professional Plus 2016 licenses need to be assigned to the device that is running the VDI desktop. If we just take Mrs. Lime in the diagram above, this is what it looks like, and she's allowed to take that machine wherever she likes and access her VDI desktop.

Figure 29: VDI Licensing – x86 Device

Licensing VDI for non-x86 Devices

Let's now extend our scenario for Spring Green Grocers and welcome Mrs. Periwinkle. Mrs. Periwinkle works on a part-time basis and has been assigned an iPad from which she needs to access her VDI desktop.

So, how's this licensed? Well, the same principles apply – the iPad needs to be licensed for Windows and Office in the same way that Mrs. Lime's laptop was. However, in this case we can't assign an ordinary Windows 10 Enterprise E3 license because this license requires that there's a qualifying underlying operating system – and the iPad can't run Windows so it won't have this license.

In this case you assign a different license for the Windows portion, and the license that's needed is the Windows Virtual Desktop Access (VDA) E3 device license which is always a Subscription License. For the purposes of the exam, you should consider this license to be exactly equivalent to a Windows 10 Enterprise E3 license in a VDI scenario, with just one important difference: there is no qualifying operating system required.

There are no restrictions on assigning an Office license to an iPad so here are the licenses required for Mrs. Periwinkle in this scenario and, again, she's allowed to use this device wherever she likes:

Figure 30: VDI Licensing – non-x86 Device

© Licensing School 2018

Licensing VDI for Multiple Devices

Let's now consider another organization deploying virtual desktops through VDI – Tangerine Truckers. Tangerine Truckers have a mix of x86 and non-x86 devices that they want to deliver Windows 10 Enterprise E3 and Office Professional Plus 2016 desktops to, but their users use multiple devices. When we looked at Spring Green Grocers we saw that each user just had one device and so it was appropriate to license the individual devices for VDI. If we have to license all the Tangerine Truckers devices for VDI this will become (probably prohibitively) expensive. The answer is, of course, user licensing for Windows and Office, so let's take a look at how we'd license one of their users, Zak Suma.

From a Windows perspective, we assign a Windows 10 Enterprise E3 User license to Zak which we know includes Software Assurance and thus gives the necessary rights to run a virtual desktop on the server. The User license also allows Zak to access the Windows part of the virtual desktop from ANY device. However, there's a condition of the User license that we need to take into account here – you may remember it from the Windows 10 section. Zak must be the primary user of a device licensed for Windows 10 Pro or Enterprise, Windows 8.1 Pro or Enterprise, or Windows 7 Professional or Enterprise, and this device must also be his primary work device. If he primarily uses an iPad or we can't define his primary device then we can't assign the Windows 10 Enterprise E3 User license to him, but we CAN assign a Windows Virtual Desktop Access E3 User license since there are no operating system or device requirements associated with that.

From an Office perspective, we need a user license for Office too, and we saw at the end of the previous section that this is a User Subscription License for Office 365 ProPlus. This license includes the rights to run Office on a server in a VDI scenario, and when we assign it to Zak again he's licensed to access the Office part of the virtual desktop from ANY device.

So, to license Zak to access his virtual desktop from any device we assign him a Windows 10 Enterprise E3 or Windows VDA E3 User Subscription License, and an Office 365 ProPlus User Subscription License.

Figure 31: VDI Licensing by User

Server Licensing Requirements

The final part of our VDI story is to consider what CALs are required to access the VDI desktops on the server. Since you're preparing for a Microsoft exam it would make sense to assume that the VDI server is a Microsoft one and, in that case, it's Windows Server 2016 and Remote Desktop Services that need to be licensed. Each user or device needs a Windows Server 2016 CAL and an RDS 2016 CAL. It's likely that Spring Green Grocers will choose Device CALs and Tangerine Truckers will choose User CALs.

© Licensing School 2018

Windows 10 Multitenant Hosting

As a final note, when an organization is considering using virtual desktops for their users they have a choice as to where those virtual desktops are hosted:

- In an on-premises Virtual Desktop Infrastructure (as we've just looked at)

- In Azure

- On a partner's multitenant (shared) infrastructure

Customers who have Windows 10 Enterprise E3/E5 User SLs acquired through a Volume Licensing agreement may choose any of the deployment options, and customers who have purchased these licenses through CSP may choose the Azure or partner multitenant solutions.

Applying your knowledge in the exam:

- Customers in the exam will either need to be licensed for VDI on a device basis or a user basis, so learn the licenses required in those situations. Don't forget to include the Windows Server and RDS CALs in your licensing recommendations, and choose User or Device CALs as appropriate. If you're confident with the summary on the Revision Card on page 78 then you'll be able to answer the exam questions

- Remember that, for the exam, you should consider the Windows 10 Enterprise E3 User SLs and the VDA E3 User SLs to have broadly the same rights, and you should make your licensing recommendation based on the type of device that a user has as his primary device

On-Premises Products Use Rights

The use rights of the on-premises products are detailed in the Product Terms document which is released every month by Microsoft. This document has a useful table for every single product where you can see the licensing programs that it's available through and the points allocations for the Select Plus and MPSA agreements. It also tells you the pool that the product falls into, the prior version, and in the case of subscription licenses, whether or not they're eligible to be reduced at anniversary.

There is also a comprehensive section on Software Assurance which explains which benefits are available through which programs and how the entitlements are calculated.

The Product Terms document also contains information that explains the licensing terms that apply to all products, such as rights to use other versions of the software or when licenses may be reassigned, and has sections for each of the different licensing models.

You can download this document from the following link:
https://www.microsoft.com/Licensing/product-licensing.

© Licensing School 2018

Licensing On-Premises Products Revision Cards

Let me introduce you to our Revision Cards. We thought it would be useful to have a recap or summary section which covers all the key points that you need to know for the exam so we decided on a series of "cards" – or tables that you can work through just to remind yourself of the key points that you need to know from this section. You'll see that the following cards have all the products that we've looked at with key notes on how they're licensed.

Revision Card 1:
Licensing Windows Server 2016

Product	Licensing Model	Virtualization Rights
Windows Server 2016 Standard	Assign a Core license to each physical core with a minimum of 8 Core licenses per processor and 16 Core licenses per server. All physical cores must be licensed	2 virtual machines when the physical server is completely licensed. License it again to run another 2 virtual machines
Windows Server 2016 Datacenter	User or Device CALs available External users can be licensed with CALs or with a single External Connector license per server	Unlimited virtual machines

Revision Card 2:
Licensing Windows Server 2016 Services

Product	Description	Licensing Model
Windows Server 2016 Remote Desktop Services	Service of Windows Server to allow an organization to install and run applications on a server	RDS CAL RDS External Connector for external users
Windows Server 2016 Active Directory Rights Management Services	Service of Windows Server giving Information Rights Management capabilities to prevent documents being forwarded or printed, for example	AD RMS CAL AD RMS External Connector for external users

© Licensing School 2018

Revision Card 3:
System Center 2016 Server Management Licenses

Product	Licensing Model	Virtualization Rights
System Center 2016 Standard	Assign a Core license to each physical core with a minimum of 8 Core licenses per processor and 16 Core licenses per server. All physical cores must be licensed	2 virtual machines may be managed when the physical server is completely licensed. License it again to manage another 2 virtual machines
System Center 2016 Datacenter		Unlimited virtual machines may be managed

Revision Card 4:
System Center 2016 Client Management Licenses

Client Management License	Availability
System Center Configuration Manager 1606 CML	Included in the Core/Enterprise CAL Suite
System Center Endpoint Protection 1606 SL	
System Center 2016 Data Protection Manager CML	Only available separately
System Center 2016 Operations Manager CML	
System Center 2016 Orchestrator CML	
System Center 2016 Service Manager CML	

Revision Card 5:
Licensing SQL Server 2016

Edition	Licensing Model	Virtualization Licensing
Standard	Server/CAL • Assign a Server license to the physical server and CALs to users and devices accessing the server	1 VM per Server license
Standard	Per Core • Assign a Core license to each physical core with a minimum of 4 Core licenses per processor	License individual VMs • Assign a Core license to each virtual core with a minimum of 4 Core licenses per VM
Enterprise	Per Core • Assign a Core license to each physical core with a minimum of 4 Core licenses per processor	License individual VMs, or License the physical server • Run SQL in 1 VM per Core license • Add SA for unlimited virtualization

© Licensing School 2018

Revision Card 6:
Licensing the Productivity Servers

Product	Description	Licensing Model
Exchange Server 2016	The email server	Server/CAL • Standard CALs • Enterprise CALs (Unified Messaging, DLP, anti-malware) External users: Server license, or Standard + Enterprise CALs for advanced access
SharePoint Server 2016	A content management, workflow, and collaboration portal, which also allows a single infrastructure for Internet, intranet and extranet sites	Server/CAL • Standard CALs • Enterprise CALs (Advanced Search, BI) External users: Server license SQL Server required
Skype for Business Server 2015	The server solution for instant messaging, presence information, web conferencing, and enterprise telephony	Server/CAL • Standard CALs (IM, presence) • Enterprise CALs (web conferencing) • Plus CALs (enterprise telephony) External users: Server license SQL Server required
Project Server 2016	A project management server solution	Server/CAL External users: CALs SQL Server and SharePoint Server required

Revision Card 7:
Licensing the Dynamics 365 On-Premises Servers

Product/ Description	Licensing Model
Dynamics 365 Server • On-premises CRM solution	Server/CAL but no Server license; CALs give rights to install server software CALs • Sales CAL (for Sales professionals) • Customer Service CAL (for Customer Service professionals) • Team Members CAL (for support staff needing light access to all functionality)
Dynamics 365 for Operations Server • On-premises ERP solution	Server/CAL CALs • Operations CAL (for access to full functionality) • Operations Activity CAL (for partial access to full functionality) • Operations Device CAL (for retail device scenarios) • Team Members CAL (for support staff needing light access to all functionality

© Licensing School 2018

Revision Card 8:
The CAL Suites

	Core Infrastructure	Productivity Servers
Core CAL Suite	• Windows Server 2016 CAL • System Center Configuration Manager 1606 Client Management License (CML) • System Center Endpoint Protection 1606 Subscription License (SL)	• Exchange Server 2016 Standard CAL • SharePoint Server 2016 Standard CAL • Skype for Business Server 2015 Standard CAL
Enterprise CAL Suite	• Windows Server 2016 Active Directory Rights Management Services CAL • Advanced Threat Analytics 2016 CML	• Exchange Server 2016 Enterprise CAL with Services • SharePoint Server 2016 Enterprise CAL • Skype for Business Server 2015 Enterprise CAL • Exchange Online Archiving for Exchange Server SL

Revision Card 9:
Windows 10 Editions

Product	Description
Windows 10 Pro	Consider this the entry level product for businesses
Windows 10 Enterprise LTSB	Adds features such as DirectAccess (enabling users to work remotely without needing a VPN connection) and App-V (for application virtualization)
Windows 10 Enterprise E3	Adds extra rights such as Virtual Desktop Access (for VDI desktops) and additional MDOP tools (such as MED-V for enterprise desktop virtualization)
Windows 10 Enterprise E5	Adds Windows Defender Advanced Threat Protection (a security service that helps organizations detect, investigate, and respond to advanced attacks on their networks)

© Licensing School 2018

Revision Card 10:
Windows 10 Pro and Windows 10 Enterprise LTSB Licenses

	OEM	Volume Licensing	
Editions	Windows 10 Pro	Windows 10 Pro Upgrade	Windows 10 Enterprise LTSB Upgrade
Qualifying Operating System	None	Windows 10 Pro or Enterprise Windows 8.1 Pro or Enterprise Windows 7 Professional or Enterprise	Windows 10 Pro or Enterprise Windows 8.1 Pro or Enterprise Windows 7 Professional or Enterprise
Licensing Model	Device	Device	Device
License Reassignment Rights	None	None	None
Downgrade Rights	Windows 8.1 Pro Windows 7 Professional	Any previous Professional version	Any previous version of any edition
Software Assurance	Not included and may not be added	Not included and may not be added	Not included and may not be added
Servicing Channels	Semi-Annual Channel	Semi-Annual Channel	Long-Term Servicing Channel

Revision Card 11:
Windows 10 Enterprise E3 and E5 Licenses

	Windows 10 Enterprise E3	Windows 10 Enterprise E5
Available Licenses	Device license User SL	Device SL User SL
Software Assurance	Included in VL agreements	Included in VL agreements
Servicing Channels	Semi-Annual Channel or Long-Term Servicing Channel	Semi-Annual Channel or Long-Term Servicing Channel
License Reassignment Rights	Yes	Yes
Downgrade Rights	Any previous version of any edition	Any previous version of any edition
Qualifying Operating System (QOS)	Windows 10 Pro or Enterprise Windows 8.1 Pro or Enterprise Windows 7 Professional or Enterprise	Windows 10 Pro or Enterprise Windows 8.1 Pro or Enterprise Windows 7 Professional or Enterprise
Other Licensing Requirements	User Licenses: the user must be the primary user of a device with a QOS and that device must be the user's primary work device	User Licenses: the user must be the primary user of a device with a QOS and that device must be the user's primary work device

© Licensing School 2018

Revision Card 12:
Windows 10 License Availability

		MPSA	EA	CSP
Device	Windows 10 Pro Device license	✔		
	Windows 10 Enterprise LTSB Device license	✔		
	Windows 10 Enterprise E3 Device license	✔	✔	
	Windows 10 Enterprise E5 Device SL	✔	✔	
User	Windows 10 Enterprise E3 User SL	✔	✔	✔
	Windows 10 Enterprise E5 User SL	✔	✔	✔
Additional	Windows 10 Enterprise E3 Add-on User SL	✔	✔	
	Windows 10 Enterprise E5 Add-on Device SL	✔	✔	
	Windows 10 Enterprise E5 Add-on User SL	✔	✔	
	Windows 10 Enterprise E5 Step-Up User SL	✔	✔	

Revision Card 13:
Editions of Office 2016

	Office Standard 2016	Office Professional 2016	Office Professional Plus 2016
Word 2016	✔	✔	✔
Excel 2016	✔	✔	✔
PowerPoint 2016	✔	✔	✔
Outlook 2016	✔	✔	✔
OneNote 2016	✔	✔	✔
Publisher 2016	✔	✔	✔
Access 2016		✔	✔
Skype for Business 2016			✔

© Licensing School 2018

Revision Card 14:
Rights of Office 2016 Device Licenses

	OEM	Volume Licensing	
Editions available	Office Professional 2016	Office Standard 2016	Office Professional Plus 2016
Can add Software Assurance	Yes, (Standard) within 90 days	Yes, at point of purchase	Yes, at point of purchase
License reassignment rights	None	Yes	Yes
Downgrade rights	None	Any previous version of Standard	Any previous version of Professional Plus
Portable Use Rights	No	Yes	Yes
Server Usage Rights	No	Yes	Yes

© Licensing School 2018

Revision Card 15:
Licensing a Virtual Desktop Infrastructure

Situation	Windows and Office Licenses Required *License all devices/users with Windows and RDS CALs*	
x86 device used anywhere		• Windows 10 Enterprise E3 Device license • Office Professional Plus 2016 device license
Non-x86 device used anywhere		• Windows VDA E3 Device license • Office Professional Plus 2016 device license
Multiple devices used anywhere by a user with a primary x86 device		• Windows 10 Enterprise E3 User license • Office 365 ProPlus User license
Multiple devices used anywhere by a user with no primary device		• Windows VDA E3 User license • Office 365 ProPlus User license

© Licensing School 2018

© Licensing School 2018

Recap Questions and Answers

Use these Recap Questions to see how much you know about the Microsoft products and their licensing. If you find any areas that you need to go over you can review the relevant topic in this section of the book. You'll find a couple of questions on each page with the answers when you turn over.

© Licensing School 2018

Questions 1 – 4

1. The IT manager at Periwinkle Packaging Solutions is looking into a document management system. What product is likely to fit his needs?
   a) SharePoint Server 2016
   b) Project Server 2016
   c) Exchange Server 2016
   d) Skype for Business Server 2015

2. Taupe Telecoms have set up an online ordering system and want to allow an unlimited number of users to access their SQL Server 2016 deployment. How would you recommend that they license this product?
   a) With Processor licenses
   b) With Core licenses
   c) With an External Connector license
   d) With Server and CAL licenses

3. Blue Lamp Ideas are about to deploy Exchange Server 2016 where they want their employees to be able to make use of the full set of features that Exchange offers. What licenses will they need to purchase? Choose three answers.
   a) Exchange Server license
   b) Exchange CALs for all users
   c) Exchange Standard CALs for all users
   d) Exchange Enterprise CALs for all users
   e) Exchange External Connector license

4. Which of the following Dynamics 365 for Operations Server CALs would you recommend for an organization that needs to license a shop floor device?
   a) Team Members CAL
   b) Operations Device CAL
   c) Operations Activity CAL
   d) Operations CAL

Answers 1 – 4

1. The IT manager at Periwinkle Packaging Solutions is looking into a document management system. What product is likely to fit his needs?

   a) SharePoint Server 2016 ✓
   b) Project Server 2016
   c) Exchange Server 2016
   d) Skype for Business Server 2015

2. Taupe Telecoms have set up an online ordering system and want to allow an unlimited number of users to access their SQL Server 2016 deployment. How would you recommend that they license this product?

   a) With Processor licenses
   b) With Core licenses ✓
   c) With an External Connector license
   d) With Server and CAL licenses

3. Blue Lamp Ideas are about to deploy Exchange Server 2016 where they want their employees to be able to make use of the full set of features that Exchange offers. What licenses will they need to purchase? Choose three answers.

   a) Exchange Server license ✓
   b) Exchange CALs for all users
   c) Exchange Standard CALs for all users ✓
   d) Exchange Enterprise CALs for all users ✓
   e) Exchange External Connector license

4. Which of the following Dynamics 365 for Operations Server CALs would you recommend for an organization that needs to license a shop floor device?

   a) Team Members CAL
   b) Operations Device CAL ✓
   c) Operations Activity CAL
   d) Operations CAL

© Licensing School 2018

Questions 5 – 7

5. The Papaya Hire Company have a physical server which is running SQL Server 2016 Standard in four virtual machines which are all configured with six virtual cores. How many SQL Server 2016 Standard Core licenses do The Papaya Hire Company need to purchase to license this server?

    a) 12
    b) 16
    c) 24
    d) 32

6. The IT manager at Almond Retail cannot remember how many virtual machines he may run Windows Server in when he licenses every physical core with Windows Server 2016 Standard Core licenses. Where should he go to confirm this?

    a) The Product Terms document
    b) The Online Services Terms document
    c) The Product List document
    d) The Product Use Rights document

7. Fuchsia Fancy Dress Hire have a server with four 4-core processors running Windows Server 2016 Standard in six virtual machines. How many Windows Server 2016 Standard Core licenses should they assign to the server?

    a) 16
    b) 32
    c) 96
    d) 192

Answers 5 – 7

5. The Papaya Hire Company have a physical server which is running SQL Server 2016 Standard in four virtual machines which are all configured with six virtual cores. How many SQL Server 2016 Standard Core licenses do The Papaya Hire Company need to purchase to license this server?

    a) 12
    b) 16
    c) 24 ✓
    d) 32

6. The IT manager at Almond Retail cannot remember how many virtual machines he may run Windows Server in when he licenses every physical core with Windows Server 2016 Standard Core licenses. Where should he go to confirm this?

    a) The Product Terms document ✓
    b) The Online Services Terms document
    c) The Product List document
    d) The Product Use Rights document

7. Fuchsia Fancy Dress Hire have a server with four 4-core processors running Windows Server 2016 Standard in six virtual machines. How many Windows Server 2016 Standard Core licenses should they assign to the server?

    a) 16
    b) 32
    c) 96 ✓
    d) 192

© Licensing School 2018

Questions 8 – 10

8. Lilac Landscaping Services are intending to deploy their website using SharePoint Server 2016 on a dedicated server. What licenses do they need for this server so that external users are licensed to access the site and the content on it? Choose three answers.
   a) SharePoint Server 2016 Hosting Processor licenses
   b) SharePoint Server 2016 for Internet Sites license
   c) SharePoint Server 2016 license
   d) Windows Server 2016 Core licenses
   e) Windows Server 2016 External Connector license

9. Ultramarine Swim Wear have some servers that are running a large number of virtual machines that all need to be managed using System Center 2016. What should they license the servers with?
   a) System Center 2016 Client Management Suite licenses
   b) System Center 2016 Client Management Licenses
   c) System Center 2016 Standard Server Management Licenses
   d) System Center 2016 Datacenter Server Management Licenses

10. Pink Champagne Limousines have deployed Exchange Server 2016 throughout their organization and have a significant number of external users who need to access the server too for basic email. How should Pink Champagne Limousines license their external users?
   a) With an Exchange Server license
   b) With an Exchange External Connector license
   c) With User CALs
   d) With Device CALs

Answers 8 – 10

8. Lilac Landscaping Services are intending to deploy their website using SharePoint Server 2016 on a dedicated server. What licenses do they need for this server so that external users are licensed to access the site and the content on it? Choose three answers.
   a) SharePoint Server 2016 Hosting Processor licenses
   b) SharePoint Server 2016 for Internet Sites license
   c) **SharePoint Server 2016 license** ✓
   d) **Windows Server 2016 Core licenses** ✓
   e) **Windows Server 2016 External Connector license** ✓

9. Ultramarine Swim Wear have some servers that are running a large number of virtual machines that all need to be managed using System Center 2016. What should they license the servers with?
   a) System Center 2016 Client Management Suite licenses
   b) System Center 2016 Client Management Licenses
   c) System Center 2016 Standard Server Management Licenses
   d) **System Center 2016 Datacenter Server Management Licenses** ✓

10. Pink Champagne Limousines have deployed Exchange Server 2016 throughout their organization and have a significant number of external users who need to access the server too for basic email. How should Pink Champagne Limousines license their external users?
    a) **With an Exchange Server license** ✓
    b) With an Exchange External Connector license
    c) With User CALs
    d) With Device CALs

© Licensing School 2018

Questions 11 – 13

11. Which of the following Client Management Licenses are included in the Enterprise CAL Suite? Choose two answers.

    a) System Center Configuration Manager 1606 CML
    b) System Center 2016 Data Protection Manager CML
    c) System Center Endpoint Protection 1606 SL
    d) System Center 2016 Operations Manager CML
    e) System Center 2016 Orchestrator CML
    f) System Center 2016 Service Manager CML

12. Apple and Pears Stairlifts have deployed a sophisticated workflow solution based on SharePoint Server 2016 throughout their organization and now need to buy the relevant CALs for their users. What CALs should they purchase?

    a) SharePoint Enterprise CALs
    b) SharePoint Standard and Enterprise CALs
    c) SharePoint CALs
    d) SharePoint Standard CALs

13. The Cobalt Bolt Company have a large data warehouse application based on SQL Server 2016 which will be accessed by many hundreds of external users. What edition of SQL Server 2016 is likely to be the best purchase for them?

    a) Standard
    b) Enterprise
    c) Datacenter
    d) Business Intelligence

Answers 11 – 13

11. Which of the following Client Management Licenses are included in the Enterprise CAL Suite? Choose two answers.

    a) System Center Configuration Manager 1606 CML ✓
    b) System Center 2016 Data Protection Manager CML
    c) System Center Endpoint Protection 1606 SL ✓
    d) System Center 2016 Operations Manager CML
    e) System Center 2016 Orchestrator CML
    f) System Center 2016 Service Manager CML

12. Apple and Pears Stairlifts have deployed a sophisticated workflow solution based on SharePoint Server 2016 throughout their organization and now need to buy the relevant CALs for their users. What CALs should they purchase?

    a) SharePoint Enterprise CALs
    b) SharePoint Standard and Enterprise CALs ✓
    c) SharePoint CALs
    d) SharePoint Standard CALs

13. The Cobalt Bolt Company have a large data warehouse application based on SQL Server 2016 which will be accessed by many hundreds of external users. What edition of SQL Server 2016 is likely to be the best purchase for them?

    a) Standard
    b) Enterprise ✓
    c) Datacenter
    d) Business Intelligence

© Licensing School 2018

Questions 14 – 16

14. The IT Manager at The Raspberry Rubicon has decided to deploy Exchange Server 2016 Enterprise and has assigned a Server license to each of four servers. How many virtual machines is he licensed to run Exchange Server in on each of the physical servers?

    a) 1
    b) 2
    c) 4
    d) Unlimited

15. Tangerine Truckers have completely licensed one of their physical servers with SQL Server 2016 Enterprise Core licenses. The server has four 8-core processors. How many virtual machines are they licensed to run SQL Server 2016 in?

    a) 4
    b) 16
    c) 32
    d) An unlimited number

16. The person in charge of buying software at The Mala Kite Shop wants to buy Office 2016 licenses through a Volume Licensing agreement that includes Access 2016. Which edition of Office 2016 should he buy?

    a) Office Standard 2016
    b) Office Professional 2016
    c) Office Professional Plus 2016
    d) Office Enterprise 2016

Answers 14 – 16

14. The IT Manager at The Raspberry Rubicon has decided to deploy Exchange Server 2016 Enterprise and has assigned a Server license to each of four servers. How many virtual machines is he licensed to run Exchange Server in on each of the physical servers?

   a) 1 ✓
   b) 2
   c) 4
   d) Unlimited

15. Tangerine Truckers have completely licensed one of their physical servers with SQL Server 2016 Enterprise Core licenses. The server has four 8-core processors. How many virtual machines are they licensed to run SQL Server 2016 in?

   a) 4
   b) 16
   c) 32 ✓
   d) An unlimited number

16. The person in charge of buying software at The Mala Kite Shop wants to buy Office 2016 licenses through a Volume Licensing agreement that includes Access 2016. Which edition of Office 2016 should he buy?

   a) Office Standard 2016
   b) Office Professional 2016
   c) Office Professional Plus 2016 ✓
   d) Office Enterprise 2016

© Licensing School 2018

Questions 17 – 19

17. Vermilion Jewellers have 495 PCs which are licensed with Office Professional Plus 2016. 25 users also want Visio 2016 and Project 2016 installed on their machines. How many additional licenses should Vermilion Jewellers purchase?

    a) No licenses – Visio and Project are part of Office Professional Plus 2016
    b) 25 Visio licenses and 25 Project licenses
    c) 25 Project licenses and no Visio licenses since it's part of Office Professional Plus 2016
    d) 495 Visio licenses and 495 Project licenses

18. Cerise Estate Management want to run an unlimited number of SQL Server 2016 virtual machines on their server which has eight 8-core processors. What licenses should they acquire?

    a) 64 Enterprise Core licenses
    b) 64 Standard Core licenses with SA
    c) 64 Enterprise Core licenses with SA
    d) 64 Standard or Enterprise Core licenses with SA

19. Pastel Pink Personal Coaches have 50 users who need to use the CRM functionality of Dynamics 365 Server. 15 users will need access to the Sales functionality, and the remaining users will support them. Which licenses should Patel Pink Personal Coaches acquire?

    a) 15 Sales CALs and 35 Team Members CALs
    b) 15 Sales CALs, 35 Team Members CALs, and 1 Dynamics 365 Server license
    c) 15 Sales CALs and 35 Customer Service CALs
    d) 15 Sales CALs, 35 Customer Service CALs, and 1 Dynamics 365 Server license

Answers 17 – 19

17. Vermilion Jewellers have 495 PCs which are licensed with Office Professional Plus 2016. 25 users also want Visio 2016 and Project 2016 installed on their machines. How many additional licenses should Vermilion Jewellers purchase?

a) No licenses – Visio and Project are part of Office Professional Plus 2016

b) 25 Visio licenses and 25 Project licenses ✓

c) 25 Project licenses and no Visio licenses since it's part of Office Professional Plus 2016

d) 495 Visio licenses and 495 Project licenses

18. Cerise Estate Management want to run an unlimited number of SQL Server 2016 virtual machines on their server which has eight 8-core processors. What licenses should they acquire?

a) 64 Enterprise Core licenses

b) 64 Standard Core licenses with SA

c) 64 Enterprise Core licenses with SA ✓

d) 64 Standard or Enterprise Core licenses with SA

19. Pastel Pink Personal Coaches have 50 users who need to use the CRM functionality of Dynamics 365 Server. 15 users will need access to the Sales functionality, and the remaining users will support them. Which licenses should Pastel Pink Personal Coaches acquire?

a) 15 Sales CALs and 35 Team Members CALs ✓

b) 15 Sales CALs, 35 Team Members CALs, and 1 Dynamics 365 Server license

c) 15 Sales CALs and 35 Customer Service CALs

d) 15 Sales CALs, 35 Customer Service CALs, and 1 Dynamics 365 Server license

© Licensing School 2018

Questions 20 – 22

20. The IT staff at Purple Paint Pot Decorators want a security service that helps them to detect, investigate, and respond to advanced attacks on their networks. Which edition of Windows 10 would you recommend?
    a) Windows 10 Pro
    b) Windows 10 Enterprise LTSB
    c) Windows 10 Enterprise E3
    d) Windows 10 Enterprise E5

21. Maroon Balloons have a SQL Server 2016 solution accessed by 275 internal users and over 100 external users. They have opted to deploy the Standard edition of SQL Server 2016. How should they license it?
    a) With Server and CAL licenses for internal users, and an External Connector license for external users
    a) With Server and CAL licenses for internal and external users
    b) With Core licenses to cover both internal and external users
    c) With Processor licenses to cover both internal and external users

22. Myrtle Beachwear have deployed Windows Server 2016 and have licensed their estate with a mixture of User and Device CALs. Are they compliant?
    a) Yes, as long as every user and device is covered by one CAL or another, it's OK to mix them
    b) Yes, as long as the total number of CALs is greater than the number of users
    c) No, they need to choose either User or Device CALs
    d) No, Device CALs are not available for Windows Server 2016

Answers 20 – 22

20. The IT staff at Purple Paint Pot Decorators want a security service that helps them to detect, investigate, and respond to advanced attacks on their networks. Which edition of Windows 10 would you recommend?
    a) Windows 10 Pro
    b) Windows 10 Enterprise LTSB
    c) Windows 10 Enterprise E3
    d) Windows 10 Enterprise E5 ✓

21. Maroon Balloons have a SQL Server 2016 solution accessed by 275 internal users and over 100 external users. They have opted to deploy the Standard edition of SQL Server 2016. How should they license it?
    a) With Server and CAL licenses for internal users, and an External Connector license for external users
    b) With Server and CAL licenses for internal and external users
    c) With Core licenses to cover both internal and external users ✓
    d) With Processor licenses to cover both internal and external users

22. Myrtle Beachwear have deployed Windows Server 2016 and have licensed their estate with a mixture of User and Device CALs. Are they compliant?
    a) Yes, as long as every user and device is covered by one CAL or another, it's OK to mix them ✓
    b) Yes, as long as the total number of CALs is greater than the number of users
    c) No, they need to choose either User or Device CALs
    d) No, Device CALs are not available for Windows Server 2016

© Licensing School 2018

Questions 23 – 25

23. Scarlet Key Cutters are about to deploy Project Server 2016 in their organization. What other products are required as part of the technology infrastructure? Choose three answers.

    a) Windows Server
    b) SQL Server
    c) Exchange Server
    d) SharePoint Server
    e) Dynamics 365 Server

24. Peach Snaps Cameras have purchased four servers and want to deploy SQL Server 2016 Standard on all of them. All of the servers have two processors with eight cores each. How many Core licenses should they purchase for all of the servers?

    a) 4
    b) 8
    c) 16
    d) 64

25. Which Windows 10 licenses are available through CSP? Choose two answers.

    a) Windows 10 Enterprise E3 User SL
    b) Windows 10 Enterprise E5 User SL
    c) Windows 10 Enterprise E3 Device license
    d) Windows 10 Enterprise E5 Device SL
    e) Windows 10 Enterprise LTSB Device license

Answers 23 – 25

23. Scarlet Key Cutters are about to deploy Project Server 2016 in their organization. What other products are required as part of the technology infrastructure? Choose three answers.

   a) **Windows Server** ✓
   b) **SQL Server** ✓
   c) Exchange Server
   d) **SharePoint Server** ✓
   e) Dynamics 365 Server

24. Peach Snaps Cameras have purchased four servers and want to deploy SQL Server 2016 Standard on all of them. All of the servers have two processors with eight cores each. How many Core licenses should they purchase for all of the servers?

   a) 4
   b) 8
   c) 16
   d) **64** ✓

25. Which Windows 10 licenses are available through CSP? Choose two answers.

   a) **Windows 10 Enterprise E3 User SL** ✓
   b) **Windows 10 Enterprise E5 User SL** ✓
   c) Windows 10 Enterprise E3 Device license
   d) Windows 10 Enterprise E5 Device SL
   e) Windows 10 Enterprise LTSB Device license

© Licensing School 2018

26. Which of the following are benefits of an Office Professional Plus 2016 license purchased through an Enterprise Agreement? Choose two answers.
    a) Rights to downgrade to and install previous versions of Office Professional Plus
    b) Rights for Office to be installed on a server and accessed through technology such as Remote Desktop Services
    c) Rights for the Office components to be split across several devices as required
    d) Rights for Office to be installed on a portable device in addition to a main device

27. Mauve Stoves have bought 250 PCs with Windows 10 Pro pre-installed. What downgrade rights do they have? Choose two answers.
    a) Windows Vista Business
    b) Windows 7 Professional
    c) Windows 7 Enterprise
    d) Windows 8.1 Pro
    e) Windows XP Pro

28. Xanthic Tractors need to give access to their server infrastructure to about 127 external users. They have licensed the relevant servers with Windows Server 2016 Datacenter Core licenses and acquired CALs to cover their internal users. How should they license these external users?
    a) With External Connector Processor licenses assigned to the processors in every server
    b) With a single External Connector license per server
    c) With User CALs
    d) External users are already covered by the Windows Server Core licenses

Answers 26 – 28

26. Which of the following are benefits of an Office Professional Plus 2016 license purchased through an Enterprise Agreement? Choose two answers.

   a) **Rights to downgrade to and install previous versions of Office Professional Plus** ✓
   b) **Rights for Office to be installed on a server and accessed through technology such as Remote Desktop Services** ✓
   c) Rights for the Office components to be split across several devices as required
   d) Rights for Office to be installed on a portable device in addition to a main device

27. Mauve Stoves have bought 250 PCs with Windows 10 Pro pre-installed. What downgrade rights do they have? Choose two answers.

   a) Windows Vista Business
   b) **Windows 7 Professional** ✓
   c) Windows 7 Enterprise
   d) **Windows 8.1 Pro** ✓
   e) Windows XP Pro

28. Xanthic Tractors need to give access to their server infrastructure to about 127 external users. They have licensed the relevant servers with Windows Server 2016 Datacenter Core licenses and acquired CALs to cover their internal users. How should they license these external users?

   a) With External Connector Processor licenses assigned to the processors in every server
   b) **With a single External Connector license per server** ✓
   c) With User CALs
   d) External users are already covered by the Windows Server Core licenses

© Licensing School 2018

Questions 29 – 31

29. The Jazzberry Jam Shop want to acquire licenses for Windows Server 2016 and System Center 2016 for around half of the servers in their server farm which is not virtualized at all. What should they acquire?

   a) Windows Server 2016 Standard and System Center 2016 Standard Core licenses
   b) Windows Server 2016 Datacenter and System Center 2016 Datacenter Core licenses
   c) Core Infrastructure Server Suite Standard Core licenses
   d) Core Infrastructure Server Suite Datacenter Core licenses

30. Honeydew Hatters need a tool that delivers content management, document collaboration, web conferencing, and enterprise telephony. Which of these will Skype for Business Server 2015 deliver for them? Choose two answers.

   a) Content management
   b) Document collaboration
   c) Web conferencing
   d) Enterprise telephony

31. Amaranth Antiques have licensed all of their devices for Windows 10 Enterprise E3, Office Professional Plus 2016 and the Core CAL Suite. All licenses include Software Assurance. What other licenses should they acquire for these devices to access VDI desktops running Windows 10 Enterprise E3 and Office Professional Plus 2016?

   a) Windows VDA E3 license
   b) Windows Server 2016 CAL
   c) Remote Desktop Services 2016 CAL
   d) VDI Suite license

29. The Jazzberry Jam Shop want to acquire licenses for Windows Server 2016 and System Center 2016 for around half of the servers in their server farm which is not virtualized at all. What should they acquire?

a) Windows Server 2016 Standard and System Center 2016 Standard Core licenses

b) Windows Server 2016 Datacenter and System Center 2016 Datacenter Core licenses

c) **Core Infrastructure Server Suite Standard Core licenses** ✓

d) Core Infrastructure Server Suite Datacenter Core licenses

30. Honeydew Hatters need a tool that delivers content management, document collaboration, web conferencing, and enterprise telephony. Which of these will Skype for Business Server 2015 deliver for them? Choose two answers.

a) Content management

b) Document collaboration

c) **Web conferencing** ✓

d) **Enterprise telephony** ✓

31. Amaranth Antiques have licensed all of their devices for Windows 10 Enterprise E3, Office Professional Plus 2016 and the Core CAL Suite. All licenses include Software Assurance. What other licenses should they acquire for these devices to access VDI desktops running Windows 10 Enterprise E3 and Office Professional Plus 2016?

a) Windows VDA E3 license

b) Windows Server 2016 CAL

c) **Remote Desktop Services 2016 CAL** ✓

d) VDI Suite license

© Licensing School 2018

Questions 32 – 34

32. The Yellow Soup Tureen is about to deploy Windows Server 2016 but is uncertain of the edition to license. Based on the fact that they are unlikely to deploy any virtual servers, which is likely to be the best recommendation for them?

    a) Standard edition
    b) Enterprise edition
    c) Datacenter edition
    d) Essentials edition

33. Powderblue Pottery have deployed Skype for Business Server 2015 and all users will make extensive use of the functionality. What CALs should Powderblue Pottery buy for their users? Choose three answers.

    a) Standard CALs
    b) Enterprise CALs
    c) Plus CALs
    d) Voice CALs
    e) Add-on CALs

34. The IT manager at Ochre Poker has a single processor server with four cores which has eight virtual machines running on it. How many System Center 2016 Datacenter Core licenses should he assign to the server to manage the virtual machines?

    a) 4
    b) 8
    c) 16
    d) 32

32. The Yellow Soup Tureen is about to deploy Windows Server 2016 but is uncertain of the edition to license. Based on the fact that they are unlikely to deploy any virtual servers, which is likely to be the best recommendation for them?

    a) **Standard edition** ✓
    b) Enterprise edition
    c) Datacenter edition
    d) Essentials edition

33. Powderblue Pottery have deployed Skype for Business Server 2015 and all users will make extensive use of the functionality. What CALs should Powderblue Pottery buy for their users? Choose three answers.

    a) **Standard CALs** ✓
    b) **Enterprise CALs** ✓
    c) **Plus CALs** ✓
    d) Voice CALs
    e) Add-on CALs

34. The IT manager at Ochre Poker has a single processor server with four cores which has eight virtual machines running on it. How many System Center 2016 Datacenter Core licenses should he assign to the server to manage the virtual machines?

    a) 4
    b) 8
    c) **16** ✓
    d) 32

© Licensing School 2018

35. Which of the following licenses are included in the Enterprise CAL Suite? Choose two answers.

    a) Windows Server 2016 AD RMS CAL
    b) Windows Server 2016 RDS CAL
    c) Advanced Threat Analytics 2016 CML
    d) Skype for Business Server 2015 Plus CAL
    e) SQL Server 2016 CAL

36. The Bondi Blue Bistro is a large international chain of restaurants which has deployed Exchange Server 2016 to give their 15,000 staff access to basic email functionality. What licenses should they purchase? Choose two answers.

    a) Exchange Server 2016 Standard Server licenses
    b) Exchange Server 2016 Enterprise Server licenses
    c) Exchange Server 2016 Standard CALs
    d) Exchange Server 2016 Enterprise CALs

37. The Software Asset Management team at The Pink Pillow Shop want to check on the use rights for the Office Professional Plus 2016 licenses that they have purchased through their Enterprise Agreement. Where should you refer them to?

    a) The Microsoft Software License Terms website
    b) The Volume Licensing Service Center
    c) The Product Use Rights document
    d) The Product Terms document

Answers 35 – 37

35. Which of the following licenses are included in the Enterprise CAL Suite? Choose two answers.
   a) **Windows Server 2016 AD RMS CAL** ✓
   b) Windows Server 2016 RDS CAL
   c) **Advanced Threat Analytics 2016 CML** ✓
   d) Skype for Business Server 2015 Plus CAL
   e) SQL Server 2016 CAL

36. The Bondi Blue Bistro is a large international chain of restaurants which has deployed Exchange Server 2016 to give their 15,000 staff access to basic email functionality. What licenses should they purchase? Choose two answers.
   a) Exchange Server 2016 Standard Server licenses
   b) **Exchange Server 2016 Enterprise Server licenses** ✓
   c) **Exchange Server 2016 Standard CALs** ✓
   d) Exchange Server 2016 Enterprise CALs

37. The Software Asset Management team at The Pink Pillow Shop want to check on the use rights for the Office Professional Plus 2016 licenses that they have purchased through their Enterprise Agreement. Where should you refer them to?
   a) The Microsoft Software License Terms website
   b) The Volume Licensing Service Center
   c) The Product Use Rights document
   d) **The Product Terms document** ✓

© Licensing School 2018

Questions 38 – 40

38. Goldfinger Food have deployed Windows Server 2016, Exchange Server 2016, SharePoint Server 2016 and SQL Server 2016. They now need to acquire CALs for all their users to access these products for basic use. How would you recommend that they do this in the most cost-effective way?

a)   Buy the Core CAL Suite for all users
b)   Buy the Enterprise CAL Suite for all users
c)   Buy the Core CAL Suite and SQL CALs for all users
d)   Buy the Enterprise CAL Suite and SQL CALs for all users

39. The Olive Oil Drum Company have licensed all of their users with the Core CAL Suite. 75 of these users have been given a corporate-owned iPad through which they will access a VDI desktop running Windows 10 Enterprise E3 and Office Professional Plus 2016. What additional licenses must they purchase? Choose three answers.

a)   Windows 10 Enterprise E3
b)   Windows VDA E3
c)   Office Professional Plus 2016
d)   Remote Desktop Services 2016 CAL
e)   Windows Server 2016 CAL

40. Which of the following products require SQL Server as part of their infrastructure? Choose three answers.

a)   Windows Server 2016
b)   System Center 2016
c)   SharePoint Server 2016
d)   Skype for Business Server 2015
e)   Exchange Server 2016

38. Goldfinger Food have deployed Windows Server 2016, Exchange Server 2016, SharePoint Server 2016 and SQL Server 2016. They now need to acquire CALs for all their users to access these products for basic use. How would you recommend that they do this in the most cost-effective way?

    a) Buy the Core CAL Suite for all users
    b) Buy the Enterprise CAL Suite for all users
    c) **Buy the Core CAL Suite and SQL CALs for all users** ✓
    d) Buy the Enterprise CAL Suite and SQL CALs for all users

39. The Olive Oil Drum Company have licensed all of their users with the Core CAL Suite. 75 of these users have been given a corporate-owned iPad through which they will access a VDI desktop running Windows 10 Enterprise E3 and Office Professional Plus 2016. What additional licenses must they purchase? Choose three answers.

    a) Windows 10 Enterprise E3
    b) **Windows VDA E3** ✓
    c) **Office Professional Plus 2016** ✓
    d) **Remote Desktop Services 2016 CAL** ✓
    e) Windows Server 2016 CAL

40. Which of the following products require SQL Server as part of their infrastructure? Choose three answers.

    a) Windows Server 2016
    b) **System Center 2016** ✓
    c) **SharePoint Server 2016** ✓
    d) **Skype for Business Server 2015** ✓
    e) Exchange Server 2016

 © Licensing School 2018

Questions 41 – 43

41. Sienna Blenders are intending to run Office 2016 on a server and then to have their users remotely access it using Remote Desktop Services. How would you recommend that Sienna Blenders purchase their Office licenses?

    a) Either via OEM or a Volume Licensing agreement
    b) Only through OEM
    c) Only through a Volume Licensing agreement
    d) It does not matter – the use rights for Office do not vary dependent on how a customer acquires the licenses

42. Coff E-Learning Solutions have purchased Windows 10 Enterprise E3 licenses for all of their devices. Some users have started using multiple devices and Coff E-Learning Solutions realize it would be better to license these users for Windows 10 Enterprise E3 on a user basis. How should they do this?

    a) By buying Windows 10 Enterprise E3 Add-on User licenses
    b) By buying Windows 10 Enterprise E3 User SLs
    c) By buying Windows VDA E3 User SLs
    d) By buying Windows 10 Enterprise E3 User Step-up licenses

43. The IT department at Copper Feel Fabrics has deployed a Virtual Desktop Infrastructure with virtual desktops containing Windows 10 Enterprise E3 and Office Professional Plus 2016. All users have a laptop but use multiple devices to access their VDI desktop. Which licenses would you recommend that Copper Feel Fabrics acquire to license the Windows part of the desktop?

    a) Windows 10 Enterprise E3 device licenses
    b) Windows 10 Enterprise E3 User licenses
    c) Windows VDA E3 device licenses
    d) Windows VDA E3 User licenses

Answers 41 – 43

41. Sienna Blenders are intending to run Office 2016 on a server and then to have their users remotely access it using Remote Desktop Services. How would you recommend that Sienna Blenders purchase their Office licenses?
    a) Either via OEM or a Volume Licensing agreement
    b) Only through OEM
    c) Only through a Volume Licensing agreement ✓
    d) It does not matter – the use rights for Office do not vary dependent on how a customer acquires the licenses

42. Coff E-Learning Solutions have purchased Windows 10 Enterprise E3 licenses for all of their devices. Some users have started using multiple devices and Coff E-Learning Solutions realize it would be better to license these users for Windows 10 Enterprise E3 on a user basis. How should they do this?
    a) By buying Windows 10 Enterprise E3 Add-on User licenses ✓
    b) By buying Windows 10 Enterprise E3 User SLs
    c) By buying Windows VDA E3 User SLs
    d) By buying Windows 10 Enterprise E3 User Step-up licenses

43. The IT department at Copper Feel Fabrics has deployed a Virtual Desktop Infrastructure with virtual desktops containing Windows 10 Enterprise E3 and Office Professional Plus 2016. All users have a laptop but use multiple devices to access their VDI desktop. Which licenses would you recommend that Copper Feel Fabrics acquire to license the Windows part of the desktop?
    a) Windows 10 Enterprise E3 device licenses
    b) Windows 10 Enterprise E3 User licenses ✓
    c) Windows VDA E3 device licenses
    d) Windows VDA E3 User licenses

© Licensing School 2018

PART 3: LICENSING ONLINE SERVICES PRODUCTS

The Microsoft Online Services are relatively new and are the alternative to traditional on-premises deployments of products. An on-premises deployment of Exchange would see Exchange Server installed on a server in an organization's premises managed by the IT staff, with users using a variety of methods to access their email. An Online Services solution removes the need for the physical Exchange Server on-site since it is now hosted on Microsoft servers. This is attractive to organizations since the costs of the server itself and those associated with managing it are removed. From an end user perspective the users typically access their email in the same ways as with an on-premises deployment.

In this section we'll cover the key Online Services products that you need to know for the exam and you'll need to be able to recommend the right product to meet a customer's needs as well as know how it's licensed.

If you already have a good knowledge of licensing the Online Services products, why not skip to the Recap Questions on page 156 and test yourself?

Licensing Online Services

Online Services are generally licensed with User Subscription Licenses (User SLs) with just a few products licensed with Device Subscription Licenses (Device SLs). The licenses are always non-perpetual, just allowing access to the service as long as the subscription is active. Licenses may be reassigned between users but, in common with the on-premises software licenses, typically no more than every 90 days.

Online Services products often have different rights to their on-premises equivalents – there are no downgrade rights for example, and you can find details of their use rights in the Online Services Terms document. This is a document that is released monthly by Microsoft and it's where you would, for example, find confirmation that a user licensed with an Office 365 ProPlus User SL may use the Office applications on up to five devices.

You can download this document from the following link: http://www.microsoft.com/licensing/products/products.aspx.

Managing Online Services Licenses

We're going to consider the licensing of the following products in this section:

- Office 365
- Enterprise Mobility + Security
- Microsoft 365
- Dynamics 365

Organizations who buy licenses for any of these products manage the licenses in the Office 365 portal at portal.office.com. This is where they can download software that needs installing locally (Office 365 ProPlus for example) and do administrative tasks such as seeing what licenses they have available and assigning them to users.

© Licensing School 2018

Applying your knowledge in the exam:

- Remember, the Product Terms document has the use rights for the on-premises products, and the Online Services Terms document is what you should choose when the question refers to use rights of the Online Services products above

- There is just one portal for managing licenses for all of the Online Services products so don't look for a special Dynamics 365 portal when you're asked where customers would go to assign licenses – it's always the Office 365 portal

- Look out for hints that an organization could find the idea of Online Services attractive – for example, a business goal that states that the IT department don't want the hassle of managing on-premises servers, or that they want to deploy a new service but don't have any experience of setting up and managing that product

- Look out for business goals that state an organization's preference for owning or renting licenses; if they like to own assets such as software licenses, then an Online Services solution will not fit their needs since all the licenses are subscription licenses

Office 365

The Office 365 family consists of hosted versions of the productivity servers (Exchange, SharePoint and Skype for Business) and other related Online Services such as Yammer and Teams. It also includes Office 365 ProPlus (the familiar Office applications) and these products are installed locally and then managed from the cloud. Organizations can either purchase licenses for the separate services, or a Plan which gives access to a variety of services. Licenses for both the individual services and the Plans are User SLs.

For the exam, you need to be familiar with all of the individual components so that you can recommend the right Plan based on the given needs. Primarily you'll be recommending one of the Enterprise Plans so let's take a look at those first.

		E1	E3	E5
Microsoft Office	Office 365 ProPlus		✔	✔
	Office Online	✔	✔	✔
Productivity Tools	Yammer, Teams, etc.	✔	✔	✔
Exchange Online	Plan 1	✔		
	Plan 2		✔	✔
SharePoint Online	Plan 1	✔		
	Plan 2		✔	✔
Skype for Business Online	Plan 1			
	Plan 2	✔	✔	✔
	Cloud PBX, PSTN Conferencing			✔
Analytics	Power BI Pro, MyAnalytics			✔
Security	Advanced Threat Protection etc.			✔
Compliance	Advanced Data Governance etc.			✔

Figure 32: Office 365 Enterprise Plans

© Licensing School 2018

Microsoft Office

All of the Enterprise Plans include rights to Office Online (browser-based versions of Word, PowerPoint, Excel and OneNote), and the Office 365 E3 and E5 Plans include Office 365 ProPlus too. Office 365 ProPlus is also available as a separate User SL and in that case would include access to Office Online as an alternative too.

So what's the difference between Office 365 ProPlus and Office Professional Plus 2016? Licenses for either give the rights to install the Office applications and users typically won't know (or care!) which one has actually been used to install the applications on their devices. However, there are some key differences you need to know.

Firstly, the licensing model is different: Office Professional Plus 2016 is a device licensing model where the products are installed on a single device and the license is assigned to that device. Office 365 ProPlus is a user licensing model where the User SL is assigned to a user and then that user is allowed to install the Office applications on up to five devices. In addition, they can use the Office Mobile software on five tablets and five smartphones too.

Another key difference is that there are no downgrade rights for Office 365 ProPlus, whereas you can install any previous version with an Office Professional Plus 2016 license. Technically, you must also make sure that you install the right software dependent on which license has been purchased: Office Professional Plus 2016 is installed via MSI files, while Office 365 ProPlus is installed via Click-to-Run technology.

As far as deployment rights are concerned, both Office Professional Plus 2016 and Office 365 ProPlus licenses allow Office to be deployed in an RDS environment or in a Virtual Desktop Infrastructure.

Productivity Tools

There are many additional productivity tools that Microsoft include in the Enterprise Plans and typically you can't acquire these individually. The following tools are included in all of the Enterprise Plans, and these are the ones you need to be confident with for the exam.

- **Yammer:** a private enterprise social network tool to help users to collaborate both internally and externally in a secure, closed network

- **OneDrive for Business:** a place for users to store and organize their work documents

- **Teams:** a hub for teamwork where teams can access items such as conversations, files and tools in one team workspace

Exchange, SharePoint, Skype for Business Online

These products are licensed with a Plan 1 or Plan 2 User SL. Plan 1 corresponds broadly to the functionality you'd have access to with a Standard CAL if you were licensing an on-premises deployment, while Plan 2 is everything in Plan 1 and then access to the functionality that would correspond to the Enterprise CAL. Note that while the on-premises licensing requires you to have the Standard AND Enterprise CALs, when you buy these Online Services Plans, you buy EITHER Plan 1 OR Plan 2.

There are also a couple of other Skype for Business branded tools and you need to understand what they do and how they're licensed:

- **Cloud PBX:** this is for organizations that want to eliminate hardware PBX systems and to have their call management system in the cloud. This is part of an Office 365 E5 license but is also available as an Add-on User SL for a user already licensed with an Office 365 E3 license

- **PSTN Conferencing:** this is audio conferencing functionality which enables organizations to provide a tolled or toll-free dial-in number to join meetings. Again, this is part of Office 365 E5 but can be purchased as an Add-on User SL to Office 365 E3

© Licensing School 2018

Analytics

The Analytics tools are only included in the Office 365 E5 Plan, so if a customer has any of the needs below, then this is a hint to recommend this Plan:

- **Power BI Pro:** this enables users to take data and transform it into rich visuals and use analytics on it, with the goal of helping them to make better decisions

- **MyAnalytics:** this shows users how they spend their time so that (if they want to!) they can create better work habits and optimize their working day

Security

Don't be misled with questions about security requirements; Office 365 E5 has the extra security components listed below, but unless a customer need is clearly referring to one of these, you should recommend Office 365 E3 since it has a good standard set of security functionality included:

- **Threat Intelligence:** this is a set of tools to help security teams understand and respond to threats

- **Advanced Threat Protection:** this helps protects against threats in end-user email focusing on attachments and URLs

- **Advanced Security Management:** gives security teams insights into suspicious activity in Office 365 so that they can investigate situations that are potentially problematic

Compliance

Look out for customers who have a stated need for compliance – perhaps they're part of a highly regulated industry. These are the components to look out for so that you can recommend Office 365 E5:

- **Advanced eDiscovery:** this searches across email and document repositories to explore large, unstructured sets of data, which is useful in the legal discovery process

- **Customer Lockbox:** this helps meet compliance obligations with procedures for data access authorization

- **Advanced Data Governance:** this applies machine learning to help find and retain important data, and eliminate trivial, redundant and obsolete data that could cause risk if compromised

PSTN Calling Plans

You'll notice that PSTN Calling Plans are not listed on the Enterprise Plans diagram in Figure 32 since they are always purchased as an Add-on User SL. There are Domestic and International Calling Plans which essentially makes Microsoft your telecoms provider and provides you with calling minutes. A Domestic Calling Plan allows a user to make calls in the country to which his Office 365 license is assigned, and the International Calling Plan includes the Domestic country and other international destinations.

The pre-requisite to buying a PSTN Calling Plan is a Cloud PBX license, so you could either add this purchase to Office 365 E5, or buy Office 365 E3, and add on both a Cloud PBX User SL and a PSTN Calling Plan User SL.

© Licensing School 2018

Firstline Worker Plan

Next we need to consider the Office 365 F1 Plan, where the F stands for "Firstline". A Firstline worker is someone who only spends a small amount of their time using technology, and thus probably does not need such a comprehensive (or expensive) set of tools as the Enterprise worker. There is just one F Plan – F1 – and as you can see below, it consists of Office Online for working with Office documents, some of the productivity tools such as Yammer and Teams, Exchange Online Kiosk and SharePoint Online Kiosk, which give basic access to Exchange and SharePoint Online, and access to the presence and instant messaging functionality of Skype for Business.

	F1
Office Online	✔
Yammer, Teams etc.	✔
Exchange Online Kiosk	✔
SharePoint Online Kiosk	✔
Skype for Business Online Plan 1	✔

Figure 33: Office 365 F1 Plan

Business Plans

So far we've looked at the Plans that larger organizations are likely to choose for their workers, whether Enterprise or Firstline types. There are also some Office 365 Business Plans (Business Essentials, Business, and Business Premium) which are limited to 300 users and thus unlikely to be the right recommendation for the organizations detailed in the exam.

Dual Access Rights

Dual Access Rights are also called CAL Equivalence Rights and are the rights to access licensed on-premises servers. The Office 365 Enterprise Plans (E1, E3, E5) give rights to Exchange, SharePoint and Skype for Business Servers, and this diagram shows the exact on-premises rights that these Enterprise plans have:

On-premises CAL	E1	E3	E5
Exchange Standard CAL	✔	✔	✔
Exchange Enterprise CAL		✔	✔
SharePoint Standard CAL	✔	✔	✔
SharePoint Enterprise CAL		✔	✔
Skype for Business Standard CAL	✔	✔	✔
Skype for Business Enterprise CAL	✔	✔	✔
Skype for Business Plus CAL			✔

Figure 34: Office 365 CAL Dual Access Rights

Applying your knowledge in the exam:

- Don't forget that the Office 365 Online Services are ALWAYS licensed by user, not device, so if you're asked to recommend the number of licenses a customer needs, you need to consider the number of users, rather than the number of devices that they are using

- Make sure that you learn the different use rights that Office Professional Plus 2016 and Office 365 ProPlus give. In particular, remember that Office 365 ProPlus does not give downgrade rights and watch out for a requirement for this in the business goals section of a customer scenario

© Licensing School 2018

- If you're asked to choose between recommending Office 365 ProPlus and Office Professional Plus 2016, remember that where there are more devices than users, Office 365 ProPlus is likely to be the most cost-effective recommendation

- Be prepared to recommend the right Office 365 Plan for a given scenario, so make sure that you're confident with the differences between them. In particular, remember that Office 365 ProPlus is included in either Office 365 E3 or E5, and learn all of the components that are in Office 365 E5. You should be able to identify all of them (analytics, security, compliance) from a description and know that if that's the functionality the customer needs then they need Office 365 E5

- It's fine to mix Plans across an organization and you should look out for this in the scenarios since this would be a good, cost-effective recommendation

- Look out for business goals that state that users need to be able to access (for example) SharePoint sites that have been deployed on on-premises servers as well as ones deployed via SharePoint Online. The Office 365 Enterprise Plan User SLs include dual access rights, so you should never recommend that a customer needs SharePoint CALs AND Office 365 User SLs. This of course applies to on-premises Exchange and Skype for Business solutions too

- Don't forget the Office F1 Plan when you're thinking about recommending Plans. If an organization is trying to minimize costs it could be a hint that the F1 Plan should be recommended

- The Office 365 E1 and F1 Plans are close in terms of what functionality they allow access to and would both be acceptable answers for a cost-effective solution to license users who need light access to Office 365. However, Office 365 F1 does not license access to the on-premises servers and so remember that as the key differentiator when trying to choose between these Plans

- There are two key reasons why the organizations described in the exam will not be interested in the Office 365 Business Plans: they are limited to 300 users and they do not allow access to on-premises servers. You should be able to pick these reasons from a list of other plausible, but incorrect, answers!

- Make sure that you recommend the most cost-effective ways to license the telephony functionality. For example, if you have worked out that the customer needs Cloud PBX, then don't just recommend Office 365 E5 unless there are other components of Office 365 E5 mentioned – it may be more appropriate to buy Office 365 E3 and then the Cloud PBX User SL as an Add-on to that

- Don't forget that the PSTN Calling Plans are not included in any of the Office 365 Plans and that users who are to be licensed for them need a Cloud PBX User SL too

© Licensing School 2018

Enterprise Mobility + Security (EMS)

EMS Technologies

User licensing for Windows and Office means that a user isn't tied to using a single device, and this is usually considered to be great for their productivity. However, if a user is using more than one device then there's likely to be an increased burden on the IT department that needs to keep the devices and the information they access secure. The Enterprise Mobility + Security suite ensures users and the devices they use are covered for a range of security and management technologies as shown in the table below:

Technology	Description
Azure Active Directory Premium	A hybrid identity management solution providing a single identity across devices, data centers and the cloud
Azure Information Protection Premium	A cloud-based solution to classify, label, and protect corporate documents and emails
Microsoft Intune	A cloud-based solution to securely manage mobile devices and mobile apps
Microsoft Cloud App Security	A cloud-based solution to discover which SaaS apps users are using, and to control which ones they have access to

Figure 35: Enterprise Mobility + Security Technologies

Licensing EMS

EMS is available in two editions – E3 and E5 – and although it's a single license assigned to a user, the devices that they use can be managed with the technologies above.

Dual Access Rights

Both the EMS E3 and E5 User SLs include equivalent rights to the core infrastructure components of the Enterprise CAL Suite, along with rights to the Microsoft Identity Manager CAL. The diagram below shows the differences between an E3 and E5 license, and the included on-premises CAL rights:

	EMS E3	EMS E5	
Azure Active Directory Premium Plan 1	✔		Rights to cloud services
Azure Active Directory Premium Plan 2		✔	
Azure Information Protection Premium Plan 1	✔		
Azure Information Protection Premium Plan 2		✔	
Microsoft Intune	✔	✔	
Cloud App Security		✔	
Windows Server 2016 CAL	✔	✔	Rights to on-premises servers
System Center Endpoint Protection 1606 SL	✔	✔	
System Center Configuration Manager 1606 CML	✔	✔	
Windows Server 2016 AD RMS CAL	✔	✔	
Advanced Threat Analytics 2016 CML	✔	✔	
Microsoft Identity Manager 2016 CAL	✔	✔	

Figure 36: EMS E3/E5 and Dual Access Rights

© Licensing School 2018

Applying your knowledge in the exam:

- Make sure you can respond to the triggers for a recommendation of EMS; perhaps an organization is issuing all users with a second device that they're worried about the extra management burden of, or perhaps they want to allow users to bring in their own devices and are worried about keeping their corporate data and resources secure

- Don't over-recommend the edition of EMS – you always need to be able to justify to yourself why you're recommending EMS E5 over EMS E3. You should look for business goals along the lines of: "Contoso need the highest level of information protection", otherwise EMS E3 is likely to be the right recommendation

- Make sure you're familiar with the dual access rights of EMS so that you don't over-recommend licenses. For example, a customer would not need to purchase the Core CAL Suite and an EMS E3 User SL, you would be looking to recommend an Add-on User SL, which we'll look at later in this section

Microsoft 365 Enterprise

Microsoft 365 Enterprise was launched in July 2017 as the new name for a collection of products previously called Secure Productive Enterprise, and before that called the Enterprise Cloud Suite.

Licensing Microsoft 365 Enterprise

Today Microsoft 365 Enterprise is available in two flavors – E3 and E5 – and is a single subscription license assigned to a user which licenses that user for Windows 10 Enterprise E3/E5, Office 365 E3/E5 and EMS E3/E5.

Dual Access Rights

Since Microsoft 365 includes both Office 365 and EMS, a Microsoft 365 User SL includes rights to both the productivity servers and the core infrastructure servers and in fact, both the E3 and E5 User SLs have rights equivalent to the Enterprise CAL Suite.

On-Premises Server Installation Rights

There is one other quirk with Microsoft 365 Enterprise E3 and E5 User SLs, which is an additional right that is granted if the licenses are purchased through an Enterprise Agreement. This additional right allows the installation of some of the server products which may then be accessed by Microsoft 365 Enterprise E3/E5 licensed users. The products are Exchange, SharePoint and Skype for Business Server and the rights allow unlimited installations of these products in both physical and virtual infrastructures with rights to previous versions if required. The only restriction is that the installations must be on hardware dedicated to the customer – so not on shared servers in a Service Provider's server farm for example

Step-up User SLs

So far in this section we've actually been talking about Full User SLs, but you also need to know about other types of User SLs, and the first one we'll look at is the Step-up. This is used when a customer has purchased a lower edition of an Online Service and now wants to make use of a higher edition. Perhaps, for instance, an organization purchased Microsoft 365 Enterprise E3 User SLs for their users using their Enterprise Agreement and now some

© Licensing School 2018

of the users need to use Microsoft 365 Enterprise E5. All users would continue to be licensed with the Microsoft 365 Enterprise E3 User SLs and then additional Microsoft 365 Enterprise E3 to E5 Step-up User SLs would be purchased for and assigned to the required users.

These are the Step-up User SLs you should know about for the exam:

- Office 365 E1 to E3 or E5, Office 365 E3 to E5

- EMS E3 to E5

- Microsoft 365 Enterprise E3 to E5

Note that if customers have Microsoft 365 Enterprise E3 User SLs and just need more functionality in Office 365, then they are eligible for the Office 365 E3 to E5 Step-up User SLs. The same applies to EMS too.

Applying your knowledge in the exam:

- Never assume that if there's a choice between recommending Microsoft 365 Enterprise E3 or E5 then the answer is always going to be E5. If you genuinely have no idea of the right answer, then E5 will always be your best guess, but otherwise make sure you can pick out something particular that validates a choice of E5

- Remember that a customer who has Microsoft 365 Enterprise E3 User SLs has rights equivalent to the Enterprise CAL Suite, as well as rights to install unlimited copies of Exchange Server, SharePoint Server, and Skype for Business Server

- Remember that there are no Windows Server installation rights in Microsoft 365 Enterprise User SLs, but you DO get Windows Server CAL rights

Dynamics 365 Online

In Part 2 of this book we looked at Dynamics 365 and saw that it's CRM or ERP functionality available as either an on-premises or an online solution, which the following diagram summarizes:

Figure 37: Dynamics 365

We looked at the specifics of the on-premises licensing in Part 2 and it's now time to look at how the online solutions are licensed

Licensing Dynamics 365 Customer Engagement

Looking at the diagram above we can see that the online CRM functionality in Dynamics 365 is called "Customer Engagement" and the following licenses are available to license users for CRM tasks:

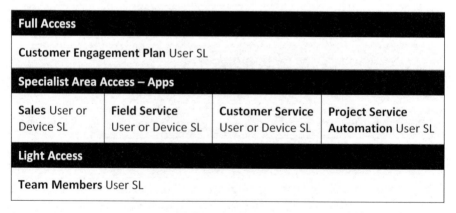

Figure 38: Dynamics 365 Customer Engagement Licenses

© Licensing School 2018

Let's start with the specialist area access in the diagram – these are the Customer Engagement Apps, and license users for functionality in a particular area. They are typically used for users whose main role is carrying out tasks specifically related to Sales, Field Service, Customer Service, or Project Service Automation. All Apps except the Project Service Automation App are available as User or Device SLs.

The Team Members User SL is aimed at users who support people in the main roles; they don't need full access to all of the functionality, but they do need to do tasks like look up a Purchase Order number or the status of a customer service request. The Team Members User SL gives light access to functionality across all of the Apps. All of the licenses for the Apps also give Team Member access to the other Apps, so if someone was licensed with a Customer Service User SL then they would also have light access to the Field Service functionality for example.

The Customer Engagement Plan User SL on the other hand, gives full access to all of the Apps and from a price perspective is aimed at those users who need to use the full functionality of two or more Apps.

Licensing Dynamics 365 Operations

The licenses available for the online ERP solution, known as "Operations", are shown in the diagram below:

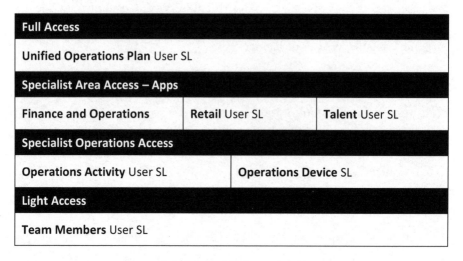

Figure 39: Dynamics 365 Operations Licenses

Let's look at the Apps again first. Here you would buy a Talent User Subscription License for people who are HR professionals and recruiters, but again there's a Team Members license available and that's what you would use for people involved in the recruiting process at a less involved level such as hiring managers or interviewers.

The Retail User SL is used to license users at the headquarters and central operations function of retailers, while employees in retail stores could be licensed via the Operations Activity license which is more functionality than the Team Members license but not the full Retail license. Alternatively, the Operations Device license could be used to license a device which behaves as a point of sale device, shop floor device, warehouse device or store manager device, and then multiple users could use this device under the single Device license.

Note that the Finance and Operations App, which covers financial, manufacturing and supply chain capabilities, is not available as a separate

© Licensing School 2018

license, it's part of the Unified Operations Plan which includes access to all Operations functionality.

Licensing Dynamics 365

To understand the full picture of the Dynamics 365 online licensing there are just two more things to understand: firstly, the Team Members User SL actually extends across both halves of the solution giving light access to both CRM and ERP functionality. And secondly, for users who need access to the complete range of functionality there's a Dynamics 365 Plan User SL available which is essentially a combination of the Customer Engagement Plan and the Unified Operations Plan.

Dual Access Rights

In common with the other Online Services the Dynamics 365 User SLs also give access to equivalent on-premises servers as shown in the table below:

Dynamics 365 SL	Dynamics 365 CAL rights
Dynamics 365 Plan SL	Sales CAL Customer Service CAL Operations CAL
Customer Engagement Plan SL	Sales CAL Customer Service CAL
Sales SL	Sales CAL
Customer Service SL	Customer Service CAL
Unified Operations Plan SL	Operations CAL
Operations Activity SL	Operations Activity CAL
Operations Device SL	Operations Device CAL
Team Members SL	Team Members CAL

Figure 40: Dynamics 365 Dual Use Rights

You may remember that there was something odd about the server licensing in an on-premises Dynamics 365 solution: there is no server license for Dynamics 365 Server, but there is for Dynamics 365 for Operations Server. The rights that are included with the Dynamics 365 SLs are again a little odd, but consistent:

- If you buy any Customer Engagement SLs then you have rights to access a Dynamics 365 Server as per the table above AND to install the server product

- If you buy any Operations SLs then you have rights to access a Dynamics 365 for Operations Server as per the table above AND to install the server product

Applying your knowledge in the exam:

- Remember that the online CRM functionality in Dynamics 365 is called "Customer Engagement" and the online ERP functionality is called "Operations"

- The Dynamics 365 User SLs are not included in any of the Office 365 or Microsoft 365 Plans so make sure that you include these User SLs as additional licensing recommendations

- Make sure that you feel comfortable about recommending the right licenses for different types of users: look out for words like "specialist" or "professional" to recommend a User SL for an App, and for "support" or "light access" to recommend the Team Members User SL

- Remember that the Team Members functionality is included in all of the Apps licenses so make sure you just recommend one or the other for a single user

- If you're given a hybrid solution to license, remember that you don't need to recommend on-premises licenses AND Online Services User SLs; the Dynamics 365 User SLs include both CAL equivalence rights and the rights to install the on-premises server software

© Licensing School 2018

Moving to the Cloud

Customers who take advantage of cloud solutions may be using the cloud for a new solution or may have an existing on-premises solution that they want to move to the cloud. If they are using the cloud for a new solution that they haven't previously licensed, then they will need Full User Subscription Licenses and those are the types of licenses that we've focused on so far in this section.

However, if a customer has an existing on-premises solution with corresponding licenses then there are different User Subscription Licenses available – either From SA or Add-on User SLs. These are available for customers with existing Software Assurance and recognize the fact that the customer has made an investment in Microsoft licenses.

Let's take an Enterprise Agreement customer who has the full Desktop Platform (Office Professional Plus, Core or Enterprise CAL Suite, and Windows 10 Enterprise E3 licenses) and is now interested in moving to Microsoft 365 Enterprise E3. They could buy the Full User SL but that wouldn't recognize their existing investment. An Add-on User SL is bought in addition to the existing traditional licenses and adds on access to all the additional Microsoft 365 Enterprise E3 functionality. With a From SA User SL, the customer stops paying for the original licenses and moves to a single User SL for the Microsoft 365 Enterprise E3 services. You can compare these options below:

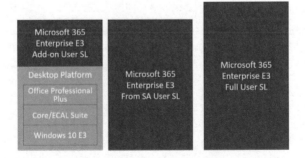

Figure 41: Options for Moving to the Cloud

The height of the bars gives a representation in terms of costs of these different options. In the real world it probably isn't as clear cut as this throughout all geographies, but for the purposes of the exam you should assume that the price of the original traditional licenses plus an Add-on User SL is equivalent to the price of a From SA User SL, both of which are cheaper than a Full User SL.

Let's now get some detail on exactly what Add-on and From SA User SLs are available and how they're transacted. The main way these licenses are sold is through the Enterprise Agreement so that will be our focus.

Add-on User SLs
We saw that the left-hand side of the diagram in Figure 41 represents a customer who is interested in Add-on User SLs to license their users for the cloud services of Microsoft 365 Enterprise. What do they buy though? Let's assume that there are (conveniently) 1,000 users and 1,000 devices in this organization. They have already purchased 1,000 Windows, Office and Enterprise CAL Suite licenses and these are considered to be qualifying licenses for the Add-ons. Add-ons are licensed by user and so they buy 1,000 Add-on User SLs giving them the licensing position shown in the first column. They continue to pay SA on the underlying licenses but they have now cloud rights as if they had purchased the Full User SLs at the right-hand side.

In a slightly more realistic scenario where there aren't the same number of users and devices, you can only buy Add-on User SLs up to the number of underlying qualifying licenses. So if the customer had 1,000 devices licensed with the Desktop Platform, and 1,200 users, then they could only buy 1,000 Add-on User SLs and would need to license the remaining users with 200 Full User SLs.

Add-on User SLs are transacted as Additional Products within an Enterprise Agreement and so there is no requirement to buy an Add-on User SL for all users across the organization. They can be added at any time during the year and the customer must pay for complete months up until the anniversary. At

© Licensing School 2018

the anniversary, the number of Add-on User SLs may be reduced if needed, and then an upfront payment is made for the required number of User SLs for the next 12 months.

We've talked about the Microsoft 365 Enterprise E3 Add-on User SLs so far, but there are more Add-on User SLs that you should be familiar with for the exam. The diagram below shows the traditional licenses a customer may have in their Enterprise Agreement and what Add-on User SLs they would be eligible for. Now, some of you may have been trained by one of us at Licensing School and may be familiar with this diagram – if not, read on to understand what it's showing you!

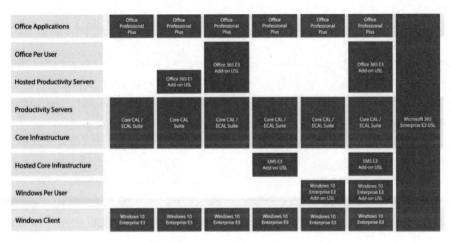

Figure 42: Online Services Add-on User SLs

Down the left-hand side are the workloads that can be licensed in an Enterprise Agreement and the first column shows the traditional licenses that customers have bought and which particular rights they give – the Office Professional Plus license licensing the Office applications, the Core or Enterprise CAL Suite licensing access to the Productivity Servers (Exchange, SharePoint and Skype for Business) and to the Core Infrastructure Servers (Windows Server and System Center), and a Windows 10 Enterprise E3 device license licensing the Windows client operating system. These are the products that a customer must commit to in an EA and

I've put a pale blue highlight on the diagram to indicate that these are the Enterprise Products.

The spaces show what this collection of licenses doesn't license and that's where customers can buy Add-ons to fill in the gaps. So you can see that a customer with the Core CAL Suite in the second column could purchase the Office 365 E1 Add-on and in this situation the Core CAL Suite license would continue to license the on-premises productivity servers, with the E1 Add-on licensing the equivalent services in the cloud. A customer with both Office Professional Plus and a CAL Suite in the third column would be eligible to purchase an Office 365 E3 Add-on User SL and you can see that that would add Office licensed per user (via Office 365 ProPlus) and access to the Office 365 hosted services.

The EMS E3 Add-on is added on to the Core or Enterprise CAL Suite in the fourth column, and a Windows 10 Enterprise E3 Add-on is added on to a Windows 10 Enterprise E3 device license in the fifth column. The sixth column shows that you could add all three Add-ons – which you would actually purchase as the Microsoft 365 Enterprise E3 Add-on User SL, and the final column shows that the traditional licenses plus all the Add-ons give access to the same services as if you had purchased the Full Microsoft 365 Enterprise E3 User SL.

Applying your knowledge in the exam:

- Remember that active SA is required to transact the Add-on User SLs so don't recommend these licenses as a way of moving to the cloud unless you're sure the customer has SA

- Always be aware that an Add-on solution, while convenient, may be a more complicated licensing position – you're likely to have multiple qualifying licenses linking to a single Add-on. If the customer is looking to simplify their licensing, this may be a steer that an Add-on is not the required solution

© Licensing School 2018

- Be ready to pick out the Add-ons that a customer would be eligible for so make sure that you learn the table above (Figure 42), taking note that Office Professional Plus 2016 on its own is never a qualifying license for an Add-on

- Remember that a customer needs to continue to pay for the SA on the underlying licenses for the Add-on User SLs to be valid, so make sure your recommendation includes both the qualifying licenses and the Add-on User SLs

- Remember that an Add-on is an Additional Product so there is no minimum number of licenses that a customer must buy, but there is a maximum – the number of Add-ons can never exceed the number of qualifying licenses

- There is no requirement for a customer to move away from Add-ons at the renewal of their Enterprise Agreement and so you should feel comfortable recommending this as a licensing solution at renewal if it seems to meet all their needs

- Add-on User SLs can be transacted at any moment in an EA and therefore if you're looking for a licensing solution midterm in the EA, these User SLs are likely to be the best recommendation

From SA User SLs

So, with Add-on User SLs a customer keeps their existing licenses and purchases these additional licenses as required. This is very convenient and easy for customers, but does give rise to a slightly complicated licensing position – you have up to three underlying licenses, at least two of which will be device licenses and an Add-on license which is user based. Add-on User SLs are great for trying the cloud services and to easily license the additional services at any time in an agreement, but at renewal it's often the case that a customer opts to simplify their licensing position by moving to From SA User SLs. In this case, they stop paying for the underlying licenses and just have a single User SL for their users.

In our original example we took a customer moving from the Desktop Platform to Microsoft 365 Enterprise E3 but again there are some additional From SA User SLs to know about for the exam. Take a look at the diagram below and then, again, read on to understand exactly what it shows.

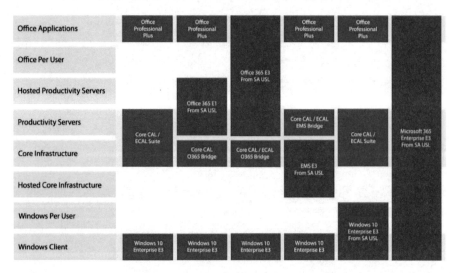

Figure 43: Online Services From SA User SLs

© Licensing School 2018

It's based on the same structure as Figure 42 so there's the traditional licensing position at the left-hand side and the complete Microsoft 365 Enterprise E3 From SA User SL at the right-hand side. Then there are some new elements – the CAL Suite Bridge licenses.

Let's take the customer in the second column to understand how and what these Bridge licenses are. He signed his Enterprise Agreement with the full desktop with the Core CAL Suite and then decided that Office 365 E1 User SLs suited his business needs better than the Core CAL Suite, and because he has active SA he is eligible for the Office 365 E1 From SA User SL. However, if he stops paying for the Core CAL Suite license as he moves to this From SA User SL you can see that there would be a gap on the diagram where he would no longer be licensed to access the Core Infrastructure servers. This could be a problem technically, but is also a problem from a licensing perspective since he committed to pay for the components of the Core CAL suite for the duration of the agreement. It's the Core CAL Suite Bridge for Office 365 which fills in this gap and maintains the commitment he made.

The table below shows the licenses the customer has before the transition (Core CAL Suite) and the different components that are contained in that license. The After Transition columns show the E1 and Core CAL Bridge licenses, and the positioning indicates the equivalence of the components.

Before Transition	After Transition	
Core CAL Suite	**Office 365 E1**	**Core CAL Bridge for Office 365**
Exchange Standard CAL	Exchange Online Plan 1	
SharePoint Standard CAL	SharePoint Online Plan 1	
SfB Standard CAL	SfB Online Plan 2	
Windows Server CAL		Windows Server CAL
SC Config Manager CML		SC Config Manager CML
SC Endpoint Protection SL		SC Endpoint Protection SL

Figure 44: Transitioning Core CAL to E1 and the Core CAL Bridge

You should learn the transitions in columns 2 to 5 in Figure 43 for the exam. Imagine that the customer always starts with the Desktop Platform at the left-hand side and then in column 3 they want to transition to Office 365 E3 – this means that they stop paying for Office Professional Plus and the CAL Suite and the Core/Enterprise CAL Suite Bridge for Office 365 fills in the gap. In the fourth column they want EMS E3 so they stop paying for their CAL Suite and the Core/Enterprise CAL Suite Bridge for EMS fills in the gap. The fifth column shows that the customer wants to move to Windows 10 Enterprise E3 user licensing and this doesn't affect the other components of the desktop.

Transacting From SA User SLs
From a transactional perspective, there are some rules you should know concerning when the From SA User SLs may be purchased by a customer: the customer must fully own the underlying licenses and the From SA User SLs can only be transacted at anniversary or renewal. Typically, this means that a customer can't buy these licenses in the first 3-year term of an EA, and actually it's generally easier to transact Add-ons if a customer wanted to move to the cloud during the second 3-year term, and then change to From SA User SLs at the start of the third 3-year term. This should be your first recommendation for customers in the exam. Note that Subscription EA customers are eligible for From SA User SLs too as long as they have paid for the qualifying licenses for a period of three consecutive years.

Special Rights to Office Professional Plus
If you look at the sixth column in Figure 42 and compare it to the last column then the licensing position is very similar, but with an Add-on User SL you retain the original Office Professional Plus license. This means that you retain the rights to downgrade to a previous version of Office, which you don't get with Office 365 ProPlus acquired through a Microsoft 365 Enterprise User SL. However, there are some special rights for customers who move to the Microsoft 365 From SA User SL; they are also allowed one installation of Office Professional Plus for use of the licensed user. This installation can be a previous version, but it may not be used in an RDS or VDI deployment.

© Licensing School 2018

Software Assurance Benefits

The other thing a customer moving from a traditional licensing position to a From SA User SL may be concerned about is losing their SA benefits on the Desktop Platform licenses. In fact, all From SA User SLs include the SA benefits of the underlying qualifying licenses.

Applying your knowledge in the exam:

- Remember that to be eligible for From SA User SLs a customer must have fully paid for underlying licenses or have been paying for the licenses for three years in a Subscription EA, so make sure that this condition is met when you recommend From SA User SLs as a solution

- Always remember that From SA User SLs can only be transacted at anniversary or renewal and, in the vast majority of cases, it's going to be easier to transact Add-on User SLs during the term of an EA and then consider From SA User SLs at renewal

- Remember the two things that a From SA User SL customer retains which are unexpected: the rights to install current, future and previous versions of Office Professional Plus, and the Software Assurance benefits of the underlying qualifying licenses

- You won't get any difficult questions on transitions in the exam, but do try and learn the From SA User SL transitions in columns 2 to 5 in Figure 43 so that you can answer the questions you do get with confidence. However, if your brain is full, then focus on Microsoft 365 Enterprise and make sure you're completely happy with the three options for moving to this shown in Figure 41

Dynamics 365 Qualified Offers

Dynamics 365 is more expensive than CRM Server 2016 and AX Server 2012 R3 were, and so Microsoft have made some special pricing available for eligible customers when they move to the cloud via Add-on or From SA User SLs. An eligible customer is one that had active SA on CRM Server 2016 or AX Server 2012 R3 at October 31, 2016, and you can identify the special pricing SKUs by looking for the words "Qualified Offer" in the SKU name. For example, the SKU below is the CSP SKU for customers who were licensed with CRM Professional CALs and want to move to Dynamics 365 Customer Engagement Plan User SLs:

- Dynamics 365 Customer Engagement Plan Enterprise Edition From SA for CRM Pro (Qualified Offer)

Equally, there were price increases over CRM Online and there are also Qualified Offers available for customers who were licensed with CRM Online at October 31, 2016. For example, the SKU below is the CSP SKU for customers who were licensed with CRM Online Professional User SLs and want to move to Dynamics 365 Sales User SLs:

- Dynamics 365 for Sales Enterprise Edition CRMOL Professional (Qualified Offer)

Applying your knowledge in the exam:

- Look out for customers who are concerned about the cost of moving to Dynamics 365 online and see if they are eligible for any of the Qualified Offers. If dates are mentioned then you need to check that they had the relevant licenses on October 31, 2016 and then either active SA on CRM Server 2016 or AX Server 2012 R3, or CRM Online licenses

© Licensing School 2018

Licensing Online Services Products Revision Cards

The following pages contain the Revision Cards for this section, providing a summary of the key points that you should know about licensing the Online Services products for the exam.

Revision Card 16:
Online Services Resources

Resource	Uses
Office 365 portal	Manage Office 365, EMS and Dynamics 365 licenses Download Office 365 ProPlus
Online Services Terms document	Find use rights for all Online Services products

Revision Card 17:
Office 365 Enterprise Plans

		E1	E3	E5
Microsoft Office	Office 365 ProPlus		✔	✔
	Office Online	✔	✔	✔
Productivity Tools	Yammer, Teams, etc.	✔	✔	✔
Exchange Online	Plan 1	✔		
	Plan 2		✔	✔
SharePoint Online	Plan 1	✔		
	Plan 2		✔	✔
Skype for Business Online	Plan 1			
	Plan 2	✔	✔	✔
	Cloud PBX, PSTN Conferencing			✔
Analytics	Power BI Pro, MyAnalytics			✔
Security	Advanced Threat Protection etc.			✔
Compliance	Advanced Data Governance etc.			✔

© Licensing School 2018

Revision Card 18:
Office 365 Components: Productivity Tools

Component	Description and Licensing Notes
Office Online	Browser-based versions of Word, PowerPoint, Excel and OneNote
Office 365 ProPlus	User SL for the Office Professional Plus 2016 applications 5 installations allowed for the licensed user
Cloud PBX	For organizations that want to eliminate hardware PBX systems and to have their call management system in the cloud Part of an Office 365 E5 license but also available as an Add-on User SL for a user already licensed with an Office 365 E3 license
PSTN Conferencing	Audio conferencing functionality which enables organizations to provide a tolled or toll-free dial-in number to join meetings Part of an Office 365 E5 license but also available as an Add-on User SL for a user already licensed with an Office 365 E3 license
Power BI Pro	Enables users to take data and transform it into rich visuals and use analytics on it, with the goal of helping them to make better decisions
MyAnalytics	Shows users how they spend their time so that they can create better work habits and optimize their working day

Revision Card 19:
Office 365 Components: Security and Compliance Tools, and Calling Plans

Component	Description and Licensing Notes
Threat Intelligence	A set of tools and dashboards to help security teams understand and respond to threats
Advanced Threat Protection	Helps protect against threats in end-user email focusing on attachments and URLs
Advanced Security Management	Gives security teams insights into suspicious activity in Office 365 so that they can investigate situations that are potentially problematic
Advanced eDiscovery	Searches across email and document repositories to explore large, unstructured sets of data, which is useful in the legal discovery process
Customer Lockbox	Helps meet compliance obligations with procedures for data access authorization
Advanced Data Governance	Applies machine learning to help find and retain important data, and eliminate trivial, redundant and obsolete data that could cause risk if compromised
PSTN Calling Plans	Domestic and International Calling Plans for making calls via the world's telephone networks (PSTN) Cloud PBX User SL required Add Calling Plan to Office 365 E3 + Cloud PBX or Office 365 E5

© Licensing School 2018

Revision Card 20:
Office 365 Firstline Worker Plan

	F1
Office Online	✔
Yammer, Teams etc.	✔
Exchange Online Kiosk	✔
SharePoint Online Kiosk	✔
Skype for Business Online Plan 1	✔

Revision Card 21:
Office 365 Business Plans

Plans	Restrictions
Business Essentials	Limited to 300 users
Business	No dual access rights to on-premises servers
Business Premium	

Revision Card 22:
Office 365 Dual Access Rights

On-premises CAL	E1	E3	E5
Exchange Standard CAL	✓	✓	✓
Exchange Enterprise CAL		✓	✓
SharePoint Standard CAL	✓	✓	✓
SharePoint Enterprise CAL		✓	✓
Skype for Business Standard CAL	✓	✓	✓
Skype for Business Enterprise CAL	✓	✓	✓
Skype for Business Plus CAL			✓

© Licensing School 2018

Revision Card 23:
EMS E3/E5 and Dual Access Rights

	EMS E3	EMS E5	
Azure Active Directory Premium Plan 1	✔		Rights to cloud services
Azure Active Directory Premium Plan 2		✔	
Azure Information Protection Premium Plan 1	✔		
Azure Information Protection Premium Plan 2		✔	
Microsoft Intune	✔	✔	
Cloud App Security		✔	
Windows Server 2016 CAL	✔	✔	Rights to on-premises servers
System Center Endpoint Protection 1606 SL	✔	✔	
System Center Configuration Manager 1606 CML	✔	✔	
Windows Server 2016 AD RMS CAL	✔	✔	
Advanced Threat Analytics 2016 CML	✔	✔	
Microsoft Identity Manager 2016 CAL	✔	✔	

Revision Card 24:
Microsoft 365 Enterprise

	Details
Editions	Microsoft 365 Enterprise E3 • Windows 10 Enterprise E3 • Office 365 E3 • EMS E3 Microsoft 365 Enterprise E5 • Windows 10 Enterprise E5 • Office 365 E5 • EMS E5
Licenses Available	Full User SL Add-on User SL From SA User SL Step-up User SL
Dual Access Rights	Equivalent to the Enterprise CAL Suite
On-Premises Server Installation Rights	Unlimited installations of Exchange Server, SharePoint Server, Skype for Business Server when User SLs acquired through an EA
Office Professional Plus Rights	From SA User SLs include rights to install Office Professional Plus
SA Benefits	From SA User SLs give equivalent SA benefits of qualifying licenses

© Licensing School 2018

Revision Card 25:
Licensing Dynamics 365 Online for CRM

Full Access

Customer Engagement Plan User SL

Specialist Area Access – Apps

Sales User or Device SL	Field Service User or Device SL	Customer Service User or Device SL	Project Service Automation User SL

Light Access

Team Members User SL

Revision Card 26:
Licensing Dynamics 365 Online for ERP

Full Access

Unified Operations Plan User SL

Specialist Area Access – Apps

Finance and Operations	Retail User SL	Talent User SL

Specialist Operations Access

Operations Activity User SL	Operations Device SL

Light Access

Team Members User SL

Revision Card 27:
Dynamics 365 Dual Access Rights

Dynamics 365 SL	Dynamics 365 CAL rights
Dynamics 365 Plan SL	Sales CAL Customer Service CAL Operations CAL
Customer Engagement Plan SL	Sales CAL Customer Service CAL
Sales SL	Sales CAL
Customer Service SL	Customer Service CAL
Unified Operations Plan SL	Operations CAL
Operations Activity SL	Operations Activity CAL
Operations Device SL	Operations Device CAL
Team Members SL	Team Members CAL

Revision Card 28:
Dynamics 365 On-Premises Server Installation Rights

Dynamics 365 SL	Server Installation Rights
Any Customer Engagement SLs	Install Dynamics 365 Server
Any Operations SLs	Install Dynamics 365 for Operations Server

© Licensing School 2018

Revision Card 29:
Options for Moving to the Cloud

Revision Card 30:
User SL Transaction Rules

User SL	Notes
Full User SL	Transact at any time No qualifying licenses required
Add-on User SL	Transact at any time Active SA on qualifying licenses required
From SA User SL	Transact at anniversary or renewal Active SA on qualifying licenses required Qualifying licenses must be fully paid perpetual licenses or subscription licenses that have been paid for three years

Revision Card 31:
Online Services Add-on User SLs

	Microsoft 365 Enterprise E3 USL					
Office Applications	Office Professional Plus	Office Professional Plus	Office Professional Plus	Office Professional Plus	Office Professional Plus	Office Professional Plus
Office Per User	Office 365 E3 Add-on USL			Office 365 E3 Add-on USL	Office 365 E1 Add-on USL	
Hosted Productivity Servers						
Productivity Servers	Core CAL / ECAL Suite	Core CAL / ECAL Suite	Core CAL / ECAL Suite	Core CAL / ECAL Suite	Core CAL Suite	Core CAL / ECAL Suite
Core Infrastructure	EMS E3 Add-on USL		EMS E3 Add-on USL			
Hosted Core Infrastructure						
Windows Per User	Windows 10 Enterprise E3 Add-on USL	Windows 10 Enterprise E3 Add-on USL				
Windows Client	Windows 10 Enterprise E3	Windows 10 Enterprise E3	Windows 10 Enterprise E3	Windows 10 Enterprise E3	Windows 10 Enterprise E3	Windows 10 Enterprise E3

© Licensing School 2018

Revision Card 32:
Online Services From SA User SLs

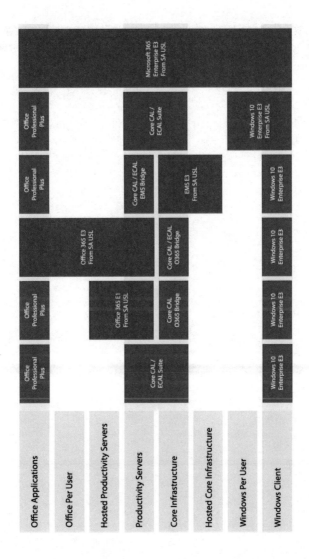

Revision Card 33:
Dynamics 365 Qualified Offers

Qualifying Licenses	Qualified Offers
CRM Server 2016 CALs with active SA at October 31, 2016	Special priced Add-on and From SA User SLs for Dynamics 365
AX Server 2012 R3 CALs with active SA at October 31, 2016	Special priced Add-on and From SA User SLs for Dynamics 365
CRM Online licenses at October 31, 2016	Special priced Customer Engagement SLs

© Licensing School 2018

Recap Questions and Answers

Use these Recap Questions to see how much you know about licensing the Online Services products. If you find any areas that you need to go over you can review the relevant topic in this section of the book. Again, you'll find a couple of questions on each page with the answers when you turn over.

© Licensing School 2018

Questions 1 – 3

1. Peach Snaps Cameras have identified that their 550 users need access to Exchange and SharePoint Online and to be able to install the Office applications on up to three devices each. Which Office 365 plan would you recommend for them?
   a) Office 365 F1
   b) Office 365 E1
   c) Office 365 E3
   d) Office 365 E5

2. Mellow Yellow Sounds want their store staff to have access to the company intranet and basic email functionality for which they are using Microsoft Online Services. They will also need to view and occasionally edit Office documents. How would you recommend they license the users most cost-effectively?
   a) With Office 365 E1 User SLs
   b) With Office 365 F1 User SLs
   c) With Office Online User SLs and Core CAL Suite licenses
   d) With Office 365 Business Essentials User SLs

3. Blacken White Solicitors want to license their users for Microsoft 365 Enterprise E3 User SLs and to be able to install unlimited copies of Exchange Server, SharePoint Server and Skype for Business Server in their on-premises data center. How should they acquire the Microsoft 365 Enterprise E3 User SLs?
   a) Through any of the Volume Licensing agreements
   b) Through CSP or an Enterprise Agreement
   c) Through CSP or an MPSA
   d) Through an Enterprise Agreement

Answers 1 – 3

1. Peach Snaps Cameras have identified that their 550 users need access to Exchange and SharePoint Online and to be able to install the Office applications on up to three devices each. Which Office 365 plan would you recommend for them?

   a) Office 365 F1
   b) Office 365 E1
   c) **Office 365 E3** ✓
   d) Office 365 E5

2. Mellow Yellow Sounds want their store staff to have access to the company intranet and basic email functionality for which they are using Microsoft Online Services. They will also need to view and occasionally edit Office documents. How would you recommend they license the users most cost-effectively?

   a) With Office 365 E1 User SLs
   b) **With Office 365 F1 User SLs** ✓
   c) With Office Online User SLs and Core CAL Suite licenses
   d) With Office 365 Business Essentials User SLs

3. Blacken White Solicitors want to license their users for Microsoft 365 Enterprise E3 User SLs and to be able to install unlimited copies of Exchange Server, SharePoint Server and Skype for Business Server in their on-premises data center. How should they acquire the Microsoft 365 Enterprise E3 User SLs?

   a) Through any of the Volume Licensing agreements
   b) Through CSP or an Enterprise Agreement
   c) Through CSP or an MPSA
   d) **Through an Enterprise Agreement** ✓

© Licensing School 2018

Questions 4 – 6

4. Aisle of White Paints have 600 users and devices and an Enterprise Agreement through which they have licensed the Enterprise Desktop. During the second year of the EA they want to move all of their users to Microsoft 365 Enterprise E3. Which licenses should they buy?

   a)   Microsoft 365 Enterprise E3 Full User SLs
   b)   Microsoft 365 Enterprise E3 Add-on User SLs
   c)   Microsoft 365 Enterprise E3 Step-up User SLs
   d)   Microsoft 365 Enterprise E3 From SA User SLs

5. Amaranth Antiques have an existing Enterprise Agreement with the Core CAL Suite licensed by Device. They want to extend their identity and access management to the cloud and have improved mobile device management. Which licenses should they acquire?

   a)   EMS E3 Add-on User SLs
   b)   Core CAL Suite to Enterprise CAL Suite Step-up licenses
   c)   Microsoft Intune User SLs
   d)   EMS E3 Full User SLs
   e)   Azure Information Protection User SLs

6. Ochre Poker have an Enterprise Agreement through which they have purchased Office Professional Plus 2016 and Core CAL Suite licenses. They are interested in moving to the cloud. Which of the following Add-on User SLs are they eligible to purchase? Choose three answers.

   a)   Office 365 E3 Add-on User SLs
   b)   Office 365 E1 Add-on User SLs
   c)   EMS E3 Add-on User SLs
   d)   Microsoft 365 Enterprise E3 Add-on User SLs
   e)   Windows 10 Enterprise E3 Add-on User SLs

Answers 4 – 6

4. Aisle of White Paints have 600 users and devices and an Enterprise Agreement through which they have licensed the Enterprise Desktop. During the second year of the EA they want to move all of their users to Microsoft 365 Enterprise E3. Which licenses should they buy?

    a) Microsoft 365 Enterprise E3 Full User SLs
    b) Microsoft 365 Enterprise E3 Add-on User SLs ✓
    c) Microsoft 365 Enterprise E3 Step-up User SLs
    d) Microsoft 365 Enterprise E3 From SA User SLs

5. Amaranth Antiques have an existing Enterprise Agreement with the Core CAL Suite licensed by Device. They want to extend their identity and access management to the cloud and have improved mobile device management. Which licenses should they acquire?

    a) EMS E3 Add-on User SLs ✓
    b) Core CAL Suite to Enterprise CAL Suite Step-up licenses
    c) Microsoft Intune User SLs
    d) EMS E3 Full User SLs
    e) Azure Information Protection User SLs

6. Ochre Poker have an Enterprise Agreement through which they have purchased Office Professional Plus 2016 and Core CAL Suite licenses. They are interested in moving to the cloud. Which of the following Add-on User SLs are they eligible to purchase? Choose three answers.

    a) Office 365 E3 Add-on User SLs ✓
    b) Office 365 E1 Add-on User SLs ✓
    c) EMS E3 Add-on User SLs ✓
    d) Microsoft 365 Enterprise E3 Add-on User SLs
    e) Windows 10 Enterprise E3 Add-on User SLs

© Licensing School 2018

Questions 7 – 9

7. Maroon Balloons want their users to be able to install Windows 10 Enterprise E3 and the latest Office applications locally, and to access applications such as SharePoint in both their on-premises data center and online. They want any devices their users use to be secure and well-managed. What is the most cost-effective way of licensing the solution they need?

   a) Microsoft 365 Enterprise E3 User SLs
   b) Office 365 E3 User SLs + Windows 10 Enterprise E3 User SLs
   c) Microsoft 365 Enterprise E5 User SLs
   d) Office 365 E3 User SLs + EMS E5 User SLs + Windows 10 Enterprise E3 User SLs

8. Turquoise Toys want to allow their users to use their own devices to access corporate data and resources but are concerned about managing these devices and keeping them secure. Which of the following should they choose to license their users with to meet these goals?

   a) Azure Information Protection Premium User SLs
   b) Enterprise Mobility + Security E3 User SLs
   c) Windows 10 Enterprise E5 User SLs
   d) Advanced Security Management User SLs

9. The sales people at Almond Retail need to use Office 365 ProPlus, Power BI Pro, and to have a calling plan to make calls around the world. Which of the following licensing solutions would meet their needs?

   a) Office 365 E5 User SLs
   b) Office 365 E3 User SLs
   c) Office 365 E5 User SLs + PSTN International Calling Plan User SLs
   d) Office 365 E5 User SLs + Cloud PBX User SLs + PSTN International Calling Plan User SLs

Answers 7 – 9

7. Maroon Balloons want their users to be able to install Windows 10 Enterprise E3 and the latest Office applications locally, and to access applications such as SharePoint in both their on-premises data center and online. They want any devices their users use to be secure and well-managed. What is the most cost-effective way of licensing the solution they need?

   a) **Microsoft 365 Enterprise E3 User SLs** ✓
   b) Office 365 E3 User SLs + Windows 10 Enterprise E3 User SLs
   c) Microsoft 365 Enterprise E5 User SLs
   d) Office 365 E3 User SLs + EMS E5 User SLs + Windows 10 Enterprise E3 User SLs

8. Turquoise Toys want to allow their users to use their own devices to access corporate data and resources but are concerned about managing these devices and keeping them secure. Which of the following should they choose to license their users with to meet these goals?

   a) Azure Information Protection Premium User SLs
   b) **Enterprise Mobility + Security E3 User SLs** ✓
   c) Windows 10 Enterprise E5 User SLs
   d) Advanced Security Management User SLs

9. The sales people at Almond Retail need to use Office 365 ProPlus, Power BI Pro, and to have a calling plan to make calls around the world. Which of the following licensing solutions would meet their needs?

   a) Office 365 E5 User SLs
   b) Office 365 E3 User SLs
   c) **Office 365 E5 User SLs + PSTN International Calling Plan User SLs** ✓
   d) Office 365 E5 User SLs + Cloud PBX User SLs + PSTN International Calling Plan User SLs

© Licensing School 2018

Questions 10 – 12

10. The IT team at Sienna Blenders want to enhance the protection they have against malicious attachments and URLs in their users' email. What technology would assist with this?

    a) Threat Intelligence
    b) Advanced Security Management
    c) Advanced Threat Protection
    d) Windows Defender Advanced Threat Protection

11. The Procurement Manager at Cyan Ida's Pharmacy would like to be sure that her Office 365 E3 User SLs purchased through the MPSA give access to SharePoint Online. Where should she go to confirm this?

    a) The Product Use Rights document
    b) The Online Services Terms document
    c) The Product Terms document
    d) The MPSA Licensing Manual

12. Which of the following rights does a user licensed for Office 365 ProPlus have? Choose two answers.

    a) Rights to use Office Online
    b) Rights to use Office on Demand
    c) Downgrade rights
    d) Rights to deploy Office in a VDI environment
    e) Rights to deploy Office on an unlimited number of machines

Answers 10 – 12

10. The IT team at Sienna Blenders want to enhance the protection they have against malicious attachments and URLs in their users' email. What technology would assist with this?
    a) Threat Intelligence
    b) Advanced Security Management
    c) Advanced Threat Protection ✓
    d) Windows Defender Advanced Threat Protection

11. The Procurement Manager at Cyan Ida's Pharmacy would like to be sure that her Office 365 E3 User SLs purchased through the MPSA give access to SharePoint Online. Where should she go to confirm this?
    a) The Product Use Rights document
    b) The Online Services Terms document ✓
    c) The Product Terms document
    d) The MPSA Licensing Manual

12. Which of the following rights does a user licensed for Office 365 ProPlus have? Choose two answers.
    a) Rights to use Office Online ✓
    b) Rights to use Office on Demand
    c) Downgrade rights
    d) Rights to deploy Office in a VDI environment ✓
    e) Rights to deploy Office on an unlimited number of machines

© Licensing School 2018

Questions 13 – 15

13. Lightshades of Grey have licensed Office Professional Plus 2016 and the Core CAL Suite through an Enterprise Agreement for five years. At anniversary they want to move to Office 365 E3. What will their licensing position be at this time?

    a) Office 365 E3 Full User SLs
    b) Office 365 E3 From SA User SLs + Core CAL Suite Bridge CALs for Office 365
    c) Office 365 E3 From SA User SLs
    d) Office 365 E3 Full User SLs + Core CAL Suite Bridge CALs for Office 365
    e) Office 365 E3 Add-on User SLs
    f) Office 365 E3 Add-on User SLs + Core CAL Suite Bridge CALs for Office 365

14. World of Magnolia have licensed their users with Customer Engagement Plan User SLs. Which of the following on-premises CALs do they have equivalent rights to? Choose two answers.

    a) Sales CAL
    b) Operations CAL
    c) Customer Service CAL
    d) Operations Activity CAL
    e) Operations Device CAL

15. Cerise Estate Management want to license their users for the finance and operations functionality in Dynamics 365 online. Which licenses should they acquire for their users?

    a) Customer Engagement Plan User SLs
    b) Operations Activity User SLs
    c) Dynamics 365 Plan User SLs
    d) Unified Operations Plan User SLs

Answers 13 – 15

13. Lightshades of Grey have licensed Office Professional Plus 2016 and the Core CAL Suite through an Enterprise Agreement for five years. At anniversary they want to move to Office 365 E3. What will their licensing position be at this time?

    a) Office 365 E3 Full User SLs
    b) Office 365 E3 From SA User SLs + Core CAL Suite Bridge CALs for Office 365 ✓
    c) Office 365 E3 From SA User SLs
    d) Office 365 E3 Full User SLs + Core CAL Suite Bridge CALs for Office 365
    e) Office 365 E3 Add-on User SLs
    f) Office 365 E3 Add-on User SLs + Core CAL Suite Bridge CALs for Office 365

14. World of Magnolia have licensed their users with Customer Engagement Plan User SLs. Which of the following on-premises CALs do they have equivalent rights to? Choose two answers.

    a) Sales CAL ✓
    b) Operations CAL
    c) Customer Service CAL ✓
    d) Operations Activity CAL
    e) Operations Device CAL

15. Cerise Estate Management want to license their users for the finance and operations functionality in Dynamics 365 online. Which licenses should they acquire for their users?

    a) Customer Engagement Plan User SLs
    b) Operations Activity User SLs
    c) Dynamics 365 Plan User SLs
    d) Unified Operations Plan User SLs ✓

© Licensing School 2018

Questions 16 – 18

16. Honeydew Hatters want to use Dynamics 365 ERP functionality both on an on-premises server and online. They have 20 users who need to use the full range of functionality. Which licenses should they acquire?

    a) Unified Operations Plan User SLs
    b) Unified Operations Plan User SLs + Dynamics 365 for Operations Server license
    c) Unified Operations Plan User SLs + Dynamics 365 for Operations Server license + Operations CALs
    d) Dynamics 365 Plan User SLs

17. Xanthic Tractors have licensed all of their users with EMS E3 User SLs. Which of the following on-premises CALs do they NOT have equivalent rights to?

    a) Windows Server 2016 CAL
    b) Windows Server 2016 AD RMS CAL
    c) Windows Server 2016 RDS CAL
    d) Advanced Threat Analytics 2016 CML
    e) Microsoft Identity Management 2016 CAL

18. The IT Manager at The Mala Kite Shop has purchased some Dynamics 365 User SLs. Where would he go to assign these licenses to specific users?

    a) The Office 365 portal
    b) The Volume Licensing Service Center (VLSC)
    c) The Microsoft Business Center (MBC)
    d) The CustomerSource portal

Answers 16 – 18

16. Honeydew Hatters want to use Dynamics 365 ERP functionality both on an on-premises server and online. They have 20 users who need to use the full range of functionality. Which licenses should they acquire?
    a) **Unified Operations Plan User SLs** ✓
    b) Unified Operations Plan User SLs + Dynamics 365 for Operations Server license
    c) Unified Operations Plan User SLs + Dynamics 365 for Operations Server license + Operations CALs
    d) Dynamics 365 Plan User SLs

17. Xanthic Tractors have licensed all of their users with EMS E3 User SLs. Which of the following on-premises CALs do they NOT have equivalent rights to?
    a) Windows Server 2016 CAL
    b) Windows Server 2016 AD RMS CAL
    c) **Windows Server 2016 RDS CAL** ✓
    d) Advanced Threat Analytics 2016 CML
    e) Microsoft Identity Management 2016 CAL

18. The IT Manager at The Mala Kite Shop has purchased some Dynamics 365 User SLs. Where would he go to assign these licenses to specific users?
    a) **The Office 365 portal** ✓
    b) The Volume Licensing Service Center (VLSC)
    c) The Microsoft Business Center (MBC)
    d) The CustomerSource portal

© Licensing School 2018

Questions 19 – 21

19. Goldfinger Food have identified that their users need to use the following components. Which one would lead you to recommend Office 365 E5?

    a) Yammer
    b) Office 365 ProPlus
    c) Web conferencing via Skype for Business
    d) Cloud PBX

20. Which of the following User SLs will license a user for the full range of CRM functionality in Dynamics 365 online in the most cost-effective way?

    a) Customer Engagement Plan User SL
    b) Sales User SL + Customer Service User SL
    c) Unified Operations Plan User SL
    d) Dynamics 365 Plan User SL

21. Pink Champagne Limousines have licensed all of their users with Office 365 E3 User SLs. Which of the following on-premises servers will these licenses allow them access to? Choose three answers.

    a) Windows Server
    b) SQL Server
    c) Exchange Server
    d) Project Server
    e) Skype for Business Server
    f) SharePoint Server

Answers 19 – 21

19. Goldfinger Food have identified that their users need to use the following components. Which one would lead you to recommend Office 365 E5?
    a) Yammer
    b) Office 365 ProPlus
    c) Web conferencing via Skype for Business
    d) Cloud PBX ✓

20. Which of the following User SLs will license a user for the full range of CRM functionality in Dynamics 365 online in the most cost-effective way?
    a) Customer Engagement Plan User SL ✓
    b) Sales User SL + Customer Service User SL
    c) Unified Operations Plan User SL
    d) Dynamics 365 Plan User SL

21. Pink Champagne Limousines have licensed all of their users with Office 365 E3 User SLs. Which of the following on-premises servers will these licenses allow them access to? Choose three answers.
    a) Windows Server
    b) SQL Server
    c) Exchange Server ✓
    d) Project Server
    e) Skype for Business Server ✓
    f) SharePoint Server ✓

© Licensing School 2018

Questions 22 – 24

22. Which of the following statements are true about Microsoft 365 Enterprise E3 From SA User SLs? Choose two answers.
    a) They can be transacted at any time in an Enterprise Agreement
    b) They are available in both an Enterprise Agreement and an Enterprise Subscription Agreement
    c) Customers with active SA on any of the Desktop Platform components are eligible for these From SA User SLs
    d) Customers may continue to deploy existing and new versions of Office Professional Plus
    e) Bridge CALs are always required with these User SLs
    f) Customers lose all the SA benefits of the qualifying licenses when they move to Microsoft 365 Enterprise E3 From SA User SLs

23. The Bondi Blue Bistro have an Enterprise Agreement with the Enterprise CAL Suite and Office Professional Plus 2016 and now want to move to Office 365 E3. What licenses will they have after the transition has taken place? Choose two answers.
    a) Enterprise CAL Suite licenses
    b) Office 365 E3 User SLs
    c) Enterprise CAL Suite Bridge CALs for Office 365
    d) Office 365 E5 User SLs

24. Mauve Stoves had the following licenses at October 31, 2016. Which of them entitle Mauve Stoves to Qualified Offer licenses as they move to Dynamics 365 online? Choose two answers.
    a) CRM Online User SLs
    b) AX 2012 R3 CALs
    c) CRM Server 2016 CALs with SA
    d) AX Online User SLs

Answers 22 – 24

22. Which of the following statements are true about Microsoft 365 Enterprise E3 From SA User SLs? Choose two answers.
    a) They can be transacted at any time in an Enterprise Agreement
    b) **They are available in both an Enterprise Agreement and an Enterprise Subscription Agreement** ✓
    c) Customers with active SA on any of the Desktop Platform components are eligible for these From SA User SLs
    d) **Customers may continue to deploy existing and new versions of Office Professional Plus** ✓
    e) Bridge CALs are always required with these User SLs
    f) Customers lose all the SA benefits of the qualifying licenses when they move to Microsoft 365 Enterprise E3 From SA User SLs

23. The Bondi Blue Bistro have an Enterprise Agreement with the Enterprise CAL Suite and Office Professional Plus 2016 and now want to move to Office 365 E3. What licenses will they have after the transition has taken place? Choose two answers.
    a) Enterprise CAL Suite licenses
    b) **Office 365 E3 User SLs** ✓
    c) **Enterprise CAL Suite Bridge CALs for Office 365** ✓
    d) Office 365 E5 User SLs

24. Mauve Stoves had the following licenses at October 31, 2016. Which of them entitle Mauve Stoves to Qualified Offer licenses as they move to Dynamics 365 online? Choose two answers.
    a) **CRM Online User SLs** ✓
    b) AX 2012 R3 CALs
    c) **CRM Server 2016 CALs with SA** ✓
    d) AX Online User SLs

© Licensing School 2018

PART 4: LICENSING MICROSOFT AZURE

The Microsoft Azure services are an ever-growing collection of thousands of Microsoft-hosted cloud services. Typical examples of these services could be having virtual machines running on Microsoft's servers, hosting an application there, or even just using it as an off-site data storage facility. Naturally you don't need to be an expert on the different services for the exam, you just need to know how customers license and pay for them. In this section we'll look at the services that are sold as Azure Plans and the remainder which are charged for on a consumption basis.

If you already have a good knowledge of licensing Microsoft Azure, why not skip to the Recap Questions on page 190 and test yourself?

Azure Plans

There are three types of Azure Plans: User, Support and Infrastructure Plans.

User Plans

These are just a few Azure User Plans which are listed below:

- Azure Active Directory Basic
- Azure Active Directory Premium Plan 1 and Plan 2
- Azure Information Protection Premium Plan 1 and Plan 2
- Microsoft MultiFactor Authentication

These Plans are all licensed with User Subscription Licenses and are transacted in exactly the same way as other User SLs such as Office 365 E3: a license is assigned to a user who may then use an unlimited amount of the associated services.

Use of Microsoft MultiFactor Authentication is included in the Azure Active Directory Premium Plans, and we saw before that the Enterprise Mobility + Security suite includes both the Azure Active Directory Premium and Azure Information Protection Premium Plans.

Support Plans

There are two Azure Support Plans: Standard and Professional Direct. They are listed on the pricelist as a monthly price and customers can buy Azure Support at any time in their agreement term by paying for the Support Plan for the complete months up to the agreement anniversary. At anniversary (assuming they want to continue) they would make an upfront payment for the 12 months of the next year.

© Licensing School 2018

Infrastructure Plans

Again, there are not many Azure Infrastructure Plans, and just one which you need to know about for the exam: the Operations Management Suite (OMS). This set of tools is designed to help organizations manage Windows Server, Linux, VMware and Hyper-V workloads across an on-premises data center, Azure and other clouds. Now, the word "manage" probably makes you think of System Center as a Microsoft product, and indeed OMS builds on traditional System Center functionality.

There are two OMS Plans: OMS E1 and E2, both available as a monthly subscription. The core functionality of OMS is provided by a set of services that run in Azure supporting a variety of different management scenarios. OMS E1 gives access to Log Analytics and Automation services, and OMS E2 includes these as well as Backup and Site Recovery services.

OMS is licensed per node where a node is what you want to manage – so a virtual machine, for example, and both OMS E1 and E2 Subscription Licenses include rights to deploy System Center Standard. But what about customers who have already got System Center licenses? There are Add-on SLs for customers who have active SA on their System Center licenses and want to add OMS functionality midterm, and From SA SLs for customers with fully paid System Center licenses with active SA who want to move from System Center to OMS at anniversary or renewal. In case you were wondering, Core Infrastructure Server Suites are eligible qualifying licenses for the Add-on and From SA User SLs too.

Both Plans include a fixed amount of the relevant Azure services which are paid for complete months up to anniversary as we've already discussed. It's also fine if a customer needs to use more of a particular service, they just pay for it as an overage payment. This overage payment is not charged via an invoice as the Plan SLs are, it's paid for out of a customer's Azure Monetary Commitment balance, which we'll cover in detail in the next section.

Applying your knowledge in the exam:

- Azure User Plans are treated in exactly the same way as licenses for Online Services and thus any questions you get about these Plans will be in the context of EMS since you are unlikely to recommend an individual component (Microsoft MultiFactor Authentication) rather than EMS E3 or E5

- Although you should be focused on the word "management" to mean System Center, Operations Management Suite should be your first thought in a hybrid environment where there's a variety of workloads to manage across a variety of infrastructures

- Remember that OMS is available as a Full, Add-on and From SA Subscription License, so make sure you recommend the right one for a particular customer, ensuring that SA is active on System Center or CIS Suite licenses if you're selecting the Add-on or From SA SLs

- Don't be caught out by the transactional details of OMS – the SLs themselves are paid for complete months up to anniversary in the usual way, but any overage (which is absolutely allowed) is paid for out of Monetary Commitment

- Remember that the Full and From SA SLs include rights to deploy System Center 2016 Standard, so you don't need to include these licenses in any customer recommendations, just the OMS SLs

© Licensing School 2018

Azure Consumption Services

We've just seen that there are only a few Azure Plans which means that the vast majority of the Azure services are sold on a consumption basis – if a customer is using a service they pay for it, and if they stop using it, they don't need to pay anything. There is one particular set of Azure services that you need to be confident with for the exam and it's the service that many customers use first when they move to Azure: virtual machines. Microsoft call this Infrastructure as a Service (or IaaS) and you should be familiar with all the different ways of paying for and licensing both Windows and SQL Server virtual machines in Azure.

Windows Server Virtual Machines: All-Inclusive

The first way to buy an Azure Windows Server virtual machine is as an all-inclusive cost: you simply decide on the resources you want the virtual machine to have in terms of the number of cores and the amount of RAM etc. in much the same way you would if you went to a hardware supplier and ordered a physical machine. As you would expect, the higher specification the Azure virtual machine has, the more it costs. The price of an Azure Windows Server virtual machine includes the cost of the compute power as well as a fee for the Windows Server license and there are no requirements for CALs. It's offered on an hourly rate, with per-minute billing, which, as we said, means organizations only pay for the server while it's up and running.

You can imagine this makes it a very attractive proposition for a development and test environment or for a short-term project, since servers can be set up and then turned off when they're no longer needed. The on-premises alternative would have been to have purchased new hardware which is unused when the project ends, and to purchase licenses which, again, could potentially end up being unused for periods of time.

Windows Server Virtual Machines: Azure Hybrid Use Benefit

The second way to license an Azure Windows Server virtual machine is to just pay for the compute power of the virtual machine on a consumption basis and then to bring your own Windows Server licenses. When you pay for just the compute power of a virtual machine you actually buy a Linux virtual machine since there is no charge for this operating system, and this is often referred to as a base instance virtual machine. You can then use existing Windows Server licenses to license that base instance for Windows Server.

You need active Software Assurance on the Windows Server licenses which means you're entitled to the Azure Hybrid Use Benefit – the right to use those licenses either in an on-premises data center, or in Azure. One thing you need to be very good at in the exam is working out how many licenses are required to license various Azure base instance virtual machines, so let's look at that in detail now.

We saw in Part 2 of this book that Windows Server 2016 is licensed with Core licenses and that they are assigned to a physical server based on the number of physical cores, and that there is a minimum of eight licenses that must be assigned to each processor. This is a good number to remember for Azure virtual machines too, since the licenses must be kept together in groups of eight as you license the virtual machines.

Let's take some examples and license the following D1-5 v2 virtual machines:

Instance	Cores
D1 v2	1
D2 v2	2
D3 v2	4
D4 v2	8
D5 v2	16

Figure 45: D1-5 v2 Virtual Machines

© Licensing School 2018

Let's start with the D4 v2 virtual machine which you can see has eight cores. We know the Windows Server Core licenses have to be kept together in groups of eight so it seems straightforward to assign eight Windows Server Core licenses to this virtual machine – and this is indeed correct. Turning to the D5 v2 virtual machine with 16 cores and following the same rules, we'd need to assign 16 Core licenses to this virtual machine – or two groups of eight licenses. It's when you get to the lower-spec virtual machines that there's a temptation to forget the rules – you don't assign four Core licenses to the D3 v2 virtual machine, you must still assign eight Core licenses to it, and indeed to all the remaining virtual machines in the table.

There is just one more thing to consider in this section, and it's the difference in rights between a Windows Server 2016 Standard Core license and a Windows Server 2016 Datacenter Core license. With a Standard Core license the Azure Hybrid Use Benefit rights are alternative – an organization can choose to use licenses in an on-premises data center following the rules we discussed in Part 2, or use them for Azure virtual machines following the "groups of eight" rule. I think this is how you would expect this benefit to work, so this hopefully feels straightforward.

The rules are different for Datacenter Core licenses though because the Azure Hybrid Use Benefit rights are additive. This means that you can use the licenses in an on-premises data center AND for Azure virtual machines. Take a look at the diagram below: the on-premises servers (bottom left) are licensed correctly with 32 Core licenses each, for a total of eight groups of eight licenses. These licenses remain assigned to the servers, but they can also be used to license some base instance virtual machines in Azure. The number of cores of each virtual machine are shown in the circles – do you agree that this customer has enough licenses for this configuration of Azure virtual machines?

Figure 46: Windows Server 2016 Datacenter Azure Hybrid Use Benefit

If you count the groups of eight licenses needed for each of the Azure virtual machines (1, 2-3-4-5, 6, 7, 8) then you should find that this is a completely compliant scenario.

SQL Server Virtual Machines: All-inclusive
Let's now look at how SQL Server virtual machines are licensed in Azure, which you'll find does have some broad similarities with what we've just looked at for Windows Server. The first option is to purchase an all-inclusive SQL Server virtual machine. This is a single fee which covers three elements: the compute power of the virtual machine, the Windows Server license, and the SQL Server license. It has all the benefits of the all-inclusive Windows Server virtual machine in that costs are only incurred while the virtual machine is up and running.

It's important not to confuse a SQL Server virtual machine with the Azure SQL Database service. If you use this service then you don't set up a virtual machine and install SQL Server in it, you just consume and pay for the SQL Database service. This means, in effect, that Microsoft does all of the management of the infrastructure for you, so you don't have to manage any virtual machines or worry about high availability or backups

                                    © Licensing School 2018

If you're interested in a Microsoft view of when you would use SQL Database and when you would use SQL Server in Azure virtual machines, then it's worth taking a look at a very useful article which you can find here: http://bit.ly/SQLOptions.

In the exam, the focus is on customers using SQL Server virtual machines.

SQL Server Virtual Machines: License Mobility

The next option to consider is when you buy an all-inclusive Windows Server virtual machine and then bring your own SQL Server licenses to license it for SQL Server. This sounds similar to the Azure Hybrid Use Benefit but in fact is a Software Assurance benefit called "License Mobility through SA" and it has a couple of important differences from the Azure Hybrid Use Benefit.

This benefit applies to other products as well as SQL Server (see the License Mobility through SA section in Part 6) and doesn't just apply to virtual machines running in Azure, but the infrastructure of any partner who has been designated an Authorized Mobility Partner by Microsoft. This does include such well-known names as Amazon Web Services as well as hundreds of other local partners all over the world.

The rules for assigning SQL Server 2016 Core licenses to an all-inclusive Windows Server virtual machine are very similar to licensing a virtual machine in an on-premises data center: you assign a Core license for each core in the virtual machine with a minimum of four Core licenses.

SQL Server Virtual Machines: License Mobility + Azure Hybrid Use Benefit

And the final option is when we bring everything together: a base instance is purchased on a consumption basis, Windows Server licenses with SA (using the Azure Hybrid Use Benefit) license the Windows Server part, and SQL Server licenses with SA (using License Mobility through SA) license the SQL Server part.

Virtual Machines Summary

Here's a summary of the virtual machine licensing options we've talked about for Windows Server and SQL Server:

Windows Server Virtual Machines

1. All-inclusive Windows Server VM

2. Base-instance VM + Windows Server Core licenses with SA (using Azure Hybrid Use Benefit)

SQL Server Virtual Machines

1. All-inclusive SQL Server VM

2. All-inclusive Windows Server VM + SQL Server licenses with SA (using License Mobility through SA)

3. Base-instance VM + Windows Server Core licenses with SA (using Azure Hybrid Use Benefit) + SQL Server licenses with SA (using License Mobility through SA)

Applying your knowledge in the exam:

- Look out for details in a customer scenario that state that an IT team want some short-term or test/development servers, since this would lead to a recommendation to pay for the all-inclusive virtual machines in Azure rather than buying new hardware and licenses and extending an on-premises solution

- If a customer is moving an existing Windows Server or SQL Server workload to the cloud, then they may well have licenses available to use and it's likely to be the best recommendation to reuse those licenses. However, remember that SA is required on the licenses and, in the case of Windows Server, the licenses may only be used in Azure and not in a partner's infrastructure

© Licensing School 2018

- Make sure you're familiar with the names of the SA benefits that allow you to use licenses in the cloud: the Azure Hybrid Use Benefit for Windows Server licenses and License Mobility through SA for SQL Server licenses

- Make sure you completely understand the "groups of eight" rules for determining the number of Windows Server 2016 Core licenses required for licensing Azure base instance virtual machines for Windows Server. If you're good at applying the rules, then these are straightforward questions to answer in the exam

- Make sure you're completely comfortable with the differences between Windows Server 2016 Standard and Datacenter Core licenses as far as the Azure Hybrid Use Benefit goes: it's not the number of virtual machines that you can license that's different (as it is in an on-premises solution), it's the fact that the Datacenter licenses can stay assigned to the on-premises solution (for unlimited virtualization) AND be assigned to Azure base instance virtual machines (following the "groups of eight" rules)

- Make sure you're confident with the number of SQL Server 2016 Core licenses that need to be assigned to an Azure virtual machine to license it for SQL Server: you need to assign a Core license for each core in the virtual machine with a minimum of four Core licenses required

The Azure Portals

There are a number of portals that customers and partners work with to provision and manage the Azure consumption services. Here are the ones you need to know about for the exam:

- **Azure Management Portal (portal.azure.com)**
  This portal is used primarily by technical people to set up resources such as virtual machines. EA customers have direct access to this portal, but the default behavior in CSP is that partners have access on behalf of their customers, although they can grant access to customers if required

- **Azure Account Portal (account.azure.com)**
  This portal is primarily used by individuals who have purchased Azure services through the Microsoft web site to track their Azure usage and manage their Subscription

- **Azure Enterprise Portal (ea.azure.com)**
  This portal is used by both EA customers and their partners to track usage and spend of the Azure consumption services. Users within a customer are likely to be procurement, management or licensing people, rather than technical people who work in the Azure Management Portal

- **Partner Center (partnercenter.microsoft.com)**
  This portal is used by CSP partners to track usage and spend of the Azure consumption services by their customers. There is no Microsoft-provided portal for customers to see this information; it is up to a partner to either provide reporting information or a portal for a customer to self-serve

Applying your knowledge in the exam:

- You'll need to choose the right portal for a particular user in an organization, which will typically be a technical user setting up resources (Azure Management portal) or a procurement person checking consumption and spend in an EA (Azure Enterprise portal)

Licensing Microsoft Azure Revision Cards

The following pages contain the Revision Cards for this section, providing a summary of the key points that you should know about licensing Microsoft Azure for the exam.

Revision Card 34:
Azure User Plans

Examples	Licensing
Azure Active Directory Basic Azure Active Directory Premium Plan 1 and Plan 2 Azure Information Protection Premium Plan 1 and Plan 2 Microsoft MultiFactor Authentication	User Subscription Licenses priced on a monthly basis, paid for upfront

Revision Card 35:
Azure Support Plans

Examples	Licensing
Azure Standard Support Azure Professional Direct Support	Subscription Licenses priced on a monthly basis, paid for upfront

© Licensing School 2018

Revision Card 36:
Azure Infrastructure Plans

Examples	Licensing
Operations Management Suite (OMS) E1 and E2	Subscription Licenses priced on a monthly basis, paid for complete months up to anniversary
	Full SLs include rights to run System Center Standard
	Add-on SLs can be added on to System Center licenses with active SA
	From SA SLs can be used to move to OMS from fully paid System Center licenses with active SA. Rights to System Center Standard included
	Additional use of Azure services outside of included quota is paid for out of Azure Monetary Commitment balance

Revision Card 37:
Licensing Azure Virtual Machines

Windows Server	
All-inclusive Windows Server virtual machine	Single fee covering compute power + Windows Server license
Base-instance virtual machine + Windows Server 2016 Core licenses	Consumption-based fee for base-instance virtual machine Active SA required to take advantage of Azure Hybrid Use Benefit Keep licenses in groups of 8 when assigning to Azure virtual machines Standard Core license rights are alternative, Datacenter Core license rights are additive
SQL Server	
All-inclusive SQL Server virtual machine	Single fee covering compute power + Windows Server license + SQL Server license
All-inclusive Windows Server virtual machine + SQL Server 2016 Core licenses	Active SA required to take advantage of License Mobility through SA Assign a minimum of 4 Core licenses to an Azure virtual machine
Base-instance virtual machine + Windows Server 2016 Core licenses + SQL Server 2016 Core licenses	Consumption-based fee for base-instance virtual machine Active SA required on Windows Server and SQL Server Core licenses

© Licensing School 2018

Revision Card 38:
Azure Portals

Portal	Typical tasks	Licensing Program
Azure Management Portal	Used by technical staff to set up virtual machines, for example	EA (customer access), Web Direct (customer access), CSP (partner access)
Azure Account Portal	Used by individuals to track usage and manage their Azure Subscription	All, although mainly Web Direct customers
Azure Enterprise Portal	Used by procurement or management staff to track Azure usage and spend	EA only, used by both customers and partners
Partner Center	Used by CSP partners to track their customers' Azure usage and spend	CSP only, used by partners

Recap Questions and Answers

Use these Recap Questions to see how much you know about licensing Microsoft Azure. If you find any areas that you need to go over you can review the relevant topic in this section of the book. Again, you'll find a couple of questions on each page with the answers when you turn over.

© Licensing School 2018

Questions 1 – 3

1. Periwinkle Packaging Solutions have a short-term project for which they need to run SQL Server 2016 in four Azure virtual machines. How would you recommend that they license these virtual machines?
   a) With the SQL Database service
   b) With all-inclusive Azure SQL Server virtual machines
   c) With all-inclusive Azure Windows Server virtual machines and SQL Server 2016 Core licenses with SA
   d) With Azure base instance virtual machines and Windows Server 2016 Core licenses with SA, and SQL Server 2016 Core licenses with SA

2. Which of the following statements is NOT true about Operations Management Suite?
   a) It is available in E1 and E2 editions
   b) It includes rights to deploy System Center Standard
   c) Both the OMS SLs and any overage are paid for out of a customer's Monetary Commitment
   d) There are From SA and Add-on SLs for customers already licensed with System Center with active SA

3. What are the differences in use rights between Windows Server 2016 Standard and Datacenter Core licenses with regards to the Azure Hybrid Use Benefit?
   a) There are no differences
   b) The rights for Windows Server 2016 Standard Core licenses are Additive, and for Datacenter Core licenses they are Alternative
   c) The rights for Windows Server 2016 Standard Core licenses are Alternative, and for Datacenter Core licenses they are Additive
   d) A minimum of 4 Windows Server 2016 Standard Core licenses must be assigned to an Azure virtual machine, and a minimum of 8 Datacenter Core licenses

Answers 1 – 3

1. Periwinkle Packaging Solutions have a short-term project for which they need to run SQL Server 2016 in four Azure virtual machines. How would you recommend that they license these virtual machines?

   a) With the SQL Database service
   b) **With all-inclusive Azure SQL Server virtual machines** ✓
   c) With all-inclusive Azure Windows Server virtual machines and SQL Server 2016 Core licenses with SA
   d) With Azure base instance virtual machines and Windows Server 2016 Core licenses with SA, and SQL Server 2016 Core licenses with SA

2. Which of the following statements is NOT true about Operations Management Suite?

   a) It is available in E1 and E2 editions
   b) It includes rights to deploy System Center Standard
   c) **Both the OMS SLs and any overage are paid for out of a customer's Monetary Commitment** ✓
   d) There are From SA and Add-on SLs for customers already licensed with System Center with active SA

3. What are the differences in use rights between Windows Server 2016 Standard and Datacenter Core licenses with regards to the Azure Hybrid Use Benefit?

   a) There are no differences
   b) The rights for Windows Server 2016 Standard Core licenses are Additive, and for Datacenter Core licenses they are Alternative
   c) **The rights for Windows Server 2016 Standard Core licenses are Alternative, and for Datacenter Core licenses they are Additive** ✓
   d) A minimum of 4 Windows Server 2016 Standard Core licenses must be assigned to an Azure virtual machine, and a minimum of 8 Datacenter Core licenses

© Licensing School 2018

Questions 4 – 7

4. The Cobalt Bolt Company have Software Assurance on their SQL Server 2016 Enterprise Core licenses. Which SA benefit will allow them to use these licenses to license Azure Windows Server virtual machines for SQL Server?

   a) Azure Hybrid Use Benefit
   b) License Mobility through SA
   c) Self Hosting Use Rights
   d) Premium Assurance

5. The IT team at Xanthic Tractors are starting to set up virtual machines in Azure to extend their on-premises data center. Which portal will they use to carry out this task?

   a) Azure Management portal
   b) Azure Enterprise portal
   c) Office 365 portal
   d) VLSC

6. Vermilion Jewellers have 64 SQL Server 2016 Standard Core licenses with SA. How many D2 v2 2-core virtual machines may they license for SQL Server?

   a) 4
   b) 8
   c) 16
   d) 32

7. Lightshades of Grey have purchased OMS E2 Subscription Licenses. What product does this allow them to install on their on-premises servers?

   a) Windows Server 2016 Standard
   b) Windows Server 2016 Datacenter
   c) System Center 2016 Standard
   d) System Center 2016 Datacenter

Answers 4 – 7

4. The Cobalt Bolt Company have Software Assurance on their SQL Server 2016 Enterprise Core licenses. Which SA benefit will allow them to use these licenses to license Azure Windows Server virtual machines for SQL Server?

   a) Azure Hybrid Use Benefit
   b) License Mobility through SA ✓
   c) Self Hosting Use Rights
   d) Premium Assurance

5. The IT team at Xanthic Tractors are starting to set up virtual machines in Azure to extend their on-premises data center. Which portal will they use to carry out this task?

   a) Azure Management portal ✓
   b) Azure Enterprise portal
   c) Office 365 portal
   d) VLSC

6. Vermilion Jewellers have 64 SQL Server 2016 Standard Core licenses with SA. How many D2 v2 2-core virtual machines may they license for SQL Server?

   a) 4
   b) 8
   c) 16 ✓
   d) 32

7. Lightshades of Grey have purchased OMS E2 Subscription Licenses. What product does this allow them to install on their on-premises servers?

   a) Windows Server 2016 Standard
   b) Windows Server 2016 Datacenter
   c) System Center 2016 Standard ✓
   d) System Center 2016 Datacenter

© Licensing School 2018

Questions 8 – 11

8. Tangerine Truckers want a tool which will help them to manage Windows Server and Linux workloads across an on-premises data center, Azure and other clouds. Which of the following would you recommend?

    a) System Center 2016 Standard
    b) System Center 2016 Datacenter
    c) Operations Management Suite
    d) System Center Global Service Monitor

9. Apple and Pears Stairlifts have Software Assurance on their Windows Server 2016 Standard Core licenses. Which SA benefit will allow them to use these licenses to license Azure base instance virtual machines for Windows Server?

    a) Azure Hybrid Use Benefit
    b) License Mobility through SA
    c) Self Hosting Use Rights
    d) Premium Assurance

10. Which of the following licenses are NOT eligible for OMS Add-on SLs?

    a) System Center 2016 Standard Core licenses with SA
    b) System Center 2016 Datacenter Core licenses with SA
    c) Core Infrastructure Server Suite Core licenses with SA
    d) Windows Server 2016 Datacenter Core licenses with SA

11. How are the Azure User Plans licensed?

    a) With a User SL
    b) With a Device SL
    c) On a consumption basis
    d) With Windows Server 2016 CALs

Answers 8 – 11

8. Tangerine Truckers want a tool which will help them to manage Windows Server and Linux workloads across an on-premises data center, Azure and other clouds. Which of the following would you recommend?

    a) System Center 2016 Standard
    b) System Center 2016 Datacenter
    c) Operations Management Suite ✓
    d) System Center Global Service Monitor

9. Apple and Pears Stairlifts have Software Assurance on their Windows Server 2016 Standard Core licenses. Which SA benefit will allow them to use these licenses to license Azure base instance virtual machines for Windows Server?

    a) Azure Hybrid Use Benefit ✓
    b) License Mobility through SA
    c) Self Hosting Use Rights
    d) Premium Assurance

10. Which of the following licenses are NOT eligible for OMS Add-on SLs?

    a) System Center 2016 Standard Core licenses with SA
    b) System Center 2016 Datacenter Core licenses with SA
    c) Core Infrastructure Server Suite Core licenses with SA
    d) Windows Server 2016 Datacenter Core licenses with SA ✓

11. How are the Azure User Plans licensed?

    a) With a User SL ✓
    b) With a Device SL
    c) On a consumption basis
    d) With Windows Server 2016 CALs

© Licensing School 2018

Questions 12 – 15

12. Mauve Stoves have 64 Windows Server 2016 Standard Core licenses with SA. How many D2 v2 2-core virtual machines may they license for Windows Server?

   a) 4
   b) 8
   c) 16
   d) 32

13. The procurement manager at The Jazzberry Jam Shop needs to keep a close eye on Azure consumption and spend through his Enterprise Agreement. Which portal will he use to carry out this task?

   a) Azure Management portal
   b) Azure Enterprise portal
   c) VLSC
   d) Azure Account portal

14. Cyan Ida's Pharmacy have 72 Windows Server 2016 Datacenter Core licenses with SA. Which of the following Azure virtual machines may they license for Windows Server?

   a) Three 4-core and six 8-core virtual machines
   b) Two 2-core, three 4-core, and three 16-core virtual machines
   c) Ten 4-core virtual machines
   d) Four 2-core and six 4-core virtual machines

15. The Olive Oil Drum Company have System Center 2016 Standard Core licenses with SA. They want to move to OMS at their EA renewal. Which of the following OMS SLs would you recommend for them?

   a) Full SL
   b) Add-on SL
   c) Step-up SL
   d) From SA SL

Answers 12 – 15

12. Mauve Stoves have 64 Windows Server 2016 Standard Core licenses with SA. How many D2 v2 2-core virtual machines may they license for Windows Server?

a) 4
b) 8 ✓
c) 16
d) 32

13. The procurement manager at The Jazzberry Jam Shop needs to keep a close eye on Azure consumption and spend through his Enterprise Agreement. Which portal will he use to carry out this task?

a) Azure Management portal
b) Azure Enterprise portal ✓
c) VLSC
d) Azure Account portal

14. Cyan Ida's Pharmacy have 72 Windows Server 2016 Datacenter Core licenses with SA. Which of the following Azure virtual machines may they license for Windows Server?

a) Three 4-core and six 8-core virtual machines ✓
b) Two 2-core, three 4-core, and three 16-core virtual machines
c) Ten 4-core virtual machines
d) Four 2-core and six 4-core virtual machines

15. The Olive Oil Drum Company have System Center 2016 Standard Core licenses with SA. They want to move to OMS at their EA renewal. Which of the following OMS SLs would you recommend for them?

a) Full SL
b) Add-on SL
c) Step-up SL
d) From SA SL ✓

© Licensing School 2018

PART 5: MICROSOFT LICENSING PROGRAMS

For the exam, you need to be able to recommend the right way to buy licenses for the organizations that are described. In the past it would just be recommending one of the Volume Licensing agreements (the Enterprise Agreement or the MPSA, for example) but now you need to know where the Cloud Solution Provider (CSP) program fits in too.

The exam focusses on commercial customers so, although many of the Volume Licensing agreements are available for academic or government customers, you don't need to know any detail about these specific agreements.

If you already have a good knowledge of the Microsoft licensing programs, why not skip to the Recap Questions on page 244 and test yourself?

Microsoft Licensing Programs Overview

The diagram below gives you a summary of all of the licensing programs that you need to know about for the exam. Here you can see whether the programs require that a larger number of licenses are purchased (the bottom row) or a smaller number (the top row). You can also see which programs require a commitment (the right-hand column) or allow customers to buy what they need when they need it, on a transactional basis (the left-hand column). The little servers and clouds indicate whether on-premises licenses and/or Online Services and Azure can be purchased through a particular agreement, the colors indicate whether the licenses are perpetual or subscription, and the SA icons indicate whether Software Assurance is available as an included or an optional purchase.

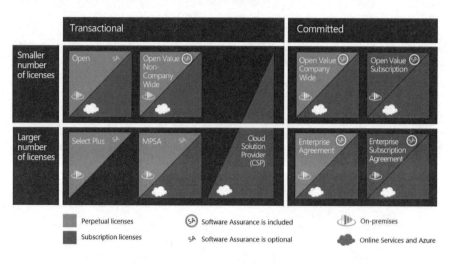

Figure 47: Microsoft Licensing Programs

You might have noticed a couple of things about the Cloud Solution Provider program: it spans both large and small customers, only Online Services and Azure are available through it, and there is no concept of Software Assurance in CSP.

The Server and Cloud Enrollment is also an important program to know about and it's part of the Enterprise Agreement shown on the diagram, where

© Licensing School 2018

a commitment must be made, SA is always included, and customers may acquire on-premises products, Online Services and Azure through it.

There are a couple of other ways to buy licenses which are not on this diagram (and thus not a focus for the exam), but let's briefly look at them so you're not tempted to choose them as correct answers in the exam:

- **FPP (Full Packaged Product):** bought through the retail channel aimed primarily at consumers and very small businesses

- **OEM (pre-installed software):** often used by businesses of all sizes to acquire Windows 10 Pro

- **Web Direct:** buying Online Services/Azure directly from the Microsoft website, aimed primarily at individuals and smaller businesses

- **SPLA (Services Provider License Agreement):** allows hosting partners to license Microsoft products on a monthly basis to provide services and hosted applications to their customers. Note that the use rights of products purchased under SPLA are governed by the SPUR (Services Provider Use Rights) document

Enterprise and Enterprise Subscription Agreements

For a long time the Enterprise Agreement was exclusively based on an enterprise-wide commitment to desktop products. Today, however, a customer can use an EA to commit to either the desktop products or to the server products, and the terms and conditions are contained in something called an Enrollment. There is an Enterprise Enrollment for the desktop products, and a Server and Cloud Enrollment for the server products. Because the Enterprise Enrollment was the only enrollment available under an EA for a long time, for many people it remains synonymous with an EA and in the exam you should consider an EA and the Enterprise Enrollment to mean the same thing, with the Server and Cloud Enrollment being called just that, or the SCE. So, in this section we'll look at how the desktop commitment works, and then a bit later we'll look at the SCE.

The Basics

The Enterprise Agreement is aimed at a larger customer who has more than 500 users or devices. It's always a three-year term, SA is compulsory on all purchases of licenses for on-premises products, and affiliates may also buy under an organization's Enterprise Agreement. For the purposes of the exam, an affiliate is defined to be a separate legal entity more than 50% owned by the organization signing the Enterprise Agreement. Affiliate organizations can be located anywhere in the world and thus the EA is ideally suited to an organization with a more complicated structure.

The following products are available in an Enterprise Agreement:

On-Premises		Online Services		Azure	
License only		Full User SLs	✔	User Plans	✔
License with SA	✔	Add-on User SLs	✔	Infrastructure Plans	✔
SA renewal	✔	From SA User SLs	✔	Support Plans	✔
		Step-up User SLs	✔	Consumption services	✔

Figure 48: Availability of Licenses in an EA

© Licensing School 2018

Purchasing On-Premises Products

In Figure 47 (which shows all of the Microsoft licensing programs) you can see that there is an Enterprise Agreement and an Enterprise Subscription Agreement. Both agreements enable customers to buy licenses for on-premises software, but they are perpetual licenses in an Enterprise Agreement and non-perpetual licenses in an Enterprise Subscription Agreement.

Perpetual licenses mean that customers are licensed to use the products that they buy through the agreement for ever – even if they don't renew the agreement. Non-perpetual licenses – also called subscription licenses – only license software to be used during the term of the agreement, and at the end of the agreement the customer can choose to renew the agreement and carry on using the software, not renew and de-install all software, or buy-out the licenses – that is, convert them to perpetual licenses and use the software for ever, as described above. Non-perpetual licenses are cheaper than perpetual licenses since customers are, in effect, just leasing the software rather than owning it.

I'll use the term "Enterprise Agreement" to refer to both of these agreements throughout this section since many of the program attributes are the same. Where there are differences I'll make sure to highlight these by using terms such as a perpetual Enterprise Agreement or the Enterprise Subscription Agreement.

Enterprise-Wide Commitment

If a customer wants to buy on-premises software through an EA then they must first qualify for the EA by counting all the "Qualified Devices" or "Qualified Users" in their organization, and then choosing an "Enterprise Product" that they are prepared to license for all of these Qualified Devices/Users. They must also meet a minimum of having 500 Qualified Devices or Users.

A Qualified Device is any device that can run Windows Pro locally in a physical or virtual operating system environment or one that's used to access a Virtual Desktop Infrastructure. A customer must count all devices as part of their Qualified Device total unless they qualify as one of the following exceptions:

- A PC that is used as a server
- An Industry Device – one that only runs hotel booking software, for example
- A device that is not managed by the organization

You need to know the definitions above for the exam but if you would like more detail on how, for example, you determine if a device is actually managed by an organization then there's a useful Volume Licensing Brief issued by Microsoft that gives a lot more detail.

For Qualified Users consider, for the purposes of the exam, that a Qualified User is anyone who uses a Qualified Device. If you're curious, or want more detail, you will find the full definitions for both Qualified Users and Qualified Devices in the Enterprise Enrollment document.

The Enterprise Products are listed below and for any chosen product, the customer must purchase the same number of licenses as they have Qualified Devices/Users:

- Windows 10 Enterprise E3/E5 or VDA E3/E5
- Office Professional Plus 2016 or Office 365 ProPlus
- Core CAL Suite or Enterprise CAL Suite

Customers who choose a single product enterprise-wide enter into what is known as a "Component EA". If they choose to license all three components – Windows, Office and a CAL Suite – then this is known as a platform, and the customer is said to have a "Platform EA".

It's also worth noting that if an organization standardizes on device licenses for Office 2016 through an EA then they must purchase Office Professional Plus 2016; if an organization DID want to standardize on Office Standard

© Licensing School 2018

2016 then they would need to purchase these licenses through an alternative agreement – the MPSA perhaps. Some of you may know customers who HAVE standardized on Office Standard 2016 through an EA – Microsoft do often grant exceptions, but you should learn the standard, programmatic elements of the EA for the exam.

Additional Products

Customers with an Enterprise Agreement can also choose to license all of the other available on-premises products through their agreement and these products (Windows Server, Visio, SQL CALs etc.) are known as Additional Products. Organizations may buy as many, or as few, of these products as they want to.

In addition, licenses for Online Services such as Project Online Professional may also be bought as Additional Products in any quantity, and we'll look at the rules for how these work in the next section.

Pricing

The Enterprise Agreement requires a level of customer commitment to standardize on Enterprise Products for the desktop, and because of that there are discounts available compared to an MPSA. For example, if a customer has 500 PCs and chooses to buy Office Professional Plus 2016 licenses with SA for all of them through an EA, then they will receive a significant discount compared to making exactly the same purchase through an MPSA. In addition, there's a further discount available if the customer signs up for the whole platform in an EA, and of course opting for subscription licenses in an Enterprise Subscription Agreement reduces the cost still further.

There are four different price levels available to an Enterprise Agreement customer, with discounts increasing between the levels. The discounts are based on the number of Qualified Devices or Qualified Users, with Level A requiring that a customer have 500 Qualified Devices/Users to sign the Enterprise Agreement. Note that the number of licenses for Additional Products has no bearing on the price level, which is governed solely by the number of Qualified Devices and/or Users.

You don't need to learn the numbers of Qualified Devices/Users for each level for the exam, but should know that if a customer has a large number of users/devices and wants the best price, then the EA is the agreement that will deliver this benefit. The price levels are shown below for your reference:

Qualified Devices/Users	Price Level
500	A
2,400	B
6,000	C
15,000	D

Figure 49: Enterprise Agreement Price Levels

Price Protection
Any licenses for products that are on a customer's initial order when they sign the Enterprise Agreement have fixed pricing for the three years of the agreement. This means that a customer knows exactly how much they will pay for any products that they have opted to pay annually for, and how much they will pay if they need to add additional licenses.

Payment
Customers usually opt to pay annually for licenses for on-premises products. For a customer with a perpetual EA, they pay a third of the license cost and a year's SA at the start of each year of the agreement. Enterprise Subscription Agreement customers pay an agreed annual fee for their products at the start of each year.

Customers can add licenses at any time for on-premises Additional Products that they have not purchased before. A single payment is made in the month of installation, which consists of the full amount of the license cost and a pro-rated amount for Software Assurance dependent on when in the agreement term the purchase was made.

© Licensing School 2018

True Up and Annual Orders

As we've said, customers signing a perpetual Enterprise Agreement do so with a stated number of Qualified Devices/Users. At the first anniversary they count up any new Qualified Devices or Users that may have been added during the year and pay for Enterprise Product licenses for those devices or users during a process known as True Up. This process is then repeated on the second anniversary and at the end of the agreement. Note that while the number of Qualified Devices/Users may go up during the agreement, it is not allowed to decrease. If customers have added licenses for any Additional Products that were on the initial order, then these are trued up in the same way.

Organizations with an Enterprise Subscription Agreement have the flexibility of increasing or decreasing the number of their Qualified Devices/Users as circumstances dictate, and at anniversary simply make an Annual Order when they pay for Enterprise Products for the number of Qualified Devices or Qualified Users for the following year. Organizations may decrease their Qualified Devices/Users at an anniversary as long as they do not go below the program minimum of 500 devices/users, and you can imagine that organizations with fluctuating numbers of devices/users often find this agreement attractive.

Applying your knowledge in the exam:

- Look out for business goals that state that the IT department want to standardize on an enterprise-wide desktop to make deployment and management of the desktops easier, or for problem statements such as an organization having file sharing compatibility issues, since a standardized desktop would be a great recommendation for them

- You may need to calculate the total Qualified Devices for an organization so make sure that you know the exceptions for the devices that don't need to be included: PCs used as a server, industry devices, and devices that aren't managed

- Make sure that you know the Enterprise Products so that you can confidently pick them out of a list and disregard any red herrings such as an organization which has "standardized" by covering all their users with the Windows CAL

- Remember that it is only the Enterprise Subscription Agreement that allows the number of Qualified Devices/Users to go down as well as up, so as soon as the business goals state that an organization needs this flexibility or has a fluctuating number of employees, then this is the agreement to recommend. Also look out for organizations that actively want to decrease licenses or employees through the term of their agreement

- Make sure that you know the options that a customer has available to them at the end of an Enterprise Subscription Agreement so that you can choose the right recommendation if their existing agreement is coming to an end. Recommend renewing the agreement if they want to continue the agreement as before, or suggest buying out the licenses if they want to convert them to perpetual licenses. The third option is that they don't renew the agreement and must de-install all their software – an unlikely correct answer in the exam!

© Licensing School 2018

Purchasing Online Services

The previous section covered a "traditional" EA where an organization commits to on-premises Enterprise Products across their Qualified Devices/Users. However, an EA may also be signed with licenses for Enterprise Online Services and in this type of EA there is no enterprise-wide commitment required.

Minimums

An Enterprise Online Services-only EA is signed with 500 User SLs of the following qualifying Enterprise Online Services:

- Office 365 E1, E3 or E5

- EMS E3 or E5

- Microsoft 365 Enterprise E3 or E5

Additional Products

When an Enterprise Online Services-only EA has been signed a customer may add both on-premises and Online Services Additional Products either to the initial order or at any time during the agreement term. On-premises Additional Products are transacted in exactly the same way as described in the previous section, and Online Services Additional Products are transacted as described in the Payment section below.

Pricing

The same price levels are available to customers signing an Enterprise Online Services-only EA based on the number of Enterprise Online Services User Subscription Licenses that are on the initial order.

Price Protection

Prices for the chosen Enterprise Online Services are fixed for the three-year term of the agreement.

Payment

Licenses for Online Services appear as a monthly price on the price list. Payment is made upfront for 12 months at the start of the agreement and at anniversaries. Additional licenses may be added at any time during the year and customers must pay for complete months remaining until the anniversary. Generally, customers may choose to pay at that moment in time or at anniversary. Licenses for Online Services Additional Products are paid for in this way too.

Adding and Reducing User SLs

As we've just said, licenses for Online Services may be added at any time and there is a commitment to pay the monthly fee for the licenses at least until the anniversary. At anniversary any licenses for Online Services Additional Products may be reduced (to zero if required) and those for Enterprise Online Services to the program minimum of 500 User SLs.

Applying your knowledge in the exam:

- Remember that customers can sign an Enterprise Agreement with 500 User SLs and no enterprise-wide commitment. However, make sure that you can pick out the Enterprise Online Services (Office 365 E1/E3/E5, EMS E3/E5, Microsoft 365 Enterprise E3/E5) since the initial order of 500 User SLs must consist of these licenses

- If you're trying to decide on the right program for a customer to purchase their Online Services licenses through, then remember that the EA gives price protection on these licenses for the full three-year term which makes it attractive

- Equally, if you get the feel that a customer needs a transactional approach to purchasing Online Services, then the EA is unlikely to be the best recommendation since although licenses can be added at any time, they can only be reduced at anniversary

© Licensing School 2018

Purchasing Azure Services

In Part 4 we saw that the Azure Services are broadly split into two categories from a purchasing point of view: Azure Plans and the Azure consumption services. All of the Azure Plan types are available in the Enterprise Agreement and Part 4 explains how they are transacted, so this section will focus on the Azure consumption services which we haven't covered in detail yet.

Monetary Commitment: Initial Order

To buy Azure consumption services in an EA, a customer must already have made a commitment to either the Enterprise Products or Enterprise Online Services. Then they estimate at the start of their agreement how much they think they are likely to spend on the Azure consumption services. This is not as difficult as it sounds – there's a calculator to help with estimating spend (https://azure.microsoft.com/en-us/pricing/calculator/) and, if you follow some recommendations, there are no penalties for not getting the estimates exactly right. The amount that a customer estimates that they will spend in the year is known as the Annual Monetary Commitment and is paid in full at the beginning of each year of the agreement.

Let's take an example to see how this works. Imagine that a customer has used the Azure calculator to find an estimated price for the Windows Server and Linux virtual machines that he wants to run. The calculator has quoted him an estimated monthly cost of $2,266.22. To translate this amount into a Monetary Commitment order you divide it by the cost of a single Monetary Commitment SKU ($100) which gives 22.6622 SKUs required per month. Clearly you need to order a whole number of SKUs, so let's take 22 and multiply that by 12 to find the yearly amount which is 264. Multiplying by $100 gives a Monetary Commitment amount of $26,400. Note that the minimum Monetary Commitment order in an EA is $1,200 – one Monetary Commitment SKU per month for 12 months.

So what happens if the customer doesn't get the Annual Monetary Commitment exactly right and either underspends or overspends in a particular year? Well, the underspend is easy – the customer forfeits the remaining funds at the end of the year. For this reason, you should always recommend that the customer makes an Annual Monetary Commitment for a lesser amount than perhaps they would originally estimate.

Monetary Commitment: Overage
Overspend of Monetary Commitment is known as overage so let's now see how that works.

For this example, let's consider the Olive Oil Drum Company in the diagram below. You can see that they made an Annual Monetary Commitment for $100,000 and consumed $25,000 of services in each of the first two quarters. Then they consumed a further $50,000 in the third quarter alone, and then $40,000 in the final quarter of the year. You'll also see something marked as the "Consumption Allowance" on the diagram:

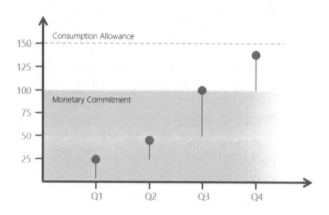

Figure 50: Azure Consumption Allowance

The Consumption Allowance is 50% of the original Monetary Commitment – so $50,000 in this case – and if the customer's overage on Azure stays within the Consumption Allowance during the year then the customer simply pays for the overage at the end of the year. So the Olive Oil Drum Company paid $100,000 at the start of the year and then at the end of the year would pay the remaining $40,000.

 © Licensing School 2018

The next example to consider is what happens when the overage exceeds the Consumption Allowance. In the example below, Cerise Estate Management made a Monetary Commitment of $60,000 which meant that their Consumption Allowance was set at $90,000. They consumed $40,000 of services in each of the first two quarters keeping them within the Consumption Allowance at $80,000 but then exceeded it in quarters three and four with continued consumption at $40,000 per quarter.

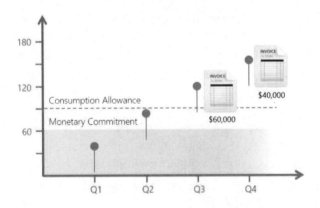

Figure 51: Azure Quarterly Billing

As soon as the Consumption Allowance is exceeded, the customer is switched to quarterly billing and at the end of the first quarter where the Consumption Allowance was exceeded they are invoiced for the full amount over the original Monetary Commitment. So, in the diagram above, there is an invoice issued at the end of Q3 for $60,000 – this is for the $120,000 that they have actually consumed minus the $60,000 they originally paid in the upfront Monetary Commitment. Another invoice is then issued at the end of the fourth quarter for the $40,000 of services they consumed in that quarter.

The final point that you need to know about overage is the fact that there is a slight difference between Direct and Indirect EAs. In a Direct EA Microsoft bills the customer directly, and in an Indirect EA the customer is billed by the reseller. It doesn't really matter if you do or don't have both Direct and Indirect EAs in your geography, you just need to know this one difference in overage: in an Indirect EA there is no Consumption Allowance and when the original Monetary Commitment is exhausted the customer is immediately switched to quarterly billing for the overage.

Monetary Commitment: Increases
In the previous example, Cerise Estate Management may be quite happy to go to quarterly billing for their Azure overage but they may prefer to be more in control of the payment schedule and therefore want to make an additional Monetary Commitment payment of a size and at a time that suits them. It's worth knowing that when an additional Monetary Commitment payment is made during the year, the next year's Monetary Commitment payment is automatically changed. You need to be able to calculate the change in the payment amount for the exam.

We know that Cerise Estate Management made an initial Monetary Commitment payment of $60,000. Let's now imagine that they make a further payment of $90,000 in month four of the year. How does this change the next year's payments? These are the steps you need to go through to calculate the adjusted amount:

Step 1: Count how many complete months there are left in the year:
We know they made the payment in month 4, so there are 8 complete months left

Step 2: Calculate the pro-rated amount added per month by dividing the added amount by the complete months left:
$90,000 ÷ 8 = $11,250

Step 3: Calculate this amount as a yearly amount by multiplying by 12:
$11,250 × 12 = $135,000

Step 4: Calculate the new Monetary Commitment by adding this new amount to the original Monetary Commitment:
$60,000 + $135,000 = $195,000

© Licensing School 2018

Pricing

There are no price levels for the Azure services in an EA, so a price per hour for a Windows Server virtual machine is the same regardless of which price level the customer is entitled to for his Enterprise Products or Enterprise Online Services.

Price Protection

Customers who buy the Azure consumptions services through an EA get best price protection for these services. This means that every month when the Azure systems are deciding how much to decrement the Monetary Commitment by for a particular service, they check the following sources and charge the customer the best price of all three:

- Baseline price – the price of the service when the EA was signed

- Negotiated price – any special price for the service that was agreed when the EA was signed

- Current price – from the current month's pricelist

Applying your knowledge in the exam:

- Make sure that you're familiar with the way overage works in a Direct and an Indirect EA. There will be some customer scenarios in the exam where you're given a customer's Monetary Commitment amount and their usage of Azure and you need to identify when and for what amount their overage payments will be

- You will also need to know how to calculate new Annual Monetary Commitment payments after a customer has made an additional payment, so brace yourself and learn the calculations in the section on page 214

- Remember that one of the benefits of paying for Azure services through an EA is best price protection for the three-year term, so if this is important to the customer then confidently recommend the EA

Server and Cloud Enrollment

The Basics
The Server and Cloud Enrollment (SCE) is the second enrollment that is available to be signed under the Enterprise Agreement. The Enterprise Enrollment covers the desktop products and the SCE focusses on the server products. A customer may choose to have either or both of these Enrollments – they're absolutely not dependent on each other. The SCE does share some characteristics with the Enterprise Enrollment: the term is three years, there's a level of commitment, and Software Assurance is mandatory.

The following products are available in a Server and Cloud Enrollment:

On-Premises		Online Services		Azure	
License only		Full User SLs	✔	User Plans	✔
License with SA	✔	Add-on User SLs	✔	Infrastructure Plans	✔
SA renewal	✔	From SA User SLs	✔	Support Plans	✔
		Step-up User SLs	✔	Consumption services	✔

Figure 52: Availability of Licenses in an SCE

Purchasing On-Premises Products
Enterprise-Wide Commitment
We saw with the Enterprise Enrollment that a customer needs to make a commitment to the Enterprise Products for a minimum number of desktops and then they can add Additional Products – either on-premises products or Online Services – and also buy Azure consumption services if they want to. The Server and Cloud Enrollment is similar: a customer makes a commitment to one of three server components for a minimum number of licenses, and then can buy Additional Products and/or Azure consumption services as needed.

 © Licensing School 2018

The table below shows the three components, the products that fall under them, and the required minimums for those products. An organization looks at all of the licenses they have in use across their installed base (acquired through any licensing program) and then commits to purchase Software Assurance for all of those licenses in any one of the components.

Components	Application Platform	Core Infrastructure	Developer Tools
Products	SQL Server + optionally BizTalk and/or SharePoint	Windows Server and System Center	Visual Studio
Minimums	**SQL:** 5 Server licenses and 250 CALs, or 50 Core licenses **SharePoint:** 5 Server licenses **BizTalk:** 24 Core licenses	**Core Infrastructure Server Suite:** 400 Core licenses	**Visual Studio Enterprise with MSDN and/or MSDN Platforms:** 20 User licenses

Figure 53: SCE Server Components

Application Platform Component

As you can see in the table above, the Application Platform component centers around SQL Server. If a customer wants to commit to SQL Server with Software Assurance across their estate then the SCE is a great mechanism for them to purchase it through. If they are prepared to commit to SQL Server then they can optionally add on SharePoint and/or BizTalk Server too, but do note that they wouldn't be able to sign an SCE with just SharePoint or BizTalk Server.

I think the best way of learning about the SCE is to take a sample customer scenario so let's first consider Cyan Ida's Pharmacy who have SQL Server 2008 and 2012 and are interested in upgrading their whole estate to SQL Server 2016. This makes them an ideal candidate for the SCE, so how would they go about signing an SCE? The first stage is to document the installed base of SQL Server, and Cyan Ida's Pharmacy's current SQL Server estate is shown below:

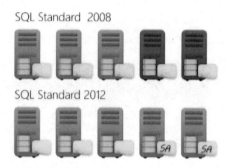

Figure 54: Cyan Ida's Pharmacy – SQL Server Estate

You can see that they have a mixed estate of SQL Server Standard 2008 and 2012 licensed with the Server/CAL model. All of the servers have licenses assigned to them, but only two of the SQL 2012 servers have licenses with active Software Assurance. Two of the SQL 2008 servers (shown in red) are currently running SQL Server but will be retired within the next 18 months.

Once the installed base is calculated, Cyan Ida's Pharmacy must sign their SCE with an initial order which covers this entire base with Software Assurance. They have a choice of three types of licenses in order to cover each server with SA: either SA renewal, a new license with Software Assurance (L&SA), or a Subscription license.

They should renew the SA for the two servers with active SA, and then purchase L&SA or Subscription licenses for the other servers. The Subscription licenses are unique to the Server and Cloud Enrollment so let's find out a bit more about these now.

There are Subscription licenses available for all of the different SQL Server licenses – so Server licenses, CALs, and Core licenses – and for all of the editions, and purchasing Subscription licenses fulfils the requirement for having active SA on licenses. The Subscription licenses are MSUs – Monthly Subscription Units – which means that they show as a monthly price on the

© Licensing School 2018

price list which makes for easy pro-rating if a customer adds them part way through an agreement. As you would expect from the name, a customer never owns a Subscription license. Customers may mix and match Subscription licenses with L&SA or SA to cover their entire estate.

Cyan Ida's Pharmacy have a choice of MSUs or L&SA to cover the servers currently without active SA. Which should they choose? Well, price may be a deciding factor for them; if they don't need or want to own perpetual licenses they may decide to move to the Subscription model since these licenses are priced at about 35% of the License price. They have eight servers that they need to cover with SA, and buying L&SA for all of them could be too high a cost.

Another reason for buying MSUs is that the number of licenses may be reduced during the term of the agreement. The two red servers indicated that the servers were due to be retired in the next 18 months or so. Because they are currently running SQL Server, they must be included in the agreement and covered with SA, but Cyan Ida's Pharmacy don't need these servers in the long term and so buying L&SA for these servers doesn't make sense if there is a Subscription alternative. As long as they buy 12 months' worth of an MSU they can reduce numbers at the next anniversary.

Cyan Ida's Pharmacy do want to own licenses long-term and so they decide to purchase L&SA for most of the servers and MSUs for the two servers that will be retired. This means that their initial order will consist of 2 x SQL Standard Server SA, 6 x SQL Standard Server L&SA, and 2 x SQL Standard Server MSU. At the first anniversary they decide whether they want to continue with the MSUs – they can decrease the number to zero if they no longer need the servers or pay another 12 months for one or both of the servers depending on their needs.

Note that there's complete flexibility with the SCE – if Cyan Ida's Pharmacy's plans change, they could add more servers and cover them with MSUs part the way through a year. At anniversary they pay for the complete months that the servers were used in the previous year and for 12 months for the following year. Once 12 months have been paid, the MSUs can be reduced again if required. Equally, since Cyan Ida's Pharmacy actually prefer to own licenses, they could add a server and then true-up the L&SA cost at the next anniversary.

Core Infrastructure Component
The Core Infrastructure component is all about Windows Server and System Center which must be purchased together as the Core Infrastructure Server (CIS) Suites. The rules are very similar to the Application Platform component that we've just considered, where the entire installed base of Windows Server and System Center licenses must be covered with SA via either SA renewal, L&SA or CSI Suite MSUs.

Developer Tools Component
The Developer Tools component is the last of the three SCE components that all behave in a very similar way. It is, of course, the mechanism for customers to acquire Visual Studio licenses and all of the rules that we've looked at apply to this component too – the installed base must meet the minimum requirements and then all licenses must be covered with SA.

Pricing
The price level of a Server and Cloud Enrollment is set by a qualifying agreement – so if a customer has a Select Plus, MPSA or Enterprise Agreement in the relevant pool then that price level is applied to the SCE. For example, if a customer has an MPSA at Level B in the servers pool then they would be eligible for Level B pricing when they signed an Application Platform SCE. If there is no qualifying agreement, then the SCE is set at Price Level A.

It's worth noting that buying SQL Server (for instance) as an Additional Product within the Enterprise Enrollment is more expensive than buying it under the Server and Cloud Enrollment. This, of course, makes sense since you're making a commitment to SQL Server when you buy it through the SCE.

 © Licensing School 2018

Price Protection, Payment, Additional Products

When on-premises products are purchased through the SCE, price protection, payment and the way Additional Products are transacted work in exactly the same way as in the Enterprise Agreement section above.

Applying your knowledge in the exam:

- Look out for business goals that specifically mention the products available through the SCE and see if the customer could commit to an SCE by being prepared to cover the whole of their installed base with SA for one, or more, products. There might be business objectives to run the latest version of the software, or a requirement for a particular SA benefit such as License Mobility, for example

- If you're asked to recommend the licenses that a customer would need on their initial order for an SCE, remember that either L&SA or Subscription licenses can cover existing licenses without SA, and if Subscription licenses are used, the amounts may be reduced after 12 months

- If a customer has stated a desire to update their core infrastructure, remember that this term refers to Windows Server and System Center and is likely to be pointing you towards recommending that customers acquire the Core Infrastructure Server Suites through an SCE. Equally though, do remember that these suites ARE available through other agreements if a customer doesn't want to commit enterprise-wide

- You should learn the minimums as shown in Figure 53 so that you don't get caught out recommending an SCE when the minimums can't be reached

- Remember that the price level for an SCE is typically inherited from an existing agreement, so look out for details of a current MPSA or Enterprise Agreement with a stated price level that would also apply to a new SCE

Purchasing Online Services

There is no option to sign a Server and Cloud Enrollment with just Online Services licenses but, as we saw in the previous section, they may be added as Additional Products once a commitment to one of the server components has been made.

Purchasing Azure Services

The Server and Cloud Enrollment gives two ways for a customer to pay for Azure consumption services dependent on whether or not they have already signed an SCE for another product. Let's take a look at the options now.

Azure as an Additional Service

When a customer signs an SCE for any of the three components that we've just looked at then they are automatically provisioned for Azure. This means that technically they're ready to use any of the Azure services and they're just invoiced quarterly for whatever they consume. This is ideal for customers who don't really want to make a commitment to Azure but are interested in trying it out.

Azure-only SCE

Alternatively, a customer can sign a Server and Cloud Enrollment by making a commitment to Azure via a Monetary Commitment payment. This works in exactly the same way as we discussed in the EA section with just a difference in the minimums: for the SCE there is a required minimum of 10 Monetary Commitment SKUs per month which equates to $10 \times 12 \times \$100 = \$12,000$ per year.

Applying your knowledge in the exam:

- Remember how the payments for Azure differ depending on how the customer buys it through the SCE: if they have an Azure-only SCE then they make an upfront Annual Monetary Commitment, if they have a non-Azure SCE then they pay quarterly in arrears based on what they have consumed

© Licensing School 2018

Microsoft Products and Services Agreement (MPSA)

The Basics

The MPSA is aimed at a larger customer who has more than 250 users or devices. The agreement is considered to be an evergreen agreement since it doesn't need re-signing every three years as an Enterprise Agreement does. Software Assurance is a completely optional purchase in an MPSA; on a license by license basis, customers can choose whether or not they buy SA. All licenses for on-premises products are perpetual licenses.

Similar to the Enterprise Agreement the MPSA enables affiliates to buy under it, but there's more flexibility than the Enterprise Agreement since an MPSA affiliate may be a business unit, division, or subsidiary as well as a more-than-50%-owned legal entity. Purchasing Accounts are set up for each affiliate which means that they can buy exactly what they need when they need it, separate to the needs of the other affiliates, but the overall purchasing is combined so that the best possible price levels are achieved.

The table below shows which products are available in the MPSA. You'll notice a couple of grey ticks: the conventional Step-up User SLs aren't available in the MPSA but there are some transition licenses that broadly do the same thing, and the Azure consumption services are no longer available to new customers.

On-Premises		Online Services		Azure	
License only	✔	Full User SLs	✔	User Plans	✔
License with SA	✔	Add-on User SLs	✔	Infrastructure Plans	
SA renewal	✔	From SA User SLs		Support Plans	
		Step-up User SLs	✔	Consumption services	✔

Figure 55: Availability of Licenses in an MPSA

Purchasing On-Premises Products

Points and Pools

Every product that Microsoft offers is categorized into one of three product pools, and these pools are key to the MPSA:

- Systems pool (Windows 10 and VDA, for example)

- Applications pool (Office and the Office family products, for example)

- Servers pool (all Server and CAL licenses)

Each product within these pools is assigned a points count and, as mentioned before, the Product Terms has an exhaustive list of all the products and how many points they are each worth, both as just a license and also with SA added.

When a customer is working out what licenses they need they should split their "shopping list" of products into these three pools since the program minimums and price levels are dependent on each pool, rather than being aggregated across all pools. This means that a customer could be eligible for the best price level in one pool, the lowest in another, and have no agreement at all for the third pool.

Price Levels

Points within an MPSA are important since they determine a customer's price level. A customer needs to buy licenses totaling at least 500 points in a particular pool each year to be eligible for an MPSA, although they don't have to purchase licenses totaling these points all on their initial order. This entitles them to Level A – the basic level – pricing. The table below shows the different numbers of points that customers have to reach each year to be eligible for that pricing, with Level D offering the best prices to customers. As with the EA, you don't need to learn these numbers for the exam, but should be aware that customers with large numbers of licenses will get a price benefit by purchasing through the MPSA.

© Licensing School 2018

Points	Price Level
500	A
4,000	B
10,000	C
25,000	D

Figure 56: MPSA Price Levels

The MPSA is targeted at customers with 250 PCs or more and although the program minimums don't refer to a specific number of PCs, if a customer with 250 PCs bought Office for all of those machines at 2 points per license, this would total 500 points – the program minimum.

Payment
Payment options for MPSA customers are dependent on whether Software Assurance is purchased with licenses: if you buy licenses without SA then the payment is due in full at the time of software installation, and if you buy licenses with SA then there is the option to spread payments. The MPSA offers a couple of different payment options, but whichever one a customer chooses they always make three payments where the cost of the license and (up to) three years of SA are split between those payments. If you know more about these options, don't worry that you need to do complicated calculations of any sort in the exam – you just need to know that spread payments are supported if SA is purchased with a license.

Price Protection
There is no price protection for on-premises products in an MPSA since customers pay for an order at that moment in time at the current pricelist price.

Commitment

A customer purchasing through an MPSA has complete flexibility in the licenses that they purchase; although they need to commit to purchasing 500 points within a particular pool each year, they do not have to buy any specific licenses or to commit to buying Software Assurance at all. This is often called a "transactional" agreement or a "pay as you go" agreement, and is ideal for a customer who wants to buy licenses as projects come up, or sees no particular benefit in, for example, standardizing the software they install on each desktop.

Applying your knowledge in the exam:

- The main reason you will recommend an MPSA in the exam is for customers who want to purchase licenses for on-premises software on ad-hoc basis, or without Software Assurance, so look out for this requirement

- It's perfectly acceptable for a customer to have an Enterprise Agreement to license their desktops and to also have an MPSA for ad hoc purchases of additional software, so bear this in mind when making a recommendation for a customer with an existing EA

- Look carefully at the business goals for an organization – if they want to upgrade just part of their estate or purchase SA on just some of their licenses, then recommend the MPSA rather than the Enterprise Agreements which require licensing commitment across the organization

- Remember that the Azure consumption services aren't available for new customers and thus you should feel happy in not recommending the MPSA where Azure is concerned

© Licensing School 2018

Purchasing Online Services

Points and Pools

Licenses for Online Services may be purchased through the MPSA, as can User SLs for the Azure User Plans which, for the purposes of the purchasing rules, can be considered to be Online Services. These licenses are placed in product pools and given a points value as we saw with the licenses for on-premises products. Typically, these User SLs are assigned a points value of 1, and the minimums for a product pool are changed to just 250 points if only User SLs are being ordered.

Payment

Online Services licenses are priced monthly and always paid for upfront in an MPSA but again there are some options in terms of exactly how many months a customer must pay for when they make their first order for Online Services. For the purposes of the exam, you need to know that it's an upfront payment for multiple months rather than a transactional payment for licenses on a monthly basis. This term is known as a Subscription.

Price Protection

There is fixed price protection available for Online Services in an MPSA: if a customer orders 100 Office 365 E3 licenses they pay upfront for those licenses at the current price list price. If they then add more Office 365 E3 licenses within the term of the Subscription then they are charged at the same price – regardless of the current price list price.

Applying your knowledge in the exam:

- Recommend the MPSA for a customer who wants a single agreement for their ad-hoc purchases of licenses for both on-premises products and Online Services products

- If a customer only wants to buy licenses for Online Services then you should consider whether the MPSA or CSP is the better option for the customer: CSP offers more options than the MPSA and is likely to be the best recommendation

Select Plus Agreements

The Basics

In July 2014 the retirement of Select Plus was announced and although this process has not yet been completed there has been no new innovation in this licensing program since then. If you look at the table below you can see that this is an older agreement where customers can only purchase perpetual licenses for on-premises products.

On-Premises		Online Services		Azure	
License only	✔	Full User SLs		User Plans	
License with SA	✔	Add-on User SLs		Infrastructure Plans	
SA renewal	✔	From SA User SLs		Support Plans	
		Step-up User SLs		Consumption services	

Figure 57: Availability of Licenses in Select Plus

As a program it works in a very similar way to the MPSA with the same points and pools and price levels etc. Customers can no longer sign a new Select Plus agreement and so although you will see Select Plus as a suggested answer in the exam, you should consider the MPSA as the replacement for Select Plus and always recommend that program in preference.

Applying your knowledge in the exam:

- You'll see questions in the exam where Select Plus is a suggested answer but due to the announced retirement of this program you should always choose MPSA in preference

© Licensing School 2018

Cloud Solution Provider Program

The Basics

The Cloud Solution Provider program is not a customer licensing agreement at all, it's a program through which partners buy licenses from Microsoft to resell to their customers. Microsoft recruit partners to sell through CSP and then it's up to the partner as to the terms and conditions that they offer their customers, so there's no standard agreement length or payment terms that partners need to impose on customers. There are some geographical restrictions within CSP, namely that a partner can only sell to a customer within the territory that they are authorized as a partner. The US and Canada are each separate territories and many European countries form another. This means that a partner based in the UK couldn't sell to subsidiaries of a UK customer based in the US. A partner also can't sell (programmatically) to a customer and its affiliates under the same agreement like they can within the EA or MPSA agreements.

Although the partner determines the terms and conditions that they go to customers with, there is a document from Microsoft which governs the use rights of products purchased through CSP. A customer must agree to the conditions of the Microsoft Cloud Agreement (they don't need to sign anything) which sometimes amends the Product Terms and thus the use rights of products purchased through CSP.

Microsoft's intention with CSP is that partners don't just sell licenses, but rather solutions. Therefore, in the exam, if a customer wants any sort of partner-managed solution, then CSP is likely to be the right recommendation.

The following products are available through CSP, where the grey ticks indicate that Add-on and From User SLs are only available for the Dynamics 365 products, and that not every single Azure consumption service is yet available in CSP:

On-Premises		Online Services		Azure	
License only		Full User SLs	✔	User Plans	✔
License with SA		Add-on User SLs	✔	Infrastructure Plans	
SA renewal		From SA User SLs	✔	Support Plans	
		Step-up User SLs		Consumption services	✔

Figure 58: Availability of Licenses in CSP

Purchasing Online Services

As I said in the introduction to this section, the partner buys licenses from Microsoft and then resells them to a customer with terms and conditions that they define. This means that Microsoft don't actually know the offers that are being made to customers which in turn means that exam questions about CSP can only test how Microsoft sell to partners with the assumption that they could pass these conditions on to their customers.

Minimums

There is no minimum order in CSP, a partner may order just one User SL if that's all that's required for a customer. Don't take this to mean that CSP is only aimed at smaller businesses, this rule is just to remove any barrier to sale, so that businesses of any size with any size requirement for Online Services can use CSP.

© Licensing School 2018

Subscriptions

When a partner orders a User SL they set up a Subscription (note the capital S!) for that Online Service. This is essentially a container to which they add licenses. So, if a customer wants 25 Office 365 E3 licenses then an Office 365 E3 Subscription is set up with 25 licenses in it.

Payment

Microsoft bill the partner monthly upfront for Online Services licenses. So, in our example above, the partner would be billed for 25 Office 365 E3 licenses at the start of their monthly billing period, and again at the start of the next one. As we've said, the partner is under no obligation to bill the customer in this way – they could bill upfront quarterly, for example – but monthly billing is an attractive option that they are able to offer their customers.

Pricing

Pricing is, of course, determined by the partner. Microsoft's intention is that it equals both Level A pricing of an EA or if a customer purchased through the Microsoft website. There is only one price level in CSP.

Price Protection

When the Subscription is set up it has a duration of 12 months. However, this is not a minimum term or commitment, it's just the term through which the price of the licenses will be fixed. If a customer needs more Office 365 E3 licenses, then the partner knows what the price will be to them and so they can guarantee a fixed price for the duration of the Subscription to their customers if they want to.

Adding and Reducing Licenses

Partners can add and reduce licenses to an existing Subscription at any time. The original customer order was for 25 Office 365 E3 licenses and we know that the partner is charged upfront at the beginning of the monthly billing period for those licenses. If the customer wants another five licenses in the middle of the month then the partner just adds those licenses to the Subscription and then they are billed, on a pro-rated daily basis, for the extra licenses at the beginning of the next billing period, as well as for 30 Office 365 E3 licenses for the next month.

Licenses may also be reduced at any time. If the same customer wanted to reduce their 30 licenses to 27 a couple of months later, then the partner would just reduce the number of licenses in the Subscription and then they would be refunded, on a pro-rated daily basis, for the reduction in the next month's bill, and would be charged for 27 Office 365 E3 licenses for the next month.

Step-up User SLs
There are no Step-up User SLs in CSP which feels a bit odd – if a partner has sold 500 Office 365 E3 User SLs to a customer who now needs Office 365 E5 for 30 of those users, how do they acquire these services? In CSP there's a simple solution: a partner simply reduces the number of Office 365 E3 User SLs to 470, and then starts a new Office 365 E5 Subscription with 30 licenses.

Applying your knowledge in the exam:

- Remember that there are no licenses for on-premises products available through CSP so avoid recommending this program when that's the customer requirement

- Don't be influenced by the size of the customer when you're considering recommending CSP – the minimum order is 1 User SL, but any size customer may find buying Online Services licenses through CSP attractive, especially if they want the option for monthly payments or being able to add and reduce licenses on a monthly basis

- Any indication that a customer wants a partner-managed solution rather than just to buy licenses is likely to lead to a recommendation for CSP

- As with the MPSA, it's perfectly acceptable for a customer to have an EA for their committed purchases and then to purchase other licenses through CSP on a more ad-hoc basis, so don't be afraid to make this recommendation

© Licensing School 2018

Purchasing Azure Services

Azure User Plans and the consumption services are available through CSP. The User Plans, purchased as User SLs, are transacted in exactly the same way as Online Services such as Office 365, and so this section focuses on the consumption services.

Subscriptions

Before a customer can use any of the Azure consumption services, an Azure Subscription must be created. This again is a container to which services (such as virtual machines) are assigned as they are set up for billing purposes.

Payment

There is no commitment required within CSP to purchase the Azure consumption services; the partner is simply invoiced at the end of the monthly billing period for whatever services the customer has consumed. Again, the partner can invoice the customer in this way, or may impose their own terms and conditions.

Pricing

As with Online Services, pricing of the Azure consumption services is determined by the partner, but again Microsoft's intention is that it equals both EA pricing or if a customer purchased through the Microsoft website. There is only one price level in CSP.

Price Protection

As with Online Services, pricing of an Azure consumption service is fixed for the duration of an Azure Subscription. However, an Azure Subscription lasts only one month (and then auto renews) and so pricing for services could potentially be different every month.

Applying your knowledge in the exam:

- To correctly recommend CSP for Azure services, look out for an organization that doesn't want to make any sort of upfront commitment to Azure and just wants to pay for the services as they use them on a monthly basis

Agreements for Small and Medium Businesses

You will find some questions in the exam that ask you to recommend a Volume Licensing agreement for Small and Medium Businesses, or SMBs. In Microsoft terms this is typically an organization with less than 250 PCs and you should use this definition for the exam. As you know, the exam is primarily focused on recommending agreements to LORGs, so you don't need a detailed knowledge of the SMB programs, you'll just need to recommend an agreement for a smaller organization, based on some simple criteria. If you know and understand the LORG agreements, then consider that an Open agreement is the SMB version of an MPSA/Select Plus agreement, an Open Value Company Wide agreement the SMB version of an Enterprise Agreement, and the Open Value Subscription agreement the equivalent of the Enterprise Subscription Agreement. Applying what you know about the LORG programs will help you to choose the right SMB agreement in the exam.

You'll find a summary table of the SMB agreements in the Revision Cards section; note that this is a simplified table of information which just gives the level of detail you need for the exam, rather than being exhaustive. You'll see that one of the major differences in the SMB and LORG agreements is the way that affiliates are treated; in the SMB programs they must all be in the same geographic territory, but in the LORG programs they can be across the world.

Applying your knowledge in the exam:

- Pay attention to the size of the organization; don't assume that because it's an exam focused on recommending licensing solutions to LORGs that all scenarios will require a recommendation of an MPSA or Enterprise Agreement. If the organization has under 250 PCs then you should be choosing an Open, Open Value, or Open Value Subscription agreement

© Licensing School 2018

The Microsoft Licensing Programs Revision Cards

The following pages contain the Revision Cards for this section, providing a summary of the key points that you should know about the Microsoft licensing programs for the exam.

© Licensing School 2018

Revision Card 39:
Microsoft Licensing Programs

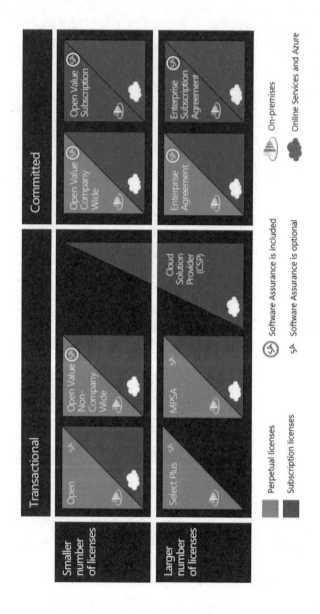

© Licensing School 2018

Revision Card 40:
On-premises Products: MPSA and Enterprise Agreements

	MPSA	Enterprise Agreement	Enterprise Subscription Agreement
Agreement Type	Transactional	Committed	Committed
Agreement Term	Evergreen	3 years	3 years
Minimums	500 points	500 Qualified Devices/Users	500 Qualified Devices/Users
License Type	Perpetual	Perpetual	Non-perpetual
Software Assurance	Optional	Included	Included
Desktop Standardization	No	Required	Required
Price Bands	4 levels	4 levels	4 levels
Other Discounts	No	Platform	Platform
Payment Terms	Upfront, or annual payments with SA	Annual payments	Annual payments
Affiliates	Across territories	Across territories	Across territories

Revision Card 41:
Online Services: MPSA, Enterprise Agreements, CSP

	MPSA	Enterprise Agreement	CSP
Minimums	250 User SLs	500 User SLs	1 User SL
Payment Terms	Upfront annually	Upfront annually	Upfront monthly
License Availability	Most User SLs	All User SLs	Primarily Full User SLs
Adding Licenses	At any time	At any time	At any time
Payment of Additional Licenses	When they are added	At anniversary	At next month
Reducing Licenses	At Subscription end	At anniversary	At any time
Price Bands	4 levels	4 levels	1 level
Price Protection	Duration of Subscription	36 months	12 months
Use Rights	Full	Full	Some limitations
Affiliates	Across territories	Across territories	Within territories

© Licensing School 2018

Revision Card 42:
Azure: Enterprise Agreements, SCE, CSP

	Enterprise Agreement	SCE	CSP
Availability of Azure Plans	All Plans	All Plans	User Plans only
Availability of consumption services	All services	All services	Most services
Payment Terms	Upfront Annual Monetary Commitment	Upfront Annual Monetary Commitment/ Quarterly in arrears	Monthly in arrears
Minimums	$1,200 per year	$12,000 per year/ None	None
Price Bands	1 level	1 level	1 level
Price Protection	Best price protection for 36 months	Best price protection for 36 months	Monthly pricing

Revision Card 43:
The Server and Cloud Enrollment: On-Premises Products

Components	Application Platform	Core Infrastructure	Developer Tools
Products	SQL Server + optionally BizTalk and/or SharePoint	Windows Server and System Center	Visual Studio
Minimums	**SQL:** 5 Server licenses and 250 CALs, or 50 Core licenses **SharePoint:** 5 Server licenses **BizTalk:** 24 Core licenses	**Core Infrastructure Server Suite:** 400 Core licenses	**Visual Studio Enterprise with MSDN and/or MSDN Platforms:** 20 User licenses
Commitment	SA on installed base	SA on installed base	SA on installed base
Licenses Available	SA-only – for existing licenses with active SA L&SA – perpetual license option for existing licenses with no SA, or new licenses MSU – subscription license option for existing licenses with no SA, or new licenses		

© Licensing School 2018

Revision Card 44:
License Availability

On-Premises		Online Services		Azure	
Enterprise Agreement/SCE					
License only		Full User SLs	✓	User Plans	✓
License with SA	✓	Add-on User SLs	✓	Infrastructure Plans	✓
SA renewal	✓	From SA User SLs	✓	Support Plans	✓
		Step-up User SLs	✓	Consumption services	✓
MPSA					
License only	✓	Full User SLs	✓	User Plans	✓
License with SA	✓	Add-on User SLs	✓	Infrastructure Plans	
SA renewal	✓	From SA User SLs		Support Plans	
		Step-up User SLs	✓	Consumption services	✓
Select Plus					
License only	✓	Full User SLs		User Plans	
License with SA	✓	Add-on User SLs		Infrastructure Plans	
SA renewal	✓	From SA User SLs		Support Plans	
		Step-up User SLs		Consumption services	
CSP					
License only		Full User SLs	✓	User Plans	✓
License with SA		Add-on User SLs	✓	Infrastructure Plans	
SA renewal		From SA User SLs	✓	Support Plans	
		Step-up User SLs		Consumption services	✓

Revision Card 45:
Open and Open Value Agreements

	Open	Open Value Company Wide	Open Value Subscription
Minimum Order	5 licenses	5 PCs	5 PCs
Agreement Term	2 years	3 years	3 years
License Type	Perpetual	Perpetual	Non-perpetual
Agreement Type	Transactional	Committed	Committed
Software Assurance	Optional	Included	Included
Desktop Standardization	No	Required	Required
Other Discounts	No	Platform	Platform
Payment Terms	Upfront	Annual payments	Annual payments
Affiliates	Same territory	Same territory	Same territory

© Licensing School 2018

© Licensing School 2018

Recap Questions and Answers

Use these Recap Questions to see how much you know about the Microsoft licensing programs. If you find any areas that you need to go over you can review the relevant topic in this section of the book. As usual, you'll find a couple of questions on each page with the answers when you turn over.

© Licensing School 2018

Questions 1 – 3

1. Purple Paint Pot Decorators have 800 PCs and they want to purchase Office Professional Plus 2016 licenses for all of them. They currently have a policy of owning all company assets and they are interested in a number of SA benefits. What licensing program is likely to be the best fit for them to purchase these licenses through?

   a) CSP
   b) Enterprise Agreement
   c) Enterprise Subscription Agreement
   d) MPSA

2. Blue Lamp Ideas need to purchase 540 Office Professional Plus 2016 licenses for their head office machines. They have 1,000 machines in total and want to cover the 540 licenses with SA to make sure that they get new version rights. How would you recommend that they purchase these 540 licenses?

   a) Select Plus
   b) Enterprise Agreement
   c) Enterprise Subscription Agreement
   d) MPSA

3. Periwinkle Packaging Solutions are a small startup company with 15 brand new machines that have Windows 10 Pro and Office Professional 2016 pre-installed. They have set up a server infrastructure and now need to buy the Core CAL Suite for all of the machines. They have decided to invest in Software Assurance but need the very lowest upfront costs. How should they purchase these Core CAL Suite licenses?

   a) OEM
   b) CSP
   c) Open Value Company Wide
   d) Open Value Subscription

Answers 1 – 3

1. Purple Paint Pot Decorators have 800 PCs and they want to purchase Office Professional Plus 2016 licenses for all of them. They currently have a policy of owning all company assets and they are interested in a number of SA benefits. What licensing program is likely to be the best fit for them to purchase these licenses through?

   a) CSP
   b) Enterprise Agreement ✓
   c) Enterprise Subscription Agreement
   d) MPSA

2. Blue Lamp Ideas need to purchase 540 Office Professional Plus 2016 licenses for their head office machines. They have 1,000 machines in total and want to cover the 540 licenses with SA to make sure that they get new version rights. How would you recommend that they purchase these 540 licenses?

   a) Select Plus
   b) Enterprise Agreement
   c) Enterprise Subscription Agreement
   d) MPSA ✓

3. Periwinkle Packaging Solutions are a small startup company with 15 brand new machines that have Windows 10 Pro and Office Professional 2016 pre-installed. They have set up a server infrastructure and now need to buy the Core CAL Suite for all of the machines. They have decided to invest in Software Assurance but need the very lowest upfront costs. How should they purchase these Core CAL Suite licenses?

   a) OEM
   b) CSP
   c) Open Value Company Wide
   d) Open Value Subscription ✓

    © Licensing School 2018

Questions 4 – 6

4. Ultramarine Swim Wear have purchased 800 PCs with Windows 10 Pro pre-installed and now want to buy Office Professional Plus 2016 licenses for these machines. They want to pay an annual fee for these licenses and, if the number of PCs goes down, they would like to pay a smaller annual fee. What licensing agreement is likely to be the best fit for them to purchase these licenses through?

    a) CSP
    b) Enterprise Agreement
    c) Enterprise Subscription Agreement
    d) Open Value Subscription

5. Maroon Balloons have signed a Server and Cloud Enrollment for the Core Infrastructure component. They have been automatically provisioned for Azure and start using the services. When are they charged for their consumption?

    a) They must make a Monetary Commitment at the time they start using the service
    b) Invoices are issued monthly
    c) Invoices are issued quarterly
    d) They true up their usage at the end of the year

6. Cyan Ida's Pharmacy have an Indirect EA and have committed to an Azure Monetary Commitment of $100,000. In each of the first two quarters of the year they use $50,000 of Azure services, and in the third quarter use $25,000. When do they pay for this overage?

    a) As soon as the services are used
    b) At the end of the month in which the services are used
    c) At the end of the quarter
    d) At anniversary

Answers 4 – 6

4. Ultramarine Swim Wear have purchased 800 PCs with Windows 10 Pro pre-installed and now want to buy Office Professional Plus 2016 licenses for these machines. They want to pay an annual fee for these licenses and, if the number of PCs goes down, they would like to pay a smaller annual fee. What licensing agreement is likely to be the best fit for them to purchase these licenses through?

   a) CSP
   b) Enterprise Agreement
   c) **Enterprise Subscription Agreement** ✓
   d) Open Value Subscription

5. Maroon Balloons have signed a Server and Cloud Enrollment for the Core Infrastructure component. They have been automatically provisioned for Azure and start using the services. When are they charged for their consumption?

   a) They must make a Monetary Commitment at the time they start using the service
   b) Invoices are issued monthly
   c) **Invoices are issued quarterly** ✓
   d) They true up their usage at the end of the year

6. Cyan Ida's Pharmacy have an Indirect EA and have committed to an Azure Monetary Commitment of $100,000. In each of the first two quarters of the year they use $50,000 of Azure services, and in the third quarter use $25,000. When do they pay for this overage?

   a) As soon as the services are used
   b) At the end of the month in which the services are used
   c) **At the end of the quarter** ✓
   d) At anniversary

© Licensing School 2018

Questions 7 – 9

7. Pink Champagne Limousines currently have an Enterprise Agreement through which they buy licenses for on-premises products with SA. They are now interested in using some of the Azure consumption services. It is important to them that they know the highest price they will pay for any service for a three-year term. Through which program would you recommend that they buy the Azure services?

    a) CSP
    b) Enterprise Agreement
    c) SPLA
    d) MPSA

8. Spring Green Grocers want to sign an MPSA and will be setting up various Purchasing Accounts to reflect the way that they want to purchase licenses as an organization. Which of the following may they set up as Purchasing Accounts? Choose three answers.

    a) The Purchasing division within Spring Green Grocers
    b) A supplier
    c) A wholly owned subsidiary
    d) A partner company of which they own 75%
    e) An associate organization of which they own 25%

9. Lightshades of Grey want to purchase some Office Professional Plus 2016 licenses with SA, some Windows Server 2016 licenses without SA, and 50 Dynamics 365 Team Members User SLs. What licensing program would you recommend that they purchase these licenses through?

    a) MPSA
    b) Enterprise Agreement
    c) CSP
    d) Enterprise Subscription Agreement

7. Pink Champagne Limousines currently have an Enterprise Agreement through which they buy licenses for on-premises products with SA. They are now interested in using some of the Azure consumption services. It is important to them that they know the highest price they will pay for any service for a three-year term. Through which program would you recommend that they buy the Azure services?

   a) CSP
   b) Enterprise Agreement ✓
   c) SPLA
   d) MPSA

8. Spring Green Grocers want to sign an MPSA and will be setting up various Purchasing Accounts to reflect the way that they want to purchase licenses as an organization. Which of the following may they set up as Purchasing Accounts? Choose three answers.

   a) The Purchasing division within Spring Green Grocers ✓
   b) A supplier
   c) A wholly owned subsidiary ✓
   d) A partner company of which they own 75% ✓
   e) An associate organization of which they own 25%

9. Lightshades of Grey want to purchase some Office Professional Plus 2016 licenses with SA, some Windows Server 2016 licenses without SA, and 50 Dynamics 365 Team Members User SLs. What licensing program would you recommend that they purchase these licenses through?

   a) MPSA ✓
   b) Enterprise Agreement
   c) CSP
   d) Enterprise Subscription Agreement

© Licensing School 2018

Questions 10 – 12

10. Fuchsia Fancy Dress Hire currently have an Enterprise Agreement and buy Office 365 E3 User SLs for their head office staff to license them for Office 365 ProPlus and the associated Online Services. They employ additional staff on a seasonal basis and would like to license them for Office 365 E1, paying for the User SLs only when the staff are employed. Through which program would you recommend that they purchase these licenses?

    a) CSP
    b) Enterprise Agreement
    c) MPSA
    d) Open Value Subscription

11. Peach Snaps Cameras have a server farm consisting of 40 dual-processor servers which they want to license with Windows Server and System Center covered with Software Assurance. How would you recommend that Peach Snaps Cameras acquire their licenses?

    a) Through an MPSA with Software Assurance Membership
    b) Through an Enterprise Subscription Agreement
    c) Through an Enrollment for Core Infrastructure
    d) Through a Server and Cloud Enrollment

12. Powderblue Pottery have a Direct EA with an annual Azure Monetary Commitment of $50,000. In month 6 of the first year they place an additional Monetary Commitment order of $30,000. How will this change their Annual Monetary Commitment payment for the next year?

    a) It will not change it at all
    b) It will decrease to $20,000
    c) It will increase to $80,000
    d) It will increase to $110,000

Answers 10 – 12

10. Fuchsia Fancy Dress Hire currently have an Enterprise Agreement and buy Office 365 E3 User SLs for their head office staff to license them for Office 365 ProPlus and the associated Online Services. They employ additional staff on a seasonal basis and would like to license them for Office 365 E1, paying for the User SLs only when the staff are employed. Through which program would you recommend that they purchase these licenses?

   a) **CSP** ✓
   b) Enterprise Agreement
   c) MPSA
   d) Open Value Subscription

11. Peach Snaps Cameras have a server farm consisting of 40 dual-processor servers which they want to license with Windows Server and System Center covered with Software Assurance. How would you recommend that Peach Snaps Cameras acquire their licenses?

   a) Through an MPSA with Software Assurance Membership
   b) Through an Enterprise Subscription Agreement
   c) Through an Enrollment for Core Infrastructure
   d) **Through a Server and Cloud Enrollment** ✓

12. Powderblue Pottery have a Direct EA with an annual Azure Monetary Commitment of $50,000. In month 6 of the first year they place an additional Monetary Commitment order of $30,000. How will this change their Annual Monetary Commitment payment for the next year?

   a) It will not change it at all
   b) It will decrease to $20,000
   c) It will increase to $80,000
   d) **It will increase to $110,000** ✓

© Licensing School 2018

Questions 13 – 15

13. Tangerine Truckers have signed a Server and Cloud Enrollment for SQL Server and opted to cover 15 servers with SQL Server 2016 Core Subscription licenses at the start of the agreement. When can they reduce the number of these Subscription licenses?
    a) At the first anniversary
    b) At the second anniversary
    c) At any time in the first year
    d) At renewal

14. World of Magnolia have 500 PCs which they want to license with non-perpetual licenses for Windows, Office and the Core CAL Suite. Which licensing program would you recommend that they purchase these licenses through?
    a) MPSA
    b) CSP
    c) Enterprise Subscription Agreement
    d) Enterprise Agreement

15. Copper Feel Fabrics want to use some Azure virtual machines in a short-term proof of concept project. How would you recommend that they pay for these Azure services?
    a) CSP
    b) Enterprise Agreement
    c) MPSA
    d) Open Value Subscription

Answers 13 – 15

13. Tangerine Truckers have signed a Server and Cloud Enrollment for SQL Server and opted to cover 15 servers with SQL Server 2016 Core Subscription licenses at the start of the agreement. When can they reduce the number of these Subscription licenses?
    a) **At the first anniversary** ✓
    b) At the second anniversary
    c) At any time in the first year
    d) At renewal

14. World of Magnolia have 500 PCs which they want to license with non-perpetual licenses for Windows, Office and the Core CAL Suite. Which licensing program would you recommend that they purchase these licenses through?
    a) MPSA
    b) CSP
    c) **Enterprise Subscription Agreement** ✓
    d) Enterprise Agreement

15. Copper Feel Fabrics want to use some Azure virtual machines in a short-term proof of concept project. How would you recommend that they pay for these Azure services?
    a) **CSP** ✓
    b) Enterprise Agreement
    c) MPSA
    d) Open Value Subscription

© Licensing School 2018

Questions 16 – 19

16. The Papaya Hire Company want to buy 10,000 Microsoft 365 Enterprise E3 User SLs and want the best possible pricing for these licenses. Which program would you recommend that they purchase them through?
    a) CSP
    b) Enterprise Agreement
    c) SPLA
    d) MPSA

17. The Cobalt Bolt Company are interested in signing an Enterprise Agreement. How many PCs must they have to sign this agreement?
    a) 100
    b) 250
    c) 500
    d) 1,000

18. Honeydew Hatters completely own three companies, all located within five miles of their head office, with a total of 1,035 PCs. They want to implement a centralized purchasing policy under a single agreement so that all organizations are licensed in exactly the same way. What agreement should they sign to achieve this?
    a) An MPSA
    b) An Open Value agreement
    c) An Enterprise Agreement
    d) The Microsoft Cloud Agreement

19. The Lemon Launderette intend to sign an MPSA. How many User SLs must they purchase in the first year to qualify for Level A pricing?
    a) 100
    b) 250
    c) 500
    d) The price level is set by the number of points not User SLs

16. The Papaya Hire Company want to buy 10,000 Microsoft 365 Enterprise E3 User SLs and want the best possible pricing for these licenses. Which program would you recommend that they purchase them through?
    a) CSP
    b) Enterprise Agreement ✓
    c) SPLA
    d) MPSA

17. The Cobalt Bolt Company are interested in signing an Enterprise Agreement. How many PCs must they have to sign this agreement?
    a) 100
    b) 250
    c) 500 ✓
    d) 1,000

18. Honeydew Hatters completely own three companies, all located within five miles of their head office, with a total of 1,035 PCs. They want to implement a centralized purchasing policy under a single agreement so that all organizations are licensed in exactly the same way. What agreement should they sign to achieve this?
    a) An MPSA
    b) An Open Value agreement
    c) An Enterprise Agreement ✓
    d) The Microsoft Cloud Agreement

19. The Lemon Launderette intend to sign an MPSA. How many User SLs must they purchase in the first year to qualify for Level A pricing?
    a) 100
    b) 250 ✓
    c) 500
    d) The price level is set by the number of points not User SLs

© Licensing School 2018

Questions 20 – 23

20. Vermilion Jewellers want to buy 500 Microsoft 365 Enterprise E3 User SLs. They want a guaranteed price for these licenses for at least three years. Which program would you recommend that they purchase them through?
    a) CSP
    b) Enterprise Agreement
    c) SPLA
    d) MPSA

21. The Yellow Soup Tureen have an Enterprise Agreement. For how long can they purchase licenses under this agreement?
    a) 1 year
    b) 2 years
    c) 3 years
    d) The agreement is evergreen so they can purchase licenses for as long as they like

22. Xanthic Tractors are about to sign an Enterprise Agreement and are counting up their Qualified Devices. Which of the following devices do not need to be included? Choose two answers.
    a) PCs that are only used to run their Hire Services software
    b) PCs that are more than five years old
    c) PCs that are not being used currently
    d) PCs that are being used as a server

23. Which of the following is a benefit of the MPSA?
    a) Discounts for an annual commitment of $1,200 to Azure services
    b) A single agreement to purchase both perpetual and non-perpetual licenses for on-premises software
    c) A single agreement to purchase both licenses for on-premises software and Online Services
    d) Discounts for committing to products deployed enterprise-wide

20. Vermilion Jewellers want to buy 500 Microsoft 365 Enterprise E3 User SLs. They want a guaranteed price for these licenses for at least three years. Which program would you recommend that they purchase them through?

    a) CSP
    b) Enterprise Agreement ✓
    c) SPLA
    d) MPSA

21. The Yellow Soup Tureen have an Enterprise Agreement. For how long can they purchase licenses under this agreement?

    a) 1 year
    b) 2 years
    c) 3 years ✓
    d) The agreement is evergreen so they can purchase licenses for as long as they like

22. Xanthic Tractors are about to sign an Enterprise Agreement and are counting up their Qualified Devices. Which of the following devices do not need to be included? Choose two answers.

    a) PCs that are only used to run their Hire Services software ✓
    b) PCs that are more than five years old
    c) PCs that are not being used currently
    d) PCs that are being used as a server ✓

23. Which of the following is a benefit of the MPSA?

    a) Discounts for an annual commitment of $1,200 to Azure services
    b) A single agreement to purchase both perpetual and non-perpetual licenses for on-premises software
    c) A single agreement to purchase both licenses for on-premises software and Online Services ✓
    d) Discounts for committing to products deployed enterprise-wide

© Licensing School 2018

Questions 24 – 26

24. Mauve Stoves have historically purchased their server licenses through an MPSA for which they have achieved Level B pricing. They now intend to sign a new Server and Cloud Enrollment since they want to upgrade their whole SQL Server estate of 50 servers to the latest version. Which price level will they be entitled to for the new SCE?
    a) Level A
    b) Level B
    c) Level C
    d) Level D

25. Lilac Landscaping Services are considering signing a Server and Cloud Enrollment to buy Azure consumption services through. What is the minimum Annual Monetary Commitment they must make if they sign this agreement?
    a) There is no minimum
    b) $1,200
    c) $12,000
    d) $120,000

26. Taupe Telecoms feel that an Enterprise Agreement will best suit their licensing needs for the next three years, and they understand that they need to license at least one of the Enterprise Products for each of their Qualified Devices. Which of the following products are valid Enterprise Products? Choose three answers.
    a) Windows 10 Enterprise E3
    b) Windows Server 2016
    c) Office Professional Plus 2016
    d) Core CAL Suite
    e) Windows Server 2016 CAL
    f) SQL Server 2016 CAL

Answers 24 – 26

24. Mauve Stoves have historically purchased their server licenses through an MPSA for which they have achieved Level B pricing. They now intend to sign a new Server and Cloud Enrollment since they want to upgrade their whole SQL Server estate of 50 servers to the latest version. Which price level will they be entitled to for the new SCE?
    a) Level A
    b) Level B ✓
    c) Level C
    d) Level D

25. Lilac Landscaping Services are considering signing a Server and Cloud Enrollment to buy Azure consumption services through. What is the minimum Annual Monetary Commitment they must make if they sign this agreement?
    a) There is no minimum
    b) $1,200
    c) $12,000 ✓
    d) $120,000

26. Taupe Telecoms feel that an Enterprise Agreement will best suit their licensing needs for the next three years, and they understand that they need to license at least one of the Enterprise Products for each of their Qualified Devices. Which of the following products are valid Enterprise Products? Choose three answers.
    a) Windows 10 Enterprise E3 ✓
    b) Windows Server 2016
    c) Office Professional Plus 2016 ✓
    d) Core CAL Suite ✓
    e) Windows Server 2016 CAL
    f) SQL Server 2016 CAL

© Licensing School 2018

Questions 27 – 29

27. Goldfinger Food have signed a Direct Azure-only Server and Cloud Enrollment and have made a Monetary Commitment of $50,000. During the third quarter they exceed their Monetary Commitment by $10,000. When do they pay for this overspend?
    a) At the point in time that they exceed the Monetary Commitment
    b) At the end of the quarter in which the overspend occurred
    c) At the end of the year
    d) There is no facility for them to overspend; they must make an additional Monetary Commitment when funds run out

28. Sienna Blenders have approximately 150 PCs. They want to standardize on Office Professional Plus 2016 on all PCs with perpetual licenses with Software Assurance. Which licensing program are they likely to find a good fit to purchase licenses through?
    a) MPSA
    b) Open Value Company-Wide
    c) Enterprise Agreement
    d) CSP

29. Apple and Pears Stairlifts want to purchase 350 Microsoft 365 Enterprise E3 User SLs. They have no licensing agreements. Through which program would you recommend that they purchase these licenses?
    a) CSP
    b) Enterprise Agreement
    c) SPLA
    d) Open Value Subscription

27. Goldfinger Food have signed a Direct Azure-only Server and Cloud Enrollment and have made a Monetary Commitment of $50,000. During the third quarter they exceed their Monetary Commitment by $10,000. When do they pay for this overspend?

    a) At the point in time that they exceed the Monetary Commitment
    b) At the end of the quarter in which the overspend occurred
    c) At the end of the year ✓
    d) There is no facility for them to overspend; they must make an additional Monetary Commitment when funds run out

28. Sienna Blenders have approximately 150 PCs. They want to standardize on Office Professional Plus 2016 on all PCs with perpetual licenses with Software Assurance. Which licensing program are they likely to find a good fit to purchase licenses through?

    a) MPSA
    b) Open Value Company-Wide ✓
    c) Enterprise Agreement
    d) CSP

29. Apple and Pears Stairlifts want to purchase 350 Microsoft 365 Enterprise E3 User SLs. They have no licensing agreements. Through which program would you recommend that they purchase these licenses?

    a) CSP ✓
    b) Enterprise Agreement
    c) SPLA
    d) Open Value Subscription

© Licensing School 2018

Questions 30 – 32

30. The Mala Kite Shop own 411 devices that employees use either in the head office or at home. They want to upgrade the version of Office on 245 of these devices and want to pay for the licenses in full at this point so that they know that they don't owe any money or have any commitment to pay anything later. They are not looking to upgrade the version for another four or five years. Through which agreement would you recommend that they purchase these licenses?

a) CSP
b) MPSA
c) Enterprise Agreement
d) Enterprise Subscription Agreement

31. How is the Consumption Allowance calculated for a customer who has made a Monetary Commitment to Azure?

a) It is $10,000 or 10% of the Monetary Commitment, whichever is greater
b) It is 25% of the Monetary Commitment
c) It is 50% of the Monetary Commitment
d) It is based on the price level of the SCE

32. Coff E-Learning Solutions have ten SharePoint Servers and CALs for 500 users. They want to sign an SCE but have been told that they can't. Why is this?

a) They do not have enough SharePoint Servers to meet the minimum requirements for the SCE
b) They can't sign an SCE for SharePoint Server without including SQL Server
c) SharePoint Server is not available to be purchased under the SCE
d) They do not have active Software Assurance on their SharePoint Servers

30. The Mala Kite Shop own 411 devices that employees use either in the head office or at home. They want to upgrade the version of Office on 245 of these devices and want to pay for the licenses in full at this point so that they know that they don't owe any money or have any commitment to pay anything later. They are not looking to upgrade the version for another four or five years. Through which agreement would you recommend that they purchase these licenses?

    a) CSP
    b) MPSA ✓
    c) Enterprise Agreement
    d) Enterprise Subscription Agreement

31. How is the Consumption Allowance calculated for a customer who has made a Monetary Commitment to Azure?

    a) It is $10,000 or 10% of the Monetary Commitment, whichever is greater
    b) It is 25% of the Monetary Commitment
    c) It is 50% of the Monetary Commitment ✓
    d) It is based on the price level of the SCE

32. Coff E-Learning Solutions have ten SharePoint Servers and CALs for 500 users. They want to sign an SCE but have been told that they can't. Why is this?

    a) They do not have enough SharePoint Servers to meet the minimum requirements for the SCE
    b) They can't sign an SCE for SharePoint Server without including SQL Server ✓
    c) SharePoint Server is not available to be purchased under the SCE
    d) They do not have active Software Assurance on their SharePoint Servers

 © Licensing School 2018

Questions 33 – 35

33. The Olive Oil Drum Company have a Windows-based server farm and want to sign a Server and Cloud Enrollment for the Core Infrastructure component. What licenses will they need if they have fifty servers, each with two 4-core processors, all licensed with Windows Server Standard with no active SA?
    a) 400 CIS Standard without Windows Server L&SA
    b) 800 CIS Standard L&SA
    c) 400 CIS Standard L&SA
    d) 800 CIS Standard SA

34. Fandango Fitness have a SQL Server Standard estate licensed with the Server/CAL model. They currently have ten servers but are expecting to retire three in the short to medium term. They have SA on two of the servers that they will not retire and prefer to own licensing assets where it makes commercial sense. What would be the best option for their initial order on an SCE?
    a) 2 SQL Server SA, 3 SQL Server MSU, 5 SQL Server L&SA
    b) 10 SQL Server L&SA
    c) 2 SQL Server SA, 8 SQL Server L&SA
    d) 2 SQL Server SA, 8 SQL Server MSU

35. Which of the following are available to be purchased through CSP? Choose three answers.
    a) Subscription licenses for Office Professional Plus 2016
    b) Perpetual licenses for Office Professional Plus 2016
    c) User SLs for Office 365 ProPlus
    d) Azure User Plans
    e) Azure Infrastructure Plans
    f) Azure consumption services

Answers 33 – 35

33. The Olive Oil Drum Company have a Windows-based server farm and want to sign a Server and Cloud Enrollment for the Core Infrastructure component. What licenses will they need if they have fifty servers, each with two 4-core processors, all licensed with Windows Standard with no active SA?
    a) 400 CIS Standard without Windows Server L&SA
    b) 800 CIS Standard L&SA ✓
    c) 400 CIS Standard L&SA
    d) 800 CIS Standard SA

34. Fandango Fitness have a SQL Server Standard estate licensed with the Server/CAL model. They currently have ten servers but are expecting to retire three in the short to medium term. They have SA on two of the servers that they will not retire and prefer to own licensing assets where it makes commercial sense. What would be the best option for their initial order on an SCE?
    a) 2 SQL Server SA, 3 SQL Server MSU, 5 SQL Server L&SA ✓
    b) 10 SQL Server L&SA
    c) 2 SQL Server SA, 8 SQL Server L&SA
    d) 2 SQL Server SA, 8 SQL Server MSU

35. Which of the following are available to be purchased through CSP? Choose three answers.
    a) Subscription licenses for Office Professional Plus 2016
    b) Perpetual licenses for Office Professional Plus 2016
    c) User SLs for Office 365 ProPlus ✓
    d) Azure User Plans ✓
    e) Azure Infrastructure Plans
    f) Azure consumption services ✓

© Licensing School 2018

Questions 36 – 38

36. Amaranth Antiques want to upgrade their server estate to the latest versions of the software and are considering a Server and Cloud Enrollment. They are interested in enrolling SharePoint Server, SQL Server, BizTalk Server, Dynamics 365 Server, and Exchange Server in the agreement. Which products may be included? Choose three answers.

    a) SharePoint Server
    b) SQL Server
    c) BizTalk Server
    d) Dynamics 365 Server
    e) Exchange Server

37. The Jazzberry Jam Shop have an Enterprise Subscription Agreement that is coming to the end of its term. They understand that one of the options that they have at the end of their ESA is to convert the subscription licenses into perpetual licenses. What is the term for this process?

    a) Buy-out
    b) Buy-in
    c) True Up
    d) True Out

38. Aisle of White Paints are interested in acquiring their licenses through a program that offers discounted pricing for standardizing on a Microsoft platform product. Which of the following programs offer this? Choose two answers.

    a) Open
    b) Enterprise Agreement
    c) MPSA
    d) Enterprise Subscription Agreement

36. Amaranth Antiques want to upgrade their server estate to the latest versions of the software and are considering a Server and Cloud Enrollment. They are interested in enrolling SharePoint Server, SQL Server, BizTalk Server, Dynamics 365 Server, and Exchange Server in the agreement. Which products may be included? Choose three answers.

    a) **SharePoint Server** ✓
    b) **SQL Server** ✓
    c) **BizTalk Server** ✓
    d) Dynamics 365 Server
    e) Exchange Server

37. The Jazzberry Jam Shop have an Enterprise Subscription Agreement that is coming to the end of its term. They understand that one of the options that they have at the end of their ESA is to convert the subscription licenses into perpetual licenses. What is the term for this process?

    a) **Buy-out** ✓
    b) Buy-in
    c) True Up
    d) True Out

38. Aisle of White Paints are interested in acquiring their licenses through a program that offers discounted pricing for standardizing on a Microsoft platform product. Which of the following programs offer this? Choose two answers.

    a) Open
    b) **Enterprise Agreement** ✓
    c) MPSA
    d) **Enterprise Subscription Agreement** ✓

© Licensing School 2018

Questions 39 – 41

39. Charcoal Chimney Sweeps are considering what they need from a Volume Licensing agreement. Which of the following would lead you to specifically recommend an MPSA? Choose three answers.
   a) They want to buy perpetual licenses for on-premises software
   b) They want to buy licenses on an ad hoc basis
   c) They want to buy Azure consumption services
   d) They want to buy SA on all licenses
   e) They want to allow affiliates to purchase under the same agreement

40. Turquoise Toys want to sign a Server and Cloud Enrollment with the SQL Server component. Which of the following represent the correct minimum requirements for SQL Server? Choose two answers.
   a) 5 Server licenses and 250 CALs
   b) 40 Core licenses
   c) 50 Core licenses
   d) 5 Server licenses and 500 CALs
   e) 50 Core licenses and 5 Server licenses

41. The Bondi Blue Bistro have purchased Windows Server 2016 Core licenses with Software Assurance through their MPSA. What payment options are available to them? Choose two answers.
   a) Payment upfront
   b) Monthly payments
   c) Payment at the end of the agreement term
   d) Annual payments

Answers 39 – 41

39. Charcoal Chimney Sweeps are considering what they need from a Volume Licensing agreement. Which of the following would lead you to specifically recommend an MPSA? Choose three answers.

a) **They want to buy perpetual licenses for on-premises software** ✓

b) **They want to buy licenses on an ad hoc basis** ✓

c) They want to buy Azure consumption services

d) They want to buy SA on all licenses

e) **They want to allow affiliates to purchase under the same agreement** ✓

40. Turquoise Toys want to sign a Server and Cloud Enrollment with the SQL Server component. Which of the following represent the correct minimum requirements for SQL Server? Choose two answers.

a) **5 Server licenses and 250 CALs** ✓

b) 40 Core licenses

c) **50 Core licenses** ✓

d) 5 Server licenses and 500 CALs

e) 50 Core licenses and 5 Server licenses

41. The Bondi Blue Bistro have purchased Windows Server 2016 Core licenses with Software Assurance through their MPSA. What payment options are available to them? Choose two answers.

a) **Payment upfront** ✓

b) Monthly payments

c) Payment at the end of the agreement term

d) **Annual payments** ✓

© Licensing School 2018

Questions 42 – 45

42. Pastel Pink Personal Coaches want to buy 125 Office 365 E1 User SLs and 140 Office 365 E3 User SLs. For which of the following agreements is this a valid initial order? Choose two answers.
    a) MPSA
    b) Enterprise Agreement
    c) CSP
    d) Server and Cloud Enrollment

43. Mellow Yellow Sounds have an Enterprise Agreement which they signed with an annual Azure Monetary Commitment of $75,000. They make an additional Monetary Commitment payment of $30,000 in the ninth month. What will their Monetary Commitment payment be at the start of the next year?
    a) $75,000
    b) $105,000
    c) $120,000
    d) $195,000

44. Which of the following is true when customers buy their Azure consumption services through CSP?
    a) Requirement to make an upfront Monetary Commitment
    b) Fixed price protection for 3 years
    c) Best price protection for 12 months
    d) Ability to pay for consumed services monthly in arrears

45. Which of the following is an eligible initial order for an EA?
    a) 250 Office Professional Plus 2016 licenses + 250 Windows 10 Enterprise E3 licenses
    b) 500 Microsoft 365 E3 User SLs
    c) 500 Dynamics 365 Sales User SLs
    d) 500 Windows Server 2016 CALs

42. Pastel Pink Personal Coaches want to buy 125 Office 365 E1 User SLs and 140 Office 365 E3 User SLs. For which of the following agreements is this a valid initial order? Choose two answers.
    a) MPSA ✓
    b) Enterprise Agreement
    c) CSP ✓
    d) Server and Cloud Enrollment

43. Mellow Yellow Sounds have an Enterprise Agreement which they signed with an annual Azure Monetary Commitment of $75,000. They make an additional Monetary Commitment payment of $30,000 in the ninth month. What will their Monetary Commitment payment be at the start of the next year?
    a) $75,000
    b) $105,000
    c) $120,000
    d) $195,000 ✓

44. Which of the following is true when customers buy their Azure consumption services through CSP?
    a) Requirement to make an upfront Monetary Commitment
    b) Fixed price protection for 3 years
    c) Best price protection for 12 months
    d) Ability to pay for consumed services monthly in arrears ✓

45. Which of the following is an eligible initial order for an EA?
    a) 250 Office Professional Plus 2016 licenses + 250 Windows 10 Enterprise E3 licenses
    b) 500 Microsoft 365 E3 User SLs ✓
    c) 500 Dynamics 365 Sales User SLs
    d) 500 Windows Server 2016 CALs

   © Licensing School 2018

PART 6: SOFTWARE ASSURANCE

For the exam (and real life!) you need to be confident with all of the SA benefits in terms of what they offer an organization and the business goals that they would meet. You should be ready to pick out the most appropriate benefit to match it to the needs of the business as a whole or an individual department. In addition, you need to know what products give entitlements to which SA benefits.

If you find you want more information outside of that required for the exam, you should refer to the Product Terms document which has lots of information about all of the SA benefits.

If you are already familiar with the SA benefits, why not skip to the Recap Questions on page 312 and test yourself?

Overview

Buying Software Assurance

Software Assurance can only be purchased through Volume Licensing agreements (and thus not CSP); it's an optional purchase in Select Plus and MPSA agreements, and compulsory in the Enterprise Agreements as we saw in Part 5 of this book. Customers who purchase licenses with Software Assurance during an agreement may choose to renew just the SA at the end of the agreement, and if they continue to renew the SA, then they will never need to purchase another license for that product again.

It's worth noting that if you buy licenses through a Volume Licensing agreement you must decide at the point of purchase if you want to include SA or not; there is no option to add on SA at a later date. This is different to purchasing licenses through the OEM channel where a customer typically (and always for the purposes of the exam) has 90 days to add SA to a license – often known as a grace period. If they don't have a Volume Licensing agreement they would need to start one and all the usual program rules would apply.

Software Assurance benefits have traditionally been allocated to customers who purchase licenses for on-premises products but are also sometimes included with Online Services subscriptions. For instance, both Dynamics 365 Server Sales CALs with SA and Dynamics 365 Sales User SLs give a customer access to the CustomerSource portal.

Managing Software Assurance Benefits

Software Assurance benefits are allocated automatically to organizations as they buy licenses through their Volume Licensing agreements. Customers then manage these benefits through one of the Volume Licensing portals by choosing individuals in their organization to be Benefits Administrators. The portal shows how many of each benefit an organization has been allocated, and it's also where the benefits are activated (where required) and assigned.

© Licensing School 2018

The Volume Licensing Service Center (VLSC) is used for all of the agreements except the MPSA which uses a different portal, the Microsoft Business Center (MBC).

Activating Software Assurance Benefits
In the past, many of the Software Assurance benefits needed to be activated in the portal before they could be used. This requirement was removed when the MBC was launched for the MPSA and now there are just three remaining benefits that need to be activated in VLSC: Training Vouchers, the Home Use Program, and E-Learning.

Software Assurance Membership
Typically, all SA benefits are available to EA customers with fewer available to MPSA customers. In particular, Training Vouchers and Planning Services are not available to MPSA customers unless they make a further level of commitment. If a customer is happy to buy SA on ALL licenses in a particular pool, then they are said to have "Software Assurance Membership", or SAM, for that pool and then gain the maximum number of SA benefits for that pool, equivalent to those the EA customer is entitled to.

Applying your knowledge in the exam:

- Remember that SA is a mandatory part of an Enterprise Agreement so even if the customer scenario doesn't mention Software Assurance specifically, you can assume that an EA customer has active SA on their licenses

- Learn the portals that customers use to manage SA benefits: VLSC for the EA, and MBC for the MPSA

- Make sure you can pick out the SA benefits that need activating in VLSC: Training Vouchers, the Home Use Program, and E-Learning

- Remember that MPSA customers don't get Training Vouchers or Planning Services unless they commit to buying SA on all licenses in a particular pool, known as having Software Assurance Membership

New Version Rights

New Version Rights are probably the most well-known of all the SA benefits: if an organization buys, for example, an Office Professional Plus license with SA then they're entitled to use any newer versions of Office released during the term of their agreement. If they haven't installed that newer version of Office by the time their agreement ends, even if they don't renew the agreement, they are still licensed for that version – as long as they have purchased perpetual Office licenses of course.

This benefit applies to all products.

Applying your knowledge in the exam:

- Look out for particular business goals that specify that it's important for the organization to always have the latest version of the software available – perhaps there's a line of business application that relies on having the latest version of SQL Server deployed, for example

- It's significantly easier to manage an estate where all devices are running the same versions of a product, so look out for business goals that express a desire for easier management of client or server devices through a consistent set of products

- Watch out for statements telling you what the software refresh cycle of an organization is; if it's five years for example, benefits such as New Version Rights are not attractive and you may need to recommend an MPSA without Software Assurance

- In the exam, as in real life, New Version Rights become even more attractive as the launch of a new product comes closer. So look out for an organization's concern that if they buy licenses now they won't be licensed for the new product that is scheduled to arrive in a couple of months' time; adding SA to their license purchase will overcome this objection

© Licensing School 2018

Step-up Licenses

Customers with Software Assurance are eligible to buy Step-up licenses – note that they don't actually receive them as an SA benefit automatically as part of their agreement. A Step-up license allows a customer to move from a lower edition of a product to a higher edition by just paying the difference in the License with SA price – this is the Step-up license price.

As an example, if a customer has SQL Server Standard Core licenses and later needs to deploy SQL Server Enterprise, they need to acquire Enterprise Core licenses. If they have no SA on the SQL Server Standard Core licenses, then they need to purchase new Enterprise Core licenses in the usual way. However, if they do have SA on the SQL Server Standard Core licenses then they can just purchase Step-up licenses and thus will just pay the difference in L&SA prices, potentially saving a significant amount of money.

Another really good example of when Step-up licenses are useful is with Windows Server 2016/System Center 2016 since it allows a customer to move from Standard to Datacenter licenses as their virtualization needs grow.

Customers can also acquire Step-up licenses for the Core CAL Suite (to the Enterprise CAL Suite), Exchange Server Standard (to Enterprise), and Office Standard (to Professional Plus).

Applying your knowledge in the exam:

- Look out for business goals that indicate that an organization is unsure which edition of a particular product that they should deploy, but want to buy licenses now with the flexibility of choosing a different edition later

- If you see details of an organization which has already bought a product with SA and now realizes that they want to actually deploy a higher edition of the product, then this should lead you to recommend purchasing Step-up licenses

Microsoft Desktop Optimization Pack (MDOP)

There have been several changes over recent years as to how to acquire the tools within the Microsoft Desktop Optimization Pack. Historically, it was something that organizations could buy if they had Software Assurance on their Windows desktop operating system licenses. Today, however, two of the tools (App-V and UE-V) are included when you buy a Windows 10 Enterprise license and the remainder are included when you buy a Windows 10 Enterprise E3 or E5 User or Device license through a Volume Licensing agreement.

MDOP is a subscription so may be used while Windows 10 Enterprise E3/E5 User or Device SLs are active, or the SA is current on a Windows 10 Enterprise E3 Device license.

Applying your knowledge in the exam:

- Look out for business goals that state the organization's desire to better manage and optimize their desktops since they will want to take advantage of the extra tools included in a Windows 10 Enterprise E3/E5 license

© Licensing School 2018

Windows 10 Servicing Channels

The Windows 10 Servicing Channels control how often feature updates are delivered to Windows 10 devices. There are two channels:

- **Semi-Annual Channel**

  This channel makes feature update releases available twice a year in March and September, and each update is supported for 18 months This channel is aimed at the typical end-user PC

- **Long-Term Servicing Channel**

  These are less frequent releases, probably every 2-3 years with the next one expected in 2019, and they are supported for 10 years. This channel is designed for special-purpose PCs such as those used in point-of-sale systems or controlling factory or medical equipment where it's not possible or desirable to have features updated regularly

Customers who buy Windows 10 Enterprise E3 or E5 User or Device licenses through a Volume Licensing agreement can choose their preferred channel for their deployments of Windows 10.

Applying your knowledge in the exam:

- Microsoft's intention is that the vast majority of PCs are on the Semi-Annual Channel so that should be your first recommendation. Look out for very specialist needs if you think you should recommend the Long-Term Servicing Channel; these will be customers who can't deploy updates rather than simply not wanting to

- Windows 10 Enterprise E3/E5 Users SLs acquired through CSP are always on the Semi-Annual Channel, and thus if you need to recommend a way to acquire Windows 10 Enterprise E3/E5 User SLs where an organization would have the flexibility to use the Long-Term Servicing Channel you must recommend one of the Volume Licensing agreements

Windows To Go

If you acquire a Windows 10 Enterprise E3 or E5 User or Device license through a Volume Licensing agreement then you receive the rights to run Windows in a Windows To Go deployment. With Windows To Go, each employee is given a USB drive which contains their corporate desktop and when they insert it into a machine their personal desktop is available to them.

This is a way of rolling out standard desktops to users without having to set up a Virtual Desktop Infrastructure and you can imagine that it's attractive because of that. Technically, a Windows To Go USB drive can only be used in a device certified for Windows 7 or later whereas a VDI desktop can be delivered to a device that can't run Windows, like an iPad.

From a licensing perspective, an organization can create one or two USB drives per license, and then if they have licensed Windows by device, those USB drives can be used by any user on any licensed device, and if they have licensed Windows by user then they may be used on any device by a licensed user.

Applying your knowledge in the exam:

- Look out for business goals that state the organization's desire to deploy corporate desktops for all users, and then decide if VDI or Windows To Go will be the best solution for the customer

- Remember that a Windows To Go USB drive can't be used in a device that can't run Windows so don't recommend it for delivering corporate desktops to non-Windows tablets for example

- Part of your recommendation will be choosing Windows 10 Enterprise E3 or E5 User or Device licenses: choose User licenses when the user will need to use multiple devices, and Device licenses when they typically just use a single device

© Licensing School 2018

Windows Local Virtualization Rights

The Windows local virtualization rights benefit is aimed at developers and testers who need to have several different environments set up to work on different projects. This SA benefit is available when Windows 10 Enterprise E3/E5 User or Device licenses are purchased and allows the user to have up to four virtual machines running Windows 10 Enterprise E3/E5 locally on their device.

Applying your knowledge in the exam:

- You are less likely to have to pick out "local virtualization rights" as an answer than you are to state how many virtual machines this benefit allows to run locally, so look out for business goals that state that users need to work with multiple virtual machines and remember that this benefit allows four of these

Virtual Desktop Access (VDA)

The VDA SA benefit can be slightly confusing since there is a separate license available for purchase with exactly the same name – the Windows VDA license. Virtual Desktop Access is the licensing right that allows organizations to set up virtual desktops on their servers and to have their users access them from their desktop machines, within an infrastructure known as a Virtual Desktop Infrastructure (VDI).

All Windows 10 Enterprise E3/E5 User or Device licenses purchased through a Volume Licensing agreement give the added deployment flexibility of being allowed to create, store and run virtual desktops on a server.

Applying your knowledge in the exam:

- If an organization wants to deploy virtual desktops in a Virtual Desktop Infrastructure, then they need VDA rights. These rights are included with all Windows 10 Enterprise E3/E5 licenses and VDA E3/E5 licenses and you'll recommend the Windows licenses if the users' devices have a qualifying operating system, and the VDA ones if they don't. There are also User and Device licenses to choose between where, as usual, if users use multiple devices then User licenses are the best recommendation. Look back at the "Virtual Desktop Infrastructure" section on page 58 if you want to refresh your knowledge on this

© Licensing School 2018

Windows Thin PC

The Windows Thin PC technology is aimed at organizations who want to move to a Virtual Desktop Infrastructure. Essentially, it allows an IT department to repurpose existing PCs as thin clients running a smaller footprint version of Windows, rather than having to buy new thin client devices. This allows an organization to try out VDI without extra hardware expense.

Windows Thin PC is available as an SA benefit to organizations buying Windows 10 Enterprise E3/E5 User or Device licenses.

Applying your knowledge in the exam:

- Look out for business goals that state an organization's desire to evaluate desktop virtualization in a Virtual Desktop Infrastructure

- Remember that this feature can remove a cost barrier since the organization does not have to invest in new hardware, so if the business goals focus on worries about how much a VDI solution will cost, this is a good benefit to recommend

Enterprise Source Licensing Program

The Enterprise Source Licensing Program provides source code for most major releases and service packs of Windows client and server products, and its main purpose is to assist in the support and development of internally deployed applications on the Windows platform.

Customers must apply to join the program and there are two main criteria that they must meet: they must have an Enterprise Agreement or have committed to Software Assurance Membership through Select Plus or the MPSA on the Systems pool, and they must have a minimum of 10,000 Windows desktops.

Applying your knowledge in the exam:

- Remember that this benefit only applies to very large customers so bear that in mind if you decide to recommend it as a desired benefit in the exam

- It's also specific to customers who have purchased their Windows 10 Enterprise E3/E5 licenses through an EA or Select Plus/MPSA with SAM, so make sure that you only recommend it for customers in this situation

© Licensing School 2018

Office Online and Office Online Server

Office Online is the name for the Microsoft-hosted browser-based versions of Word, PowerPoint, Excel and OneNote. The experience is very similar to the familiar desktop products although there is less functionality available. Office Online Server allows organizations to deliver these browser-based versions of the Office products from their on-premises servers.

If a device is licensed with Office Standard 2016 or Office Professional Plus 2016 licenses with Software Assurance, then that device can be used by any user to access both Office Online and Office Online Server to edit documents. The primary user of the licensed device, however, can edit documents in Office Online or Office Online Server from any device.

Applying your knowledge in the exam:

- Look out for an organization that has licensed its users' devices for Office Standard/Professional Plus 2016 with SA, and then needs a cost-effective way for those users to view and edit Office documents from any licensed or unlicensed device

Home Use Program

The Home Use Program benefit is available to customers who purchase Software Assurance on qualifying licenses. For the purposes of the exam, consider these qualifying products to be Office Standard 2016 and Office Professional Plus 2016. The users of a licensed device are then able to purchase a copy of Office Professional Plus 2016 for home use for installation on one home computer. They may use this software as long as their organization's SA is active. One of the attractions of the Home Use Program is that it's a very cheap license to purchase and thus is an extremely cost-effective way of enabling users to use the same product at home as they do at work.

The Home Use Program is one of the benefits which must be activated in VLSC, after which the administrator receives a Program Code. This is shared with employees who then purchase the software through the Home Use Program online store.

Applying your knowledge in the exam:

- Look for business goals where the organization is deploying a new version of Office and they want to make the transition easier for users so that they're using the same products at home as they are at work

- Look out also for business goals relating to an HR director who's interested in giving his employees some additional benefits – it's perceived to be of value to employees to not have to purchase high-cost software for home use

- Also be on the lookout for business goals that state that end user productivity is important to the organization – the assumption being that users who use the same versions of products in both their work and home environments will be more productive with the tools

© Licensing School 2018

Office Roaming Rights

Roaming Rights are available when a customer adds Software Assurance to Office Standard/Professional Plus 2016 licenses. They are useful when Office is installed on and run from a server in a Remote Desktop Services deployment. Every machine that accesses Office via RDS needs to be licensed with an individual Office license and if users use multiple devices this obviously has the potential to be extremely expensive. Roaming Rights relax this condition and give the primary user of the device licensed with Office Standard/Professional Plus 2016 and SA the rights to access Office through RDS on any third party-owned device outside of the corporate premises.

Historically, this right was also an important part of licensing a virtual desktop through VDI when a user needed to use a variety of different devices. Today (and certainly for the purposes of the exam) it's easier to license a user with an Office 365 ProPlus User SL so that they can access Office on devices of their choice both inside and outside of the corporate premises.

Applying your knowledge in the exam:

- Since this SA benefit is very specific, look for a very specific set of business goals – an organization wants to allow the primary users of devices licensed with Office Standard/Professional Plus 2016 to access Office via RDS on third party-owned devices outside of the corporate premises

Fail-over Server Rights

SQL Server 2016 and Dynamics 365 for Operations Server licenses with Software Assurance include fail-over rights. This means that the products can be configured to provide redundancy so that if one server fails, its processing will be picked up, recovered, and continued by another server without the need for additional licenses. There are two rules to bear in mind: the fail-over server must be a passive server, which means that it can't be running active workloads or serving data to clients, and if the Core licensing model is being used for SQL Server then the fail-over server must have the same or fewer cores than the active server.

Applying your knowledge in the exam:

- Look for organizations that have important applications running in their business and are worried about the cost of licensing a server for fail-over, since adding SA to the license purchase will be more cost-effective than buying additional licenses for the fail-over server

- For the products covered in the exam it is only SQL Server 2016 and Dynamics 365 for Operations Server that have fail-over server rights, so this makes it easy to pick out when the benefit might be appropriate

© Licensing School 2018

Disaster Recovery Rights

This SA benefit is available when server products and their CALs (where available) are purchased with Software Assurance. It allows customers to deploy the same product on a "cold" – that is, a turned off – backup server for the purposes of disaster recovery; if the main server fails, then the organization is licensed to turn on the cold server and run the product from there without being concerned about license reassignment rules.

Applying your knowledge in the exam:

- Look for business goals which state a need for a disaster recovery option for server products

- Also look out for an organization's concerns about how much it costs to license backup servers; if they have cold backups, then buying SA is a much more cost-effective option than purchasing additional server licenses. However, do check that the backup solution is cold before you choose this option

Power BI Report Server

Organizations using Power BI to analyze and report on their business data need to license both the users who publish reports and those who consume them. However, Power BI Report Server is an on-premises server that enables licensed Power BI Pro users to publish Power BI reports and distribute them across the organization and, importantly, removes the need to license individual report consumers.

Rights to run Power BI Report Server are available for organizations with active Software Assurance on their SQL Server 2016 Enterprise Core licenses.

Applying your knowledge in the exam:

- Look out for organizations that are using Power BI to analyze business data and want a cost-effective way of making reports available to users across the business

© Licensing School 2018

Unlimited Virtualization Rights

Unlimited virtualization rights are only available for a handful of products and it's only SQL Server 2016 that you need to know about for the exam. If a physical server is licensed with SQL Server 2016 Enterprise Core licenses with Software Assurance, then an unlimited number of virtual machines running SQL Server may be deployed on that physical server.

If a customer has a server farm with a high degree of virtualization with virtual machines that move between physical servers then this is a cost-effective way of licensing these products. It also adds considerably to the ease of management of the licensing of the virtual machines across the server farm.

Applying your knowledge in the exam:

- Be prepared to recommend the right number of licenses for a given server so that it is correctly licensed for unlimited virtualization

- Remember that (for the exam) it's only SQL Server 2016 that can be licensed for unlimited virtualization, so don't be tempted by answers that imply all products can be licensed for unlimited virtualization. Equally, remember that it's only the Enterprise edition of SQL Server 2016 that is eligible for this benefit

- There IS unlimited virtualization licensing for Windows Server 2016 but this is a right of the Datacenter license rather than a Software Assurance benefit. So, don't be misled if you need to pick out products which have unlimited virtualization rights as a benefit of adding Software Assurance – it's only SQL Server!

License Mobility across Server Farms

With all of the server applications licensed with the Server/CAL model that we looked at in the On-Premises Product Licensing section, you assign a Server license to a physical server and that gives the rights to run the product in a single virtual machine. If you have a server farm where, say, a virtual machine running Exchange Server 2016 can move between physical servers this gives some licensing challenges due to the fact that a Server license cannot be reassigned to another physical server any sooner than every 90 days.

The License Mobility across Server Farms SA benefit relaxes this restriction so that, in effect, a license can follow a virtual machine around the server farm so that it's always correctly licensed.

The productivity servers (Exchange, SharePoint and Skype for Business) and SQL Server and Dynamics 365 for Operations Server all have this right when SA is purchased with the license but it's also worth noting what products do NOT have these rights. The main ones to remember for the exam are the Core Infrastructure products – that's Windows Server 2016 and System Center 2016. When these licenses are assigned in a server farm, they cannot be moved between servers any more frequently than every 90 days even with active Software Assurance.

Applying your knowledge in the exam:

- Look out for customers with a virtualized server farm since this SA benefit is likely to be a good recommendation

- Remember the products that do NOT have this benefit – the key ones being Windows Server 2016 and System Center 2016

© Licensing School 2018

License Mobility through SA

This SA benefit is aimed at organizations who want to take licenses that have been purchased through their Volume Licensing agreement and assign them to a Service Provider's hardware or to Azure. This means that they can pay the Service Provider (or Microsoft) a fee for the base virtual machine and then use existing SQL Server (for example) licenses to license that virtual machine for SQL Server.

There is a process that needs to be followed – it's not simply a case of just mentally assigning the licenses to the Service Provider's server farm. The License Verification Form must be completed and this gathers information such as the nominated Service Provider and the number of licenses that are being assigned, and then it's sent to Microsoft to be verified. Microsoft returns the form, and both the Service Provider and the customer should retain this document.

This SA benefit is available when SA is added to server product licenses (System Center 2016, Exchange Server 2016, SharePoint Server 2016, Skype for Business Server 2015, SQL Server 2016, and Dynamics 365 for Operations Server) and, where available, customers must purchase SA on the CALs as well as the Server licenses. Not all servers are eligible for this benefit, the most notable of which is Windows Server 2016. There is an alternative benefit available for Windows Server – the Azure Hybrid Use Benefit which is covered in the next section.

Applying your knowledge in the exam:

- Look for business goals that reflect an organization's desire to use a Service Provider or Azure to scale their business solutions

- Remember that Windows Server 2016 does not have this SA benefit so don't get carried away and recommend that a customer assign these licenses to a Service Provider

- Make sure you're clear on the differences between the "License Mobility through SA" benefit and the "License Mobility across Server Farms" one so that you can choose the correct benefit from a list

Azure Hybrid Use Benefit

The Azure Hybrid Use Benefit applies only to Windows Server 2016 Standard and Datacenter Core licenses. It allows an organization to choose whether they use the licenses in an on-premises data center or in Azure. If they choose to use the licenses in Azure they pay for the base instance virtual machine (the compute power) on a consumption basis and then assign Windows Server Core licenses with SA to it to license it for Windows Server.

This SA benefit is covered in detail in the "Windows Server Virtual Machines: Azure Hybrid Use Benefit" section on page 177 onwards, so work through this information and check that you know how many Core licenses you would have to assign to a given Azure virtual machine, and how the rights for Windows Server 2016 Standard and Datacenter Core licenses differ.

Applying your knowledge in the exam:

- Remember that this SA benefit only allows customers to take their Windows Server 2016 licenses to Azure, rather than other Service Providers' infrastructures

- Be prepared to recommend that a customer uses their existing Windows Server 2016 licenses if they are moving a current workload to Azure, but consider an all-inclusive Windows Server virtual machine if it's a short-term or a dev/test workload

© Licensing School 2018

System Center Global Service Monitor

System Center Global Service Monitor is a Microsoft cloud service that allows organizations to monitor the availability, performance and function of their external-facing web applications. It's innovative since it can do this from multiple locations around the world by using Azure points of presence. These locations are correlated to customer geographies, which means that IT administrators can get an insight into the complete customer experience from problems which relate to external factors (such as Internet or network problems) to specific application or service problems.

System Center Global Service Monitor integrates with the System Center Operations Manager console so that IT administrators can monitor these web applications in the same place they monitor other applications

Note that customers must specifically have Software Assurance on System Center 2016 Server Management Licenses to be eligible for this benefit.

Applying your knowledge in the exam:

- Look out for organizations that have customers who use an important web application – it's going to be critical to know the state of that application and that's what this benefit can help with

Self Hosting Use Rights

Certain server products have the Self Hosting Use Rights Software Assurance benefit. This benefit allows ISVs to build a Unified Solution based on one or more of these products and to allow their customers to access it. There are, of course, a few rules to follow: to qualify as a Unified Solution the ISV must add significant functionality to the base product, and the solution itself must be provided as a hosted service through the Internet.

This benefit applies to the following products: Windows Server 2016, System Center 2016, Exchange Server 2016, SQL Server 2016, and Dynamics 365 for Operations Server.

Applying your knowledge in the exam:

- The exam focuses on licensing for large customer organizations and you don't need to know how ISVs license and distribute their products, so expect this SA benefit to appear only as a wrong answer in a question about Software Assurance

© Licensing School 2018

Training Vouchers

Organizations are given an allocation of Training Vouchers dependent on the number of licenses they buy for Windows 10 Enterprise E3/E5 and/or Office Standard/Professional Plus 2016. As an example, within an Enterprise Agreement they would be allocated 30 Training Vouchers with a purchase of 2,500 Office Professional Plus 2016 licenses.

Training Vouchers are exchanged with qualified Microsoft Learning Partners for attendance on technical training courses – one voucher equates to one training day. There is a list of authorized training courses that vouchers can be exchanged for.

The Training Vouchers allocation is shown in the Volume Licensing portals and the Benefits Administrator is responsible for activating the benefit and then assigning the vouchers to individuals who book training courses with the Learning Partners directly. Note that the vouchers expire 180 days after they have been created.

Training Vouchers are available as an SA benefit through the Enterprise Agreements and for Select Plus or MPSA customers who have SAM on the Applications or Systems pools.

Applying your knowledge in the exam:

- Look out for business goals that state that an organization wants to get their technical teams up to speed on certain products BEFORE they are deployed; benefits such as the 24x7 Problem Resolution Support, which we'll cover shortly, are typically associated with support AFTER the products are deployed

- If you're asked to pick out SA benefits that demonstrate a high return on investment, then strongly consider Training Vouchers; these are tangible, high value benefits that are easy to see the worth of

- Remember that Training Vouchers are not eligible for end user training, so disregard any answers that suggest that Training Vouchers could be exchanged for basic training to get end users up to speed on a new deployment of Office 2016, for example

- Also remember that Training Vouchers are not available through an MPSA or Select Plus agreement without SAM, so you can potentially disregard these programs as an option if you're recommending a Volume Licensing agreement for an organization where it's been established that Training Vouchers are important

© Licensing School 2018

E-Learning

It's good to consider E-Learning just after the Training Vouchers benefit since you need to be clear on the differences. Whilst the Training Vouchers benefit only applies to technical training, the E-Learning benefit is aimed at both technical users in the IT department and ordinary end users, offering online training courses across the three product pools – Systems, Applications, and Servers. Organizations receive access to the E-Learning courses in a particular pool dependent on the number of qualifying licenses with SA that they have purchased. Buying 575 Office Professional Plus 2016 licenses, for example, gives them access to all of the courses in the Applications pool for 575 users.

E-Learning is another benefit which must be activated, after which the administrator receives an Access Code which is shared with employees who can then use the code to access the training through the Microsoft Online Learning Portal.

Applying your knowledge in the exam:

- Look out for business goals where end users need access to training, or ALL users (both technical and end user) need access to training

- Look out for concerns where an organization is dubious about moving to the new versions of Office or Windows because of the perceived high cost of retraining users; the E-Learning benefit can help overcome this concern

Planning Services

Planning Services are a collection of engagements offered by certified partners to help organizations to plan for, and thus to ultimately deploy, Microsoft products. Today there is a whole range of Planning Services for all the traditional on-premises products as well as Dynamics 365 and Azure deployments.

Customers who purchase SA on qualifying Application and Server licenses receive an allocation of Planning Services days which the SA Benefits Administrator can see and exchange for vouchers in the Volume Licensing portals for spending with appropriate partners. Note that the vouchers expire after 180 days.

Customers who have unused Training Vouchers may convert them to Planning Services days at a ratio of 3:1, so three Training Vouchers may be exchanged for one Planning Services day.

Planning Services are available as an SA benefit through the Enterprise Agreements and for Select Plus and MPSA customers who have SAM on the Applications or Servers pools and, for the purposes of the exam, assume that the qualifying licenses are Office Standard/Professional Plus 2016 and all of the server products.

Applying your knowledge in the exam:

- Look for business goals that state a concern around planning for the deployment of a Microsoft product and a desire for external consultancy – skilling up internal staff would lead you towards recommending Training Vouchers rather than Planning Services

- Make sure that the business goals are referring to activities before deployment, rather than support after the deployment – where the Problem Resolution benefits will come into play

- Note that the Planning Services vouchers must be used for the partners to generate a deployment plan rather than for them to actually deploy the software, so check that the business goals requirement is for the planning phase before you select this benefit

 © Licensing School 2018

CustomerSource

CustomerSource is a password-protected site for customers who are licensed for the Dynamics products with active Software Assurance. Customers can find answers to their product questions using self-help resources such as troubleshooters, searching the Knowledge Base, and using how-to articles and videos. They also get unlimited access to online training courses and resources such as fact sheets and presentations, as well as access to user groups in the Dynamics Community. This is also where deployment teams would go to download software and updates.

Applying your knowledge in the exam:

- Remember that this benefit only applies to the Dynamics products rather than the whole range of server products, so make sure you only choose it as a correct answer in that context

Premium Assurance

Microsoft products are generally eligible for five years of Mainstream Support and five years of Extended Support, and this Software Assurance benefit allows customers to add a further six years of product support. Premium Assurance only applies to Windows Server and SQL Server and may only be purchased through an Enterprise Agreement.

It is sold as an Add-on license and must be purchased for all Windows and/or SQL Server licenses with active Software Assurance in an EA. The Add-on licenses follow the same model as the underlying licenses so there are Windows Server Standard and Datacenter Core Premium Assurance Add-on licenses, SQL Server Standard and Enterprise Core Premium Assurance Add-on licenses, and SQL Server Standard and Enterprise Server Add-ons.

To support a specific product version, the relevant Premium Assurance offering must be purchased before the end of Extended Support. For example, to support Windows Server 2008, customers have until the end of December 2019 to purchase Premium Assurance, and to support SQL Server 2008, until the end of June 2019.

Applying your knowledge in the exam:

- Look out for organizations that have an older infrastructure that they are worried about supporting going forward, but remember that this benefit only applies to Windows Server and/or SQL Server

© Licensing School 2018

24x7 Problem Resolution Support

The 24x7 Problem Resolution Support SA benefit provides assistance for organizations that are experiencing problems with Microsoft products. There are two types of support – through the web and via the phone. Organizations with SA on their server licenses purchased through both Select Plus/MPSA and Enterprise Agreements have unlimited web-based incidents. The number of phone incidents allocated to customers is based on how much they spend on SA (for Select Plus and Enterprise Agreements) or on a points system for MPSA.

Applying your knowledge in the exam:

- Look for business goals where an organization is worried about running into problems with their deployed software and getting support from Microsoft, as this benefit could alleviate this concern

- Watch out for particular mention of a requirement for out-of-hours support since that would lead you to recommend this SA benefit too

Software Assurance Revision Cards

The following pages show the Revision Cards for the Software Assurance benefits where you'll find each benefit with a description. They are arranged in categories of benefits:

- General SA benefits

- Windows 10 deployment benefits

- Office deployment benefits

- On-premises server deployment benefits

- Cloud server deployment benefits

- Training and support benefits

As well as this making it easier for you to remember them for the exam, it's also a great way to talk to customers about them; if you focus on a specific area of benefits, rather than trying to explain all of them, it will be much easier for your customer to digest the benefits that may be of particular interest to them.

At the end there's a final card reminding you of the benefits that are not available to Select Plus or MPSA customers unless they sign up for Software Assurance Membership, and the specific benefits that need to be activated within VLSC.

© Licensing School 2018

Revision Card 46:
General SA Benefits

Benefit Name	Description
New Version Rights	Allows organizations to use a newer version of a product released during the term of an agreement **Applies to:** *All products*
Step-up Licenses	Allows organizations to move from a lower edition of a product to a higher edition by just paying the difference in the License with SA price **Applies to:** *Core CAL Suite, Windows Server 2016 Standard, System Center 2016 Standard, Exchange Server 2016 Standard, SQL Server 2016 Standard, Office Standard 2016*

Revision Card 47:
Windows 10 Deployment SA Benefits

Benefit Name	Description
Microsoft Desktop Optimization Pack (MDOP)	A collection of tools to help organizations deploy and manage their desktops *Applies to:* Windows 10 Enterprise E3/E5
Windows 10 Servicing Channels	Rights to choose either the Semi-Annual Channel or the Long-Term Servicing Channel to receive feature updates *Applies to:* Windows 10 Enterprise E3/E5
Windows To Go	Allows organizations to deploy corporate desktops via a USB drive *Applies to:* Windows 10 Enterprise E3/E5
Windows Local Virtualization Rights	Allows a user to install and use up to four virtual machines running Windows 10 Enterprise on his local device *Applies to:* Windows 10 Enterprise E3/E5
Virtual Desktop Access	Allows organizations to create, store and run virtual desktops on a server in a Virtual Desktop Infrastructure *Applies to:* Windows 10 Enterprise E3/E5
Windows Thin PC	Enables organizations to repurpose existing PCs as thin clients to access a Virtual Desktop Infrastructure *Applies to:* Windows 10 Enterprise E3/E5
Enterprise Source Licensing Program	Gives access to Windows source code to support applications deployed on the Windows platform *Applies to:* Windows 10 Enterprise E3/E5

© Licensing School 2018

Revision Card 48:
Office Deployment SA Benefits

Benefit Name	Description
Office Online and Office Online Server	Office Online gives access to Microsoft-hosted browser-based versions of Word, PowerPoint, Excel and OneNote. Office Online Server allows organizations to deliver the experience from their own on-premises servers *Applies to: Office Standard/Professional Plus 2016*
Home Use Program	Allows end users to purchase Office for use on a home PC *Applies to: Office Standard/Professional Plus 2016*
Office Roaming Rights	Allows the primary user of a device licensed with Office Standard/Professional Plus 2016 and SA to access Office delivered via RDS on any third party-owned device outside the corporate premises *Applies to: Office Standard/Professional Plus 2016*

Revision Card 49:
On-Premises Server Deployment SA Benefits

Benefit Name	Description
Fail-over Server Rights	Rights to configure a product to provide redundancy so that if one server fails, its processing will be picked up, recovered, and continued by another server without the need for additional licenses *Applies to: SQL Server 2016, Dynamics 365 for Operations Server*
Disaster Recovery Rights	Server (and CAL) licenses covered with SA allow customers to deploy the software on a cold backup server for the purposes of disaster recovery *Applies to: all server products*
Power BI Report Server	Rights to run Power BI Report Server to publish Power BI reports in an on-premises environment with no further licenses required for users to view the reports *Applies to: SQL Server 2016 Enterprise Core licenses*
Unlimited Virtualization Rights	Available for SQL Server 2016 when a physical server is completely licensed with Enterprise Core licenses with Software Assurance *Applies to: SQL Server 2016 Enterprise Core licenses*
License Mobility across Server Farms	Relaxes the 90-day license reassignment rule so that virtual machines may move freely around a server farm and the server licenses may be reassigned as required *Applies to: Exchange Server 2016, SharePoint Server 2016, Skype for Business Server 2015, SQL Server 2016, and Dynamics 365 for Operations Server* ***Notable exceptions:*** *Windows Server 2016 and System Center 2016*

© Licensing School 2018

Revision Card 50:
Cloud Server Deployment SA Benefits

Benefit Name	Description
License Mobility through SA	Allows an organization to assign server licenses to a Service Provider's shared hardware, or Azure, to license a base virtual machine for a particular product *Applies to: System Center 2016, Exchange Server 2016, SharePoint Server 2016, Skype for Business Server 2015, SQL Server 2016, Dynamics 365 for Operations Server* *Notable exceptions: Windows Server 2016*
Azure Hybrid Use Benefit	Rights to use Windows Server licenses to license Azure base instance virtual machines for Windows Server *Applies to: Windows Server 2016*
System Center Global Service Monitor	A Microsoft cloud service that allows organizations to monitor their external-facing web applications *Applies to: System Center 2016*
Self Hosting Use Rights	Allows ISVs who have built a unified solution around a Microsoft product to deploy that product and their solution for delivery over the Internet *Applies to: Windows Server 2016, System Center 2016, Exchange Server 2016, SQL Server 2016, Dynamics 365 for Operations Server*

Revision Card 51:
Training and Support SA Benefits

Benefit Name	Description
Training Vouchers	Training Vouchers are exchanged with Microsoft Learning Partners for technical training courses **Applies to:** *Windows 10 Enterprise E3/E5 and Office Standard/Professional Plus 2016*
E-Learning	Allows access to online training courses aimed at both technical users and end users **Applies to:** *all products*
Planning Services	Planning Services are delivered by certified partners to help organizations to plan for the deployment of Microsoft products **Applies to:** *Office Standard/Professional Plus 2016 and all the server products*
CustomerSource	Rights to a secure site that gives access to resources such as unlimited training courses and support via the Knowledge Base **Applies to:** *Dynamics 365 Server, Dynamics 365 for Operations Server*
Premium Assurance	Option to add a further six years of product support after Extended Support ends **Applies to:** *Windows Server, SQL Server*
24x7 Problem Resolution Support	Provides web-based or phone support to solve problems relating to Microsoft products **Applies to:** *all server products*

© Licensing School 2018

Revision Card 52:
SA Benefits Exceptions

Benefits	Exception
Training Vouchers Planning Services	Only available to MPSA and Select Plus customers if Software Assurance Membership (SAM) is taken
Training Vouchers **H**ome Use Program **E**-Learning	Remember **THE** benefits that need to be activated in VLSC!

Recap Questions and Answers

Use these Recap Questions to see how much you know about the Software Assurance benefits. If you find any areas that you need to go over you can review the relevant topic in this section of the book. As usual, you'll find a couple of questions on each page with the answers when you turn over.

© Licensing School 2018

Questions 1 – 3

1. Blue Lamp Ideas are considering deploying Exchange Server but do not have any in-house IT expertise around the installation and setup of Exchange Server. If they purchase Software Assurance with their Exchange Server licenses through their Enterprise Agreement, which SA benefits could help them with this? Choose two answers.

   a) Disaster Recovery Rights
   b) Training Vouchers
   c) Step-up licenses
   d) Planning Services

2. The Papaya Hire Company are concerned about support for their older installations of Windows Server and SQL Server. They have active SA on all licenses throughout their estate. Which SA benefit will help them?

   a) Self Hosting Use Rights
   b) Premium Assurance
   c) CustomerSource
   d) Planning Services

3. Cyan Ida's Pharmacy have an Enterprise Agreement. Where should they go to manage and activate their SA benefits?

   a) MVLC
   b) explore.ms
   c) MBC
   d) VLSC

Answers 1 – 3

1. Blue Lamp Ideas are considering deploying Exchange Server but do not have any in-house IT expertise around the installation and setup of Exchange Server. If they purchase Software Assurance with their Exchange Server licenses through their Enterprise Agreement, which SA benefits could help them with this? Choose two answers.

    a) Disaster Recovery Rights
    b) **Training Vouchers** ✓
    c) Step-up licenses
    d) **Planning Services** ✓

2. The Papaya Hire Company are concerned about support for their older installations of Windows Server and SQL Server. They have active SA on all licenses throughout their estate. Which SA benefit will help them?

    a) Self Hosting Use Rights
    b) **Premium Assurance** ✓
    c) CustomerSource
    d) Planning Services

3. Cyan Ida's Pharmacy have an Enterprise Agreement. Where should they go to manage and activate their SA benefits?

    a) MVLC
    b) explore.ms
    c) MBC
    d) **VLSC** ✓

© Licensing School 2018

Questions 4 – 6

4. The Cobalt Bolt Company are concerned about supporting their IT department once they have deployed SharePoint Server. They have Software Assurance on all of their licenses. Which of the following benefits is likely to prove most beneficial to the IT department?
   a) 24x7 Problem Resolution Support
   b) Training Vouchers
   c) E-Learning
   d) Planning Services

5. Goldfinger Food have always deployed their software on-premises and managed it themselves. They are now considering using a Service Provider's shared hardware for a new deployment of SQL Server. They have been told that they should include SA on their new SQL licenses. Why have they been told this?
   a) This is an error – as long as they purchase the licenses through a Volume Licensing agreement then they can deploy the software either on their own hardware or on a Service Provider's
   b) They need the Roaming Rights benefit
   c) They need the License Mobility through SA benefit
   d) They need the Self Hosting Use Rights benefit

6. Blacken White Solicitors have purchased 25,000 Windows 10 Enterprise E3 User licenses through their Enterprise Agreement. Which of the following SA benefits are they entitled to? Choose three answers.
   a) Enterprise Source Licensing Program
   b) License Mobility through SA
   c) Rights to the Long-Term Servicing Channel
   d) Premium Assurance
   e) Unlimited Virtualization Rights
   f) Azure Hybrid Use Benefit
   g) Complete set of MDOP tools

Answers 4 – 6

4. The Cobalt Bolt Company are concerned about supporting their IT department once they have deployed SharePoint Server. They have Software Assurance on all of their licenses. Which of the following benefits is likely to prove most beneficial to the IT department?
   a) 24x7 Problem Resolution Support ✓
   b) Training Vouchers
   c) E-Learning
   d) Planning Services

5. Goldfinger Food have always deployed their software on-premises and managed it themselves. They are now considering using a Service Provider's shared hardware for a new deployment of SQL Server. They have been told that they should include SA on their new SQL licenses. Why have they been told this?
   a) This is an error – as long as they purchase the licenses through a Volume Licensing agreement then they can deploy the software either on their own hardware or on a Service Provider's
   b) They need the Roaming Rights benefit
   c) They need the License Mobility through SA benefit ✓
   d) They need the Self Hosting Use Rights benefit

6. Blacken White Solicitors have purchased 25,000 Windows 10 Enterprise E3 User licenses through their Enterprise Agreement. Which of the following SA benefits are they entitled to? Choose three answers.
   a) Enterprise Source Licensing Program ✓
   b) License Mobility through SA
   c) Rights to the Long-Term Servicing Channel ✓
   d) Premium Assurance
   e) Unlimited Virtualization Rights
   f) Azure Hybrid Use Benefit
   g) Complete set of MDOP tools ✓

© Licensing School 2018

Questions 7 – 9

7. Aisle of White Paints have purchased Office Standard 2016 licenses with SA. Which of the following benefits are they entitled to? Choose two answers.

    a) Roaming Rights
    b) CustomerSource
    c) Premium Assurance
    d) Home Use Program
    e) Virtual Desktop Access

8. Cerise Estate Management have bought Windows Server licenses through their Enterprise Agreement. To which of the following SA benefits are they entitled? Choose two answers.

    a) Self Hosting Use Rights
    b) Fail-over Server Rights
    c) License Mobility across Server Farms
    d) Azure Hybrid Use Benefit
    e) Unlimited Virtualization Rights

9. Peach Snaps Cameras are concerned about the task of training up their end users as they move to Office Professional Plus 2016, purchasing licenses through an Enterprise Agreement. Which SA benefit may help them?

    a) Training Vouchers
    b) E-Learning
    c) Home Use Program
    d) Office Online Server

Answers 7 – 9

7. Aisle of White Paints have purchased Office Standard 2016 licenses with SA. Which of the following benefits are they entitled to? Choose two answers.

   a) **Roaming Rights** ✓
   b) CustomerSource
   c) Premium Assurance
   d) **Home Use Program** ✓
   e) Virtual Desktop Access

8. Cerise Estate Management have bought Windows Server licenses through their Enterprise Agreement. To which of the following SA benefits are they entitled? Choose two answers.

   a) **Self Hosting Use Rights** ✓
   b) Fail-over Server Rights
   c) License Mobility across Server Farms
   d) **Azure Hybrid Use Benefit** ✓
   e) Unlimited Virtualization Rights

9. Peach Snaps Cameras are concerned about the task of training up their end users as they move to Office Professional Plus 2016, purchasing licenses through an Enterprise Agreement. Which SA benefit may help them?

   a) Training Vouchers
   b) **E-Learning** ✓
   c) Home Use Program
   d) Office Online Server

© Licensing School 2018

Questions 10 – 12

10. The IT manager at Ultramarine Swim Wear wants to monitor the performance of some of his customer-facing web applications. Which SA benefit is likely to be of interest to him?

   a) Azure Hybrid Use Benefit
   b) Premium Assurance
   c) System Center Global Service Monitor
   d) Fail-over Server Rights

11. Scarlet Key Cutters are looking to implement a disaster recovery infrastructure for their latest deployment project. Which of the following represents the best advice to them?

   a) They should add SA to their license purchases so that they are entitled to Disaster Recovery Rights
   b) They should add SA to their license purchases so that they are entitled to Step-up licenses meaning that they can purchase additional licenses for disaster recovery servers at a discount
   c) They should buy licenses for both the production servers and the disaster recovery servers
   d) They should add SA to their license purchases so that they are entitled to rights to the Enterprise editions of the product which include Disaster Recovery Rights

12. Which editions of SQL Server 2016 are entitled to unlimited virtualization rights when SA is purchased with the license?

   a) Standard and Enterprise Core licenses
   b) All editions of SQL Server 2016
   c) Enterprise Core licenses
   d) Enterprise Core and Server licenses

Answers 10 – 12

10. The IT manager at Ultramarine Swim Wear wants to monitor the performance of some of his customer-facing web applications. Which SA benefit is likely to be of interest to him?

    a) Azure Hybrid Use Benefit
    b) Premium Assurance
    c) **System Center Global Service Monitor** ✓
    d) Fail-over Server Rights

11. Scarlet Key Cutters are looking to implement a disaster recovery infrastructure for their latest deployment project. Which of the following represents the best advice to them?

    a) **They should add SA to their license purchases so that they are entitled to Disaster Recovery Rights** ✓
    b) They should add SA to their license purchases so that they are entitled to Step-up licenses meaning that they can purchase additional licenses for disaster recovery servers at a discount
    c) They should buy licenses for both the production servers and the disaster recovery servers
    d) They should add SA to their license purchases so that they are entitled to rights to the Enterprise editions of the product which include Disaster Recovery Rights

12. Which editions of SQL Server 2016 are entitled to unlimited virtualization rights when SA is purchased with the license?

    a) Standard and Enterprise Core licenses
    b) All editions of SQL Server 2016
    c) **Enterprise Core licenses** ✓
    d) Enterprise Core and Server licenses

© Licensing School 2018

Questions 13 – 15

13. To which of the following products does the Premium Assurance SA benefit apply? Choose two answers.
    a) Windows Server
    b) SQL Server
    c) Dynamics 365 for Operations Server
    d) BizTalk Server
    e) System Center

14. CustomerSource gives access to a whole host of training and other self-help resources. On which licenses do customers need to have active SA to gain access to this secure site? Choose two answers.
    a) SQL Server 2016
    b) Dynamics 365 for Operations Server
    c) Dynamics 365 Server
    d) Windows Server 2016
    e) System Center 2016

15. The HR Manager at Spring Green Grocers is interested in knowing if there are any SA benefits that will help users' productivity. What would you recommend?
    a) Allowing users access to CustomerSource
    b) Allowing users to use multiple virtual desktops
    c) Enabling users to buy software for home use through the Home Use Program
    d) Deploying user desktops using MDOP

Answers 13 – 15

13. To which of the following products does the Premium Assurance SA benefit apply? Choose two answers.
    a) Windows Server ✓
    b) SQL Server ✓
    c) Dynamics 365 for Operations Server
    d) BizTalk Server
    e) System Center

14. CustomerSource gives access to a whole host of training and other self-help resources. On which licenses do customers need to have active SA to gain access to this secure site? Choose two answers.
    a) SQL Server 2016
    b) Dynamics 365 for Operations Server ✓
    c) Dynamics 365 Server ✓
    d) Windows Server 2016
    e) System Center 2016

15. The HR Manager at Spring Green Grocers is interested in knowing if there are any SA benefits that will help users' productivity. What would you recommend?
    a) Allowing users access to CustomerSource
    b) Allowing users to use multiple virtual desktops
    c) Enabling users to buy software for home use through the Home Use Program ✓
    d) Deploying user desktops using MDOP

© Licensing School 2018

Questions 16 – 18

16. Which of the following SA benefits apply to SQL Server 2016 Enterprise Core licenses? Choose two answers.
    a) Rights to deploy Power BI Report Server
    b) Unlimited Virtualization
    c) Azure Hybrid Use Benefit
    d) Enterprise Source Licensing Program
    e) CustomerSource

17. World of Magnolia want to ensure that their IT support team feel fully supported when they have deployed SharePoint Server. Which SA benefit will be useful to them?
    a) Training Vouchers
    b) 24x7 Problem Resolution Support
    c) Disaster Recovery Rights
    d) Planning Services

18. The IT Manager at Powderblue Pottery is not sure whether his upcoming SQL Server deployment will require SQL Server Standard or SQL Server Enterprise edition. How will Software Assurance help him in this situation?
    a) SA allows a one-time edition swap
    b) SA allows him to deploy any edition of a product
    c) SA allows him to buy Step-up licenses
    d) SA allows him to spread payments

Answers 16 – 18

16. Which of the following SA benefits apply to SQL Server 2016 Enterprise Core licenses? Choose two answers.

    a) Rights to deploy Power BI Report Server ✓
    b) Unlimited Virtualization ✓
    c) Azure Hybrid Use Benefit
    d) Enterprise Source Licensing Program
    e) CustomerSource

17. World of Magnolia want to ensure that their IT support team feel fully supported when they have deployed SharePoint Server. Which SA benefit will be useful to them?

    a) Training Vouchers
    b) 24x7 Problem Resolution Support ✓
    c) Disaster Recovery Rights
    d) Planning Services

18. The IT Manager at Powderblue Pottery is not sure whether his upcoming SQL Server deployment will require SQL Server Standard or SQL Server Enterprise edition. How will Software Assurance help him in this situation?

    a) SA allows a one-time edition swap
    b) SA allows him to deploy any edition of a product
    c) SA allows him to buy Step-up licenses ✓
    d) SA allows him to spread payments

© Licensing School 2018

Questions 19 – 21

19. The Pink Pillow Shop are about to start a project to deploy SharePoint Server 2016. Their technical team need some assistance in working out the best way to deploy this product in their organization. Which SA benefit is likely to be a good fit for them?

   a) Training Vouchers
   b) Planning Services
   c) E-Learning
   d) Deployment Services

20. Periwinkle Packaging Solutions are keen on trialing a Virtual Desktop Infrastructure and want eventually to deploy it using thin client hardware. However, the hardware cost is currently delaying the trial. Which SA benefit could you recommend to help this project?

   a) Virtual Desktop Access
   b) Windows Thin PC
   c) MDOP
   d) Roaming Rights

21. There are a team of developers at The Olive Oil Drum Company who want to be able to run Windows in virtual machines installed on their laptops to simulate different departments' test environments. They know that the Windows 10 Enterprise E3 local virtualization rights SA benefit will allow them to do this, but how many virtual machines will they be able to run on each device?

   a) 1
   b) 2
   c) 4
   d) Unlimited

Answers 19 – 21

19. The Pink Pillow Shop are about to start a project to deploy SharePoint Server 2016. Their technical team need some assistance in working out the best way to deploy this product in their organization. Which SA benefit is likely to be a good fit for them?
    a) Training Vouchers
    b) Planning Services ✓
    c) E-Learning
    d) Deployment Services

20. Periwinkle Packaging Solutions are keen on trialing a Virtual Desktop Infrastructure and want eventually to deploy it using thin client hardware. However, the hardware cost is currently delaying the trial. Which SA benefit could you recommend to help this project?
    a) Virtual Desktop Access
    b) Windows Thin PC ✓
    c) MDOP
    d) Roaming Rights

21. There are a team of developers at The Olive Oil Drum Company who want to be able to run Windows in virtual machines installed on their laptops to simulate different departments' test environments. They know that the Windows 10 Enterprise E3 local virtualization rights SA benefit will allow them to do this, but how many virtual machines will they be able to run on each device?
    a) 1
    b) 2
    c) 4 ✓
    d) Unlimited

© Licensing School 2018

Questions 22 – 24

22. The HR manager at Sienna Blenders has seen that her organization has an allocation of 35 Training Vouchers and wants to know what sort of training they can be used for. Which of the following would she be allowed to use the vouchers for?

    a) Technical training – how to deploy SQL Server, for example
    b) End user training – Excel basics, for example
    c) Soft skills training – time management, for example
    d) Any of the above

23. The IT manager at The Mala Kite Shop is considering a desktop virtualization project. Which of the following SA benefits will be of interest to him as he plans this virtualization project?

    a) E-Learning
    b) Virtual Desktop Access
    c) Premium Assurance
    d) Step-up licenses

24. Which of the following products does NOT have License Mobility across Server Farms rights even with active SA?

    a) SQL Server 2016
    b) Windows Server 2016
    c) SharePoint Server 2016
    d) Dynamics 365 Server

Answers 22 – 24

22. The HR manager at Sienna Blenders has seen that her organization has an allocation of 35 Training Vouchers and wants to know what sort of training they can be used for. Which of the following would she be allowed to use the vouchers for?

    a) **Technical training – how to deploy SQL Server, for example** ✓
    b) End user training – Excel basics, for example
    c) Soft skills training – time management, for example
    d) Any of the above

23. The IT manager at The Mala Kite Shop is considering a desktop virtualization project. Which of the following SA benefits will be of interest to him as he plans this virtualization project?

    a) E-Learning
    b) **Virtual Desktop Access** ✓
    c) Premium Assurance
    d) Step-up licenses

24. Which of the following products does NOT have License Mobility across Server Farms rights even with active SA?

    a) SQL Server 2016
    b) **Windows Server 2016** ✓
    c) SharePoint Server 2016
    d) Dynamics 365 Server

© Licensing School 2018

Questions 25 – 27

25. Maroon Balloons have a virtualized server farm where virtual machines move freely amongst the physical hosts. Which Software Assurance benefit is of particular use to them?

    a) License Mobility through SA
    b) License Mobility across Server Farms
    c) Disaster Recovery Rights
    d) Fail-over Server Rights

26. Which of the following products have Fail-over Server Rights as an SA benefit? Choose two answers.

    a) SQL Server 2016
    b) Windows Server 2016
    c) System Center 2016
    d) BizTalk Server 2016
    e) Dynamics 365 for Operations Server

27. Tangerine Truckers are keen to virtualize their desktops and run them from a server. What Software Assurance benefit will allow them to do this?

    a) VDA
    b) VDI
    c) MDOP
    d) Roaming Rights

Answers 25 – 27

25. Maroon Balloons have a virtualized server farm where virtual machines move freely amongst the physical hosts. Which Software Assurance benefit is of particular use to them?
    a) License Mobility through SA
    b) License Mobility across Server Farms ✓
    c) Disaster Recovery Rights
    d) Fail-over Server Rights

26. Which of the following products have Fail-over Server Rights as an SA benefit? Choose two answers.
    a) SQL Server 2016 ✓
    b) Windows Server 2016
    c) System Center 2016
    d) BizTalk Server 2016
    e) Dynamics 365 for Operations Server ✓

27. Tangerine Truckers are keen to virtualize their desktops and run them from a server. What Software Assurance benefit will allow them to do this?
    a) VDA ✓
    b) VDI
    c) MDOP
    d) Roaming Rights

© Licensing School 2018

Questions 28 – 31

28. The IT Manager at Copper Feel Fabrics has a server which he wants to license for unlimited virtualization for SQL Server 2016 Enterprise edition. The server has four processors each with four cores. What licenses should he purchase?

   a) 8 SQL Server 2016 Enterprise Core licenses
   b) 16 SQL Server 2016 Enterprise Core licenses with SA
   c) 8 SQL Server 2016 Enterprise Core licenses with SA
   d) 4 SQL Server 2016 Enterprise Processor licenses with SA

29. Where should an MPSA customer go to manage SA benefits?

   a) MBC
   b) VLSC
   c) explore.ms
   d) MVLC

30. Amaranth Antiques want to roll out corporate desktops to all of their users by giving them a USB drive. Which Software Assurance benefit gives them the right to do this?

   a) Virtual Desktop Access
   b) Windows To Go
   c) License Mobility through SA
   d) Roaming Rights

31. Which SA benefit allows users to view and edit documents through a browser on an on-premises server?

   a) Office Web Apps
   b) Virtual Desktop Access
   c) Office Roaming Rights
   d) Office Online Server

28. The IT Manager at Copper Feel Fabrics has a server which he wants to license for unlimited virtualization for SQL Server 2016 Enterprise edition. The server has four processors each with four cores. What licenses should he purchase?

   a) 8 SQL Server 2016 Enterprise Core licenses
   b) 16 SQL Server 2016 Enterprise Core licenses with SA ✓
   c) 8 SQL Server 2016 Enterprise Core licenses with SA
   d) 4 SQL Server 2016 Enterprise Processor licenses with SA

29. Where should an MPSA customer go to manage SA benefits?

   a) MBC ✓
   b) VLSC
   c) explore.ms
   d) MVLC

30. Amaranth Antiques want to roll out corporate desktops to all of their users by giving them a USB drive. Which Software Assurance benefit gives them the right to do this?

   a) Virtual Desktop Access
   b) Windows To Go ✓
   c) License Mobility through SA
   d) Roaming Rights

31. Which SA benefit allows users to view and edit documents through a browser on an on-premises server?

   a) Office Web Apps
   b) Virtual Desktop Access
   c) Office Roaming Rights
   d) Office Online Server ✓

© Licensing School 2018

PART 7: FINAL PREPARATIONS FOR THE EXAM

The Exam Syllabus

There are three key areas covered in the exam. Let's take a look at these areas to explore in a little more detail what they mean and which sections of the book will help you with the knowledge that you'll need.

Recommend the Appropriate Technology Solution (60-65%)

Questions relating to this area will require you to determine the right on-premises, Online Services or Azure product to meet a customer's needs, and then to identify the best licensing solution. Use "Part 2: Licensing On-Premises Products", "Part 3: Licensing Online Services Products" and "Part 4: Licensing Microsoft Azure" for the information that you'll need to answer questions in this area.

Recommend the Appropriate Software Assurance Benefits (15-20%)

Questions relating to this area will require you to identify SA benefits that match a particular customer need. You'll find the information that you need for this area in "Part 6: Software Assurance".

Recommend a Licensing Solution (20-25%)

Questions relating to this area will require you to work out the best way for the customer to acquire the licenses that they need. You'll need to be able to recommend either the best Volume Licensing Agreement for the customer, or that they should purchase licenses via a partner and the Cloud Solution Provider (CSP) program. "Part 5: Microsoft Licensing Programs" contains the information that you'll need to answer questions in this area.

The Exam Structure

As I mentioned right at the beginning of this book, the exam has two main sections: one section will have a whole series of around 35 individual questions and the other, two customer scenarios with about eight associated questions.

The Exam Scenario

The information that you'll be given in the scenario will be split into a number of sections. First of all, there will be an Overview section where you'll be told details such as the name of the company, where it's located, how long it's operated for, and how many employees there are. Then there will be a section on the Existing Environment and this will contain information on the current IT infrastructure and how the company purchases its existing licenses. You may find some problem statements in this section too. And finally there is a Requirements section where the future plans for the company are documented which, again, are typically either IT infrastructure related or are to do with improving license acquisition and management.

The questions that follow will ask you to recommend products, licensing models, SA benefits, and the programs through which the customer should be acquiring the required licenses. One thing to note is that the questions you're given are randomized – there could be a bank of 20 questions for the scenario and you'll be given about eight of them to answer. This does mean that the questions themselves are completely independent of each other within a single scenario. So, if you've decided that CSP is the way to go in question 1, but the answer to question 3 is clearly an Enterprise Subscription Agreement, don't doubt your answer to question 1 – the questions are completely separate!

Timewise, you should aim to spend up to 25 minutes in tackling the reading of a scenario and answering the associated questions. You'll have the opportunity to review, check and change any answers that you want to, and then you need to commit by submitting the scenario.

© Licensing School 2018

Question Types

There are several different question types which you'll come across both in the scenarios and in the general questions section, and so in this part of the book I've mocked up some sample questions to give you an idea of what to expect. And, as usual, these are not actual questions from the exam but conjured from my head.

Multiple Choice

Most of the questions will be multiple choice and you'll always be told how many answers to select if there are multiple parts to the answer.

Underlined Text

In this type of question you'll be given a statement with some underlined text in it and you need to decide if it's correct or not. If it is indeed correct, then you need to choose the "No change needed" option, otherwise you need to choose the option that would replace the underlined text to make the statement correct:

> If a customer has bought Office Professional Plus 2016 licenses, they may run Office Standard 2016 in its place.
>
> To answer, choose the option "No change needed" if the underlined text is correct. If the underlined text is not correct, choose the correct answer.
>
> A ○ No change needed
>
> B ○ Office Professional Plus 2013
>
> C ○ Office 365 ProPlus
>
> D ○ Office Professional 2010

Figure 59: Underlined Text Question

In this example, the question is testing knowledge of downgrade rights for Office Professional Plus so you should choose answer B.

Multiple Yes/No Options

The Multiple Yes/No questions give you a series of statements on the same topic and you need to evaluate whether each of them is true by choosing Yes or No. In this example, all of the statements are about ordering licenses for Online Services in CSP:

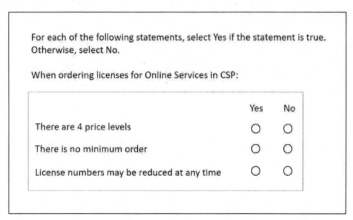

Figure 60: Multiple Yes/No Options Question

You should choose No for the first statement, and then Yes for the other two. Note that if there are several statements, then you may need to scroll down in the box.

© Licensing School 2018

Drop Down Options

The Drop Down Options questions require you to choose the correct answer from a drop down box. In this example, you have to choose how many Windows Server 2016 Standard licenses you would need to license each of the servers detailed:

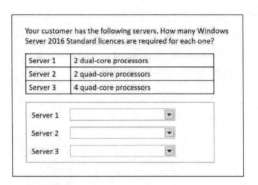

Figure 61: Drop Down Options Question

You should choose 16, 16, and 32 to score full marks. Note that if you want to choose 0 from the list then you need to actively select it – it won't be the default option.

Drag and Drop

The Drag and Drop questions give you a list of choices on the left-hand side which you need to match to the items on the right-hand side. In this example, you need to choose the correct licensing model for each of the products listed and you would do this by dragging the relevant licensing model to the boxes next to the products:

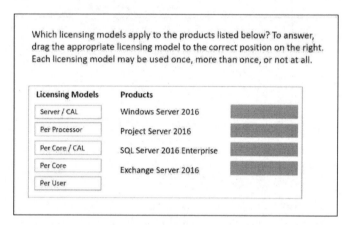

Figure 62: Drag and Drop Question

Here you would drag "Per Core/CAL" to the box next to Windows Server 2016, "Server/CAL" next to Project Server 2016 and "Per Core" next to SQL Server 2016 Enterprise. You would then drag "Server/CAL" next to Exchange Server 2016 as well since you are allowed to drag an option multiple times to the right-hand boxes if required.

© Licensing School 2018

"Sudden Death"

This is a new type of question for the 70-705 exam and is a little bit odd if you're not expecting it. In this type of question, you'll be given a goal statement and then a possible solution for which you have to choose whether or not it meets the goal. If you believe that it does, then you choose the "Yes" option. At this point, no more solutions will be presented to you so there's no opportunity at all to change your mind. For example, in the question sample below, you're being asked to recommend the right way to buy Office 365 E3 User SLs on a monthly basis. If you believe the EA is the right answer, you choose "Yes" and the question comes to an end. If you choose "No" then you're given another option – perhaps CSP, and the same thing happens: if you choose "Yes" the question comes to an end, and if you choose "No" then another option – perhaps the MPSA – is presented. If, at this point, you realize you should have chosen CSP then there's no way to go back.

Note: This question is part of a series of questions that present the same scenario. Each question in the series contains a unique solution that might meet the stated goals. Some question sets might have more than one correct solution, while others might not have a correct solution.

After you answer a question in this section, you will NOT be able to return to it. As a result, these questions will not appear in the review screen.

A customer wants to pay for Microsoft Office 365 E3 User Subscription Licenses (User SLs) on a monthly basis, reducing and increasing numbers as required.

Solution: You instruct the customer to buy the licenses through an Enterprise Agreement.

Does this meet the goal?

○ Yes

○ No

Figure 63: "Sudden Death" Question

Exam Hints

One of the most helpful hints I can give you for the exam is not to over-complicate things. When you're reading the questions don't look for hidden agenda or meaning that will make the question significantly more difficult to answer. Don't delve too deeply from a technical perspective either – if a company wants to deploy a network infrastructure, then the answer will be to deploy Windows Server. Don't worry that you might have read something in the business goals or current infrastructure that would make this technically impossible, for example.

When you just don't know the right answer you should, of course, take a guess, but make sure it's a calculated one – eliminate any suggested answers that you know are wrong and then choose from the answers that are left.

The Language of the Exam

One of the things that people find hardest about taking the exam is not the licensing knowledge, or learning about the programs and SA benefits, it's interpreting the questions and working out what the intent of the question is. Use the "applying your knowledge in the exam" points in the main sections so that you're comfortable with the sorts of things you need to look out for.

Your Final Preparations

Make sure that you're completely comfortable with the five key areas that make up Parts 2 to 6 of this book; use the Revision Cards and learn all of the facts as well as you can.

Finally, put all your knowledge into practice and work through the sample scenario that you'll find in the next section.

And when the exam is all over, email us at info@licensingschool.co.uk to let us know you've passed – we're always interested!

© Licensing School 2018

PART 8: SAMPLE SCENARIO

This scenario is designed to give you a feel for one of the scenarios that you'll be presented with in the exam. It is not one of the actual exam scenario reworded, it's simply in the same style and is genuinely made up out of my head! So, don't learn the answers, just use it to get into the mindset of the exam and to see if you still have gaps in your knowledge.

My advice would be to read the scenario through completely and then to tackle the questions. The answers are then given on the following pages along with an explanation as to why a particular answer is correct. I've given you 8 questions to tackle and this will be similar to what you'll find in the real exam.

Sample Exam Scenario: Fandango Fitness

Company Background

- Fandango Fitness are headquartered in the UK with 1,500 staff working in fitness centers all over the country. They own five subsidiary companies located in the US, Australia and mainland Europe to carry out local operations in those geographies

- The business started ten years ago and has grown steadily. Although the management team has adopted a cautious approach to growing the company, they feel they are now ready for a more aggressive expansion and envisage doubling the turnover of the business in the next two years

Existing Environment

- Fandango Fitness have an existing MPSA through which they have purchased perpetual licenses for their 1,250 PCs. All of the subsidiary companies have used their own Open agreements or OEM software to license the devices and servers that they use. There are 480 PCs in total across these organizations. All PCs are running a variety of editions and versions of Windows

- All of the PCs in the head office (150) are licensed for Microsoft Office Professional Plus 2013 through the MPSA. 75 of these PCs are due for retirement and will be replaced by new laptops

- All organizations are running a client-server network running Windows Server 2008 Enterprise, and access to the servers is licensed with Windows Server 2008 Device CALs

- Email and basic intranet sites are provided by Exchange Server 2010 and SharePoint Server 2010

© Licensing School 2018

Business Goals

- The senior management team at Fandango Fitness would like to consolidate the various existing licensing agreements that have been signed across the main organization and its subsidiaries

- The IT department has put forward a proposal which shows the benefits of standardizing the desktop across the entire organization including subsidiaries. They propose always using the latest versions of the desktop software and to roll out a single image across all desktops

- They would like to upgrade their entire server infrastructure and start using Unified Messaging capabilities throughout the wider organization. Their goal is to keep the whole infrastructure current once it has been upgraded. They will move to a virtualized environment where they will run approximately 20 virtual machines on each server at any one time, with the intention of extending the server farm to Azure within 12 months

- Fandango Fitness plan to initiate a number of global projects which will require that employees from all offices are in regular communication with each other and able to share documents, presentations and spreadsheets easily. They are worried, however, about the cost of phone calls spiraling out of control and would like to be able to control this

- Fandango Fitness would like to enable users to work at home on the same software that they use in the office. Employees will also need to access SharePoint sites and use their corporate email from home

- Fandango Fitness will start to use self-employed fitness instructors at their centers and will give them basic email capability and access to the company intranet through Microsoft Online Services. These users don't need to access any on-premises servers and should be licensed only while their three or six-month contracts with Fandango Fitness are active

Questions

1. You need to recommend a way for Fandango Fitness to purchase their licenses to meet their business goal of agreement consolidation. What would you recommend?

    a) An Enterprise Agreement for Fandango Fitness and a Select Plus agreement for the affiliates
    b) A single Enterprise Agreement for all organizations
    c) A single MPSA agreement for all organizations
    d) An Enterprise Subscription Agreement for Fandango Fitness and an MPSA agreement for the affiliates

2. How should you recommend that Fandango Fitness acquire the Online Services licenses for the fitness instructors?

    a) CSP
    b) MPSA
    c) Open Value Subscription
    d) SPLA

3. How would you recommend that Fandango Fitness license the fitness instructors in the most cost-effective way?

    a) Exchange Server 2016 Standard CALs
    b) Exchange Online Plan 1 User SLs
    c) Office 365 E1 User SLs
    d) Office 365 F1 User SLs

4. Fandango Fitness sign an Enterprise Agreement to make license purchases for their upcoming projects. Where should the procurement team go to get a single view of all of the licenses that have been purchased as the projects progress?

    a) Microsoft Volume Licensing Center
    b) eAgreements
    c) Volume Licensing Service Center
    d) Microsoft Business Center

© Licensing School 2018

5. Fandango Fitness decide to purchase SA on all their desktop licenses. Why is this important for them when you consider their business goals? Choose two answers.

a) They need to be able to purchase Step-up licenses
b) They always want to use the latest versions of the software
c) They want users to use the same software at home as at work through the Home Use Program
d) They intend to refresh much of their hardware

6. Which of the following SA benefits will meet the business goals of the IT department? Choose two answers.

a) License Mobility through Software Assurance
b) Unlimited Virtualization Rights
c) License Mobility across Server Farms
d) Roaming Rights

7. Which product would you recommend to help Fandango Fitness stop the costs of employee to employee phone calls rising as the need for collaboration increases?

a) Exchange Server 2016
b) BizTalk Server 2016
c) SharePoint Server 2016
d) Skype for Business Server 2015

8. As Fandango Fitness start to consider consolidating all of their licenses, they want to check the use rights of licenses acquired through the older Open and MPSA agreements. What would you recommend that they use?

a) The Volume Licensing Service Center
b) The Product Use Rights document
c) The Microsoft Software License Terms website
d) The Product Terms document

Answers with Explanations

1. You need to recommend a way for Fandango Fitness to purchase their licenses to meet their business goal of agreement consolidation. What would you recommend?

   - **Answer:** A single Enterprise Agreement for all organizations
   - **Reason:** The subsidiary organizations meet the requirements to be affiliates under a single Enterprise Agreement for Fandango Fitness, since all subsidiaries are completely owned. They want to standardize the desktop across all organizations and upgrade the server infrastructure which everyone will access, making a Platform EA attractive

2. How should you recommend that Fandango Fitness acquire the Online Services licenses for the fitness instructors?

   - **Answer:** CSP
   - **Reason:** They need the flexibility to add and reduce licenses on an ad-hoc basis for the fitness instructors

3. How would you recommend that Fandango Fitness license the fitness instructors in the most cost-effective way?

   - **Answer:** Office 365 F1 User SLs
   - **Reason:** We are told that the fitness instructors will need basic email capability and access to the company intranet through Microsoft Online Services which indicates Exchange Online and SharePoint Online. The Exchange CALs and Plan 1 don't include SharePoint, and of the remaining options, the F1 User SL is the most cost-effective since we know they don't need access to any on-premises servers

© Licensing School 2018

4. Fandango Fitness sign an Enterprise Agreement to make license purchases for their upcoming projects. Where should the procurement team go to get a single view of all of the licenses that have been purchased as the projects progress?

    - **Answer:** Volume Licensing Service Center
    - **Reason:** VLSC is the tool that EA customers should use to get access to this information

5. Fandango Fitness decide to purchase SA on all their desktop licenses. Why is this important for them when you consider their business goals? Choose two answers.

    - **Answer:** They always want to use the latest versions of the software
    - **Answer:** They want users to use the same software at home as at work through the Home Use Program
    - **Reason:** Although the ability to purchase Step-up licenses is an SA benefit, there is no particular business goal stated that makes this benefit attractive to Fandango Fitness. Equally, although they do intend to refresh some of their hardware, this does not map to a specific SA benefit. The other two answers are both valid SA benefits and map to stated requirements of Fandango Fitness

6. Which of the following SA benefits will meet the business goals of the IT department? Choose two answers.

    - **Answer:** License Mobility through Software Assurance
    - **Answer:** License Mobility across Server Farms
    - **Reason:** All of the choices are valid SA benefits, however there is no stated business goal that would lead to a requirement for Unlimited Virtualization Rights or Roaming Rights. They are virtualizing the server farm where there will be up to 20 virtual machines on a physical server at any one time – indicating that virtual machines will move between servers, and so will need License Mobility across Server Farms. Also, they will extend the server farm to Azure which requires License Mobility through SA

7. Which product would you recommend to help Fandango Fitness stop the costs of employee to employee phone calls rising as the need for collaboration increases?

- **Answer:** Skype for Business Server 2015
- **Reason:** Fandango Fitness will be able to make use of the Skype for Business Server enterprise telephony features to keep the cost of phone calls down

8. As Fandango Fitness start to consider consolidating all of their licenses, they want to check the use rights of licenses acquired through the older Open and MPSA agreements. What would you recommend that they use?

- **Answer:** The Product Terms document
- **Reason:** Use rights for all licenses for on-premises products are documented in the Product Terms document

© Licensing School 2018

Acknowledgements

Thanks to Simon Taylor for proof reading with the beadiest eyes in the business; if there are still errors then the fault is mine as I had the final say. Thanks also to Simon for coming up with all the fictional company names that are used throughout.

Thanks to Simona Millham, the creative brain behind the graphics used in this book. Again, if any are less than perfect it's due to my tweaking.

A special thank you to Paul Burgum, a business partner in a million, without whose guidance, support, and endless supply of good ideas I would not have been able to put this book together.

Louise Ulrick